INTERCULTURAL INTERVENTIONS

INTERCULTURAL INTERVENTIONS

Politics, Community, and Environment in the Otavalo Valley

John Stolle-McAllister

CAMBRIA
PRESS

Amherst, New York

Requests for permission should be directed to
permissions@cambriapress.com, or mailed to:
Cambria Press
University Corporate Centre
100 Corporate Parkway, Suite 128
Amherst, New York 14226, USA

Library of Congress data on file.

ISBN 978-1-62196-425-4

For Don Luis de la Torre and Doña Anita Chávez,
whose sharp intellects, unshakable commitment,
and bottomless generosity made so many lives richer
and our diverse world more just and understanding.

TABLE OF CONTENTS

LIST OF PHOTOGRAPHS

ACKNOWLEDGEMENTS

Although my name goes on the cover of the book, its contents would not be possible without the support of a large community of people in both Ecuador and Baltimore. I cannot express enough thanks for people in Otavalo, Cotacachi, Cayambe, Quito and all the places in between who took time to talk to me, show me parts of their lives, share meals, adventures, and friendships. María, César, Sisa, Isaac, Jazmín, Nallely, Aaron, Marcelo, Vanessa, Abuelita, Luis, Anita, Marianela, Rumi, Amaru, Randi, Giselle, Fabi, Edwin, Sarita, Graciela, and Luis all at various times took my family and me in, made us part of their families, and made Otavalo a true second home for us. The administration, faculty, students, and families at *Valle del Amanacer* who lovingly accepted and educated us and our children academically, socially, and culturally. All the individuals and leaders of organizations, too numerous to mention here, who took time out of their busy schedules to sit for interviews with me, helped me understand the situation in Otavalo, and provided me with wonderful insights into everyday life, hopes, frustrations, and visions of a better future. I also need to especially point out the always generous guidance of Luis de la Torre, who helped me get started, provided me with an orientation about the Indigenous movement in general and its manifestations in the Otavalo Valley, introduced me to dozens of others, and opened my eyes to the theoretic possibilities of interculturality while helping to keep my work grounded—and, most of all, provided friendship over these past dozen years.

This kind of work also takes institutional support and I am grateful to the Fulbright Scholars Program, for the Fellowship in 2006 that allowed me to start this project and this chapter in my life. The Universidad Andina Simón Bolívar in Quito and the Universidad de Otavalo also offered me an institutional home in 2006 and 2007. The Office of the Provost and the Dean of the College of Arts, Humanities and Social Sciences at UMBC provided substantial and sustained funding for my travels and stays in Ecuador, without which I would not have been able finish. Intellectual and collegial support came from my department, Modern Languages, Linguistics and Intercultural Communication, particularly Jack Sinnigen, Ana María Schwartz, Judith Schneider, Ana Oskoz, Omar Ka, Sara Poggio, and Adriana Medina Portillo, who covered for me in my absences and always offered encouraging insights into my work. I am also very appreciative of the support from the editorial staff at Cambria Press and the anonymous manuscript reviewers for their patience, flexibility, and helpful critique of my work. The book is much better for their efforts.

Finally, I am eternally grateful to my family, Kathy, Georgia, and Rowan, who were always happy travelers to Ecuador. Georgia and Rowan's bravery being students in new schools and a new language made it easier for me to push myself and build new relationships, too. They were always wonderful ambassadors and the foundation to finding new family far from home. Kathy, who is truly my partner in life, always encouraged me to take risks when it would have been easier not to, and to persevere (in life in general, and not just this project). I would have given up on this book many times if not for her. Thank you, all.

INTERCULTURAL
INTERVENTIONS

Chapter 1

Introduction

In May 2007, as we sat in the conference room of the offices of the *Unión de Organizaciones Campesinas de Cotacachi* (Union of Campesino Organizations of Cotacachi–UNORCAC), a whiteboard with a flow chart of responsibilities and deadlines for an upcoming grant proposal left over from a previous meeting hung on the wall behind him, Rumiñahui Anrango, who would soon be named president of the organization, patiently explained to me the UNORCAC's organizational history and goals. I asked him what interculturality, a word that ricocheted around all of my interviews and readings about Indigenous organizing, meant to him. He paused for a minute and then answered:

> I live interculturality: I'm Indigenous[1]; my wife is Mestiza—what does that make our children? I speak Kichwa to my kids and she speaks to them in Spanish. They wear white pants and *anacos*[2] to school, but usually they dress like everybody else. Being Indigenous does not mean wearing your hair a certain way or dressing a certain way, although having the right to do those things is part of it. It is having and using ancestral knowledge to make a better world. Of course, we use the latest technology, too—I can't imagine not having a cell phone, and don't know many Indigenous people without one[3]. Does that make us less Indigenous (he joked,

as our interview had been interrupted several times by phone calls and text messages)? It is about having and preserving that ancestral knowledge to make a more sustainable way of living and building on the communities that we have always had. Of course we change, nobody wants to go back to the way we used to be, but we have the right to say how we want to live. Being Indigenous to me means holding onto and making use of our ancestral knowledges[4]: how to grow medicinal plants; take care of the earth; have responsibility to each other. But it doesn't mean not participating in the modern world or interacting with the rest of society" (Cotacachi, May 10, 2007).

Although clearly a complicated subject, Anrango's explanation of his intercultural insertion into contemporary Ecuadorian life condensed many of the issues faced by Indigenous people as they negotiated their participation with social others. On the one hand, they fought for the right to participate in public affairs, as they also struggled to change those social, political, and cultural systems that historically marginalized them. Many activists, such as Anrango, believed that their particular cultural heritage and social positioning provided them with perspectives that not only improved the lives of Indigenous people, but also made society as a whole more sustainable and equitable. On the other hand, Indigenous people, intricately woven into the modern world struggled with appropriating technology, practices and beliefs from other cultures, while still maintaining a distinct vision of themselves.

Intercultural Interventions examines cultural and political changes in Ecuador, and particularly in the Otavalo Valley of the Northern Sierra, in the wake of the country's Indigenous movement of the late twentieth and early twenty-first centuries. In particular, I focus on the decade between 2006 and 2016. This period represents an important juncture, as people in Indigenous communities began constructing the "new normal" after a time of profound political, cultural, and social change, brought about by the concerted effort of their organizations. The election of Rafael Correa on a very progressive platform also represented, ironically, the decline of the national Indigenous organizations as institutional political actors.

That is not to say their disappearance, but rather their transformation into something else. The "new normal" also does not imply a complete break with the past and the forging together of something completely different. Rather, it was the weaving together of different strands of the cultural tapestry of collective life. Many Kichwa people in this period continued to live and rework their traditional practices and belief in a context of greater exposure to and contact with other cultural groups. Although these communities were never isolated from others, their relationship changed as a result of the mobilizations from 1990s onward. Those mobilizations themselves, of course, were part of a much longer historic trajectory of resistance, autonomous development, and internal and external negotiations. The construction of this new normal did not happen simply as the manifestation of some collective will. Rather it was the result of multiple and constant negotiations as individuals and groups asserted new or transformed identities and practices while they navigated drastically changed landscapes, some of their own doing and some well beyond their control.

The movement's fight for the rights of Indigenous peoples, while focused on issues of land rights, political participation, autonomy and cultural difference, never called for separation from its majority Mestizo population. Instead, the movement articulated its demands around a call for interculturality: that is, a process through which the country's different cultural groups ought to seek out new relationships built on equality, respect, coexistence, and mutual learning to create the conditions for a more just and sustainable country. While on the surface such a proposal might seem little different than multiculturalism, it staked out a decolonial position by recognizing that not only were cultural groups different, but that their relationships were built on historic and continuing inequality. They demanded, therefore, a profound transformation of cultural, political, and epistemological structures. In this book, I document and analyze how the concept of interculturality intervened in theoretical discussions of social change, the disruption of colonial-era political institutions in Otavalo and Cotacachi, the reconstitution of the idea of Kichwa community, and how intercultural strategies were used to define and implement solutions to environmental problems. By paying attention to the often uneven and ambiguous ways in which interculturality intervened in people's public lives as a result of the success of the Indigenous movement, this book contributes to decolonial theory by connecting that critique to the complex changes that took place in Andean Kichwa Ecuador of the first part of the twenty-first century.

The Indigenous movement had a tremendous impact on its base communities, Ecuador, and the world. At the same time, national and global processes outside of its control shaped and limited the direction of the movement. Indigenous culture was not (and is not) a homogenous entity, but like all cultures was a dynamic process, which was constantly engaged with and altered by other cultural processes. After a half millennium of unequal interaction with European colonialism and modern nation-state building, it would be impossible to point to a "pure" Indigenous culture. The converse, of course, is also true; the European-dominated culture of national Ecuador could not claim to be free of Andean influence either. At the same time, however, there were epistemological and organizational differences related to the unequal distribution of power that were not subsumed into a wholly consensual national mestizaje (Benavides 2004; Roitman 2009; Stolle-McAllister 2014). This tension between different standpoints and interpenetrated social relationships with different histories provided the context to explore the ambiguities and possibilities of a different, intercultural Ecuador. What did it mean, for example, for Indigenous politicians to run for office and win as Indigenous people while opposing Pachakutik, the national Indigenous party? Was it possible to build inter-ethnic coalitions, without sacrificing one's own ethnic identity, while advocating for the needs of the majority of one's ethnic group? Could communities, which historically relied on family ties and face-to-face knowledge, transform themselves to thrive in a wider society characterized by mobility and social relationships increasingly mediated by technology? Was it possible to advocate an alternative to development, which sought harmony between humans and the natural world, while seeking to improve the physical living standards of the most marginalized? Would a national society, while more accepting of cultural difference than it was a generation previous, accept that local communities ought to have some degree of autonomy and control over their own natural resources and internal governing structures?

Two inextricable links run through all of these questions. The first connects the ideas of social control and social change and the materiality of those processes. Many analysts have argued that the Ecuadorian Indigenous movement ought to be seen as an attempt to decolonize Ecuadorian life (Alaminos Chica and Penalva Verdú 2017; Albó 2008; Canelón Silva 2017; Kowii 2006; C. Walsh 2009, 2012). The movement not only sought the inclusion of Indigenous people, but also explicitly argued that exclusion was a fundamental part of the dominant system of accumulation and a continuing legacy of colonialism. In order to foster a more just and inclusive society, existing epistemological, cultural, and economic foundations should have been recognized as part of the colonial/modernist legacy and other ways of thinking allowed into the discussion (de Sousa Santos 2016; Mignolo 2017; Polo Blanco 2018). This strategy challenged the bases of governing elites' privilege by stripping them of their ability to set the public agenda and administer the economic system to their advantage. It required, therefore, a critical standpoint that went beyond inclusion to question of *why* the system of exploitation lasted as long as it had.

The second link was the increasingly fused and contested connections between local, regional, national, and global fields of knowledge and sociability. With the exception of small groups living in voluntary isolation in very remote areas, high levels of sharing and interaction characterized the relationships between multiple cultural groups at the turn of the century. In general terms, national education systems, for instance, serve as a means for individuals from small communities to pursue their aspirations for economic advancement and integration into national and global systems, but they also seek to create a more homogenous national citizenry. Transnational agricultural corporations paying salaries attract rural workers by providing a source of income for them and their families, but in that process dramatically alter the social and economic structures of small communities. Agroecological practices of small landholders, however, might respond to these pressures by offering alternatives to monocultural practices of agribusiness. These practices build coalitions across regions and around the world that seek a different relationship between producers and consumers, people and the land. This sharing across cultural groups provides both opportunities and challenges for all those involved because they interact with and become increasingly integrated into national and global systems.

The protests and proposals of the Indigenous movement arose within and contributed to this dynamic and fluid system. While political leaders, sympathetic intellectuals, and movement activists might have drawn clear lines between Western and Indigenous discourses and practices in an attempt to better mobilize their supporters and sharpen their analyses, the lines between those very real differences were often blurry and contextually driven. Those spaces of ambiguity and liminality provide the richest opportunities to analyze and understand the promises and limitations of resistance movements and intercultural initiatives for change. Identity politics, for instance, while perhaps a helpful mobilization strategy and an analytical shortcut, are also self-limiting. While emphasizing difference, they may elide the processes that created those differences and obscure the interconnections between groups, making it difficult to articulate a coherent and holistic alternative. The particular cases examined in this book, municipal level politics, and community re-construction and effective resource management, while acutely embedded in struggles over identity and group empowerment, pointed to the strategy through which groups and individuals negotiated both among themselves and between groups to secure the resources or the political space that they needed to carry out their projects. Kichwa politicians in Otavalo, for instance, could not win elections or secure resources from the national government without building meaningful alliances with Mestizos or national power-brokers, even when this hurt them with their "natural" base of support. Similarly, the changing life circumstances, particularly urbanization and mobility among young Kichwa-Otavalos, meant that their strategies for building a Kichwa community incorporated their experiences of the world, their participation in technologically mediated relationships, and their desires for certain levels of material accumulation, which often put them in tension with more "traditional" organization and thought.

Despite shortcomings in the implementation of particular and sometimes utopian visions and political and organizational setbacks, the transformations brought about by Indigenous peoples and their organizations were both significant and complex. Moving beyond the limited horizon of neoliberal, multicultural reforms, the intercultural proposition provided an invitation to consider the material reconstitution of society. By questioning the naturalness of the colonial/modern/developmentalist worldview and practices imposed by the particularity of Northern and European hegemony, intercultural discourse, that is the plurality of debate and dialogue of multiple cultural heritages, destabilized the supposed universality of the logic of individualistic models of accumulation and sociability. Recognizing that racism, discrimination, and marginalization were not the results of incomplete incorporation into an economic system based on inequality but rather formed an integral part of the functioning of a system that depended on the appropriation of lands, resources, and labor of others, Indigenous and other activists not only critiqued the inefficiencies of the system to fairly distribute wealth, but also questioned the system itself. There was no way to incorporate Indigenous peoples, their worldview, and practices, as distinct peoples, into a system predicated on their exploitation and transformation into individual units of production and consumption. That certainly does not mean that Indigenous individuals, or even entire communities, did not participate in dominant economic, political, and cultural relations. Rather, it suggests that the more profound transformation of Ecuador through intercultural debates and processes that envisioned a society that questions the logics of domination to create viable alternatives remained incomplete (Radcliffe 2015).

INTERCULTURALITY AS ANALYTICAL FRAMEWORK AND POLITICAL DISCOURSE

This book is framed around interculturality as a critical theoretical construct for social analysis, informed primarily by Ecuadorian and other Latin American activists and academics involved in decolonial political projects. Emanating from social sectors marginalized by the processes of modernity, interculturality provides a grounded critique of the ethnic, class, gender, and epistemic exclusions of modern liberal hegemony. Assuming a decolonial standpoint, intercultural theorists argue that a just and sustainable society can only be built by working to rid social institutions of structural inequalities and exclusionary practices. They reject the notion that any one tradition has all of the answers to social problems, instead insisting that solutions are created in the spaces between cultures. So long as inequality and exclusion exist, however, knowledge, practice, and cooperation can never be truly shared.

Circulating for some time throughout Latin America, the notion of interculturality first appeared in the context of bilingual education programs aimed ostensibly at facilitating Indigenous children's learning and ability to integrate into Spanish/Mestizo dominated societies (Bartolome 2006; Moya and Moya 2004; Vélez Verdugo 2006; Zúñiga Paredes 2011). Ecuador's Indigenous movement transformed this term into a more combative political discourse aimed not only at permitting Indigenous people to function in both Indigenous and Mestizo public spheres, but more importantly as a means to fundamentally change the unequal relationships between dominant and subaltern groups. Indigenous activists were not fighting to belong to institutions that systematically and deliberately excluded them (Canelón Silva 2017; Ramón 2005; Salazar Medina 2011; Whitten and Whitten 2011). Rather, they were fighting to change those institutions so that their ideals, values, organizations, and histories could join in dialogue with those from dominant and other subaltern groups. They argued that, as Indigenous peoples, they could not simply become part of the system without ceasing to be Indigenous. At the same time, they were not seeking to separate themselves from national society. Instead they were looking for ways to alter national society to be open to a genuine dialogue between cultural groups and to disavow the unitary construction of the colonial and liberal state to allow for the construction of a plurinational one that would recognize and benefit from the country's diverse population.

Proponents of interculturality as a liberating discourse and analytical framework argue that, at its core, it represents a challenge to the political, economic, and epistemological bases of Western modernity founded in European colonialism (Cruz Rodriguez 2016; Escobar 2010b; Kowii Maldonado 2011, Torres 2011; C. Walsh 2009). They contend that because this proposal comes from those traditionally marginalized sectors, it is fundamentally different than neoliberal multiculturalism because it seeks to alter dominant frames rather than simply include "minorities" in a system of exclusion (Aman 2014; de Sousa Santos 2016; Esteva 2015). According to Edwin Cruz Rodriguez (2013), interculturality is based on "respect, coexistence (*convivencia*), dialogue and mutual learning" (92). Multiculturalism, however, despite its respect of difference, ultimately seeks to integrate cultural others into the dominant system. The insistence on a genuinely dialogic relationship among equals decenters liberal/modernist/developmentalist hegemony, which posits itself as the end goal of a unified, linear history (Mignolo 2011). In order for different cultural groups to be able to engage in dialogue, however, they must also fundamentally alter the asymmetric relationships that currently characterize their interactions. Power, in other words, occupies a central point of reflection in intercultural theory, something that is often obscured in other ways of discussing cultural diversity.

Interculturality also assumes that all cultures are necessarily incomplete. No one group has all of the answers to social issues; solutions need to be constructed in response to ever changing circumstances, based on the constant learning that can occur between different groups. This proposition is in many ways, of course, utopic and should be seen more as a process than an attainable goal. Catherine Walsh (2009), for instance, writes about *interculturalizing* political systems, education, and social relations. Understanding interculturality as a dynamic process creates a framework to analyze not just the immediate demands of the movement, but also the more profound challenges of reorganizing society and critiquing the often-limited reforms proposed by politicians once they gain power. It also provides a base for a wider examination of dominant epistemologies and narratives of the good life and the way things ought to be. Interculturality advances the dialogue beyond simplistic binaries of Western versus non-Western by recognizing that cultures are relational and mutually constructed through interaction with other cultures.

As a contentious political discourse, there is much debate over the meaning and, therefore, the practices of interculturality. While social movements use interculturality to argue for a radical realignment of cultural groups, interculturality is also deployed by political actors as a way of *not* talking about the power differences between groups but rather a continuation of neoliberal multicultural policies. Peruvian philosopher Fidel Tubino (2013, 608) refers to this as "functional" rather than "liberating" interculturality, as it seeks to provide a means for state agencies to manage cultural diversity and, in many cases, assimilate those subaltern sectors, rather than engaging them in dialogue that would lead to changes in dominant discourses. In the case of Ecuador, disputes between the leftist government of Rafael Correa and Indigenous organizations pointed to this kind of contention (Conaghan 2017; Ellner 2014; Karg 2014). Correa's governing strategy, for instance, appropriated language and concepts from Indigenous proposals, but failed to abandon the premises of capitalist development, thereby subordinating local autonomy to national initiatives, particularly around natural resources extraction (Stolle-McAllister 2015). Even though the 2008 Constitution mentions the word "intercultural" twenty-three times (Sinnigen 2013, 605), the *meaning* of the word continues to be bitterly debated. Interculturality is, therefore, the uneven, contentious process of defining the good life, fighting against structural inequality, and using all of the country's cultural resources. It is not the superficial tolerance of difference, often advocated by proponents of multiculturalism, but rather the more difficult process of constructing productive relationships across cultural groups to create a more just, sustainable, and deeply shared society.

NATIONAL CONTEXT IN ECUADOR

Through the lens of interculturality, the story of political change in Ecuador illustrates both the promises and the frustrations of moving beyond acceptance and tolerance of others, toward a more profound transformation. On the one hand, as protagonists in their own efforts for change at the turn of the century, Indigenous activists and their organizations not only advocated for themselves, but also led an effective multicultural coalition that resisted and ultimately derailed Ecuadorian elites' neoliberal aspirations. Under the movement's constant pressure, the traditional political parties imploded, and the country's constitution was rewritten twice, in 1998 and again in 2008, in order to be more inclusive. On the other hand, however, the country's political reality, as well as limitations within the *Confederación Nacional de las Nacionalidades Indígenas del Ecuador* (National Confederation of Indigenous Nationalities of Ecuador, CONAIE) and other Indigenous organizations, suggested that external constraints coupled with internal fault lines shaped the ways in which intercultural debates occurred and changes were enacted. An ideal arc of Ecuador's Indigenous movement would have been a displacement of the colonial institutions by more inclusive, democratic, and sustainable ones. At the very least supporters would have hoped that, as in the case of Bolivia, an Indigenous leader would have won national office to articulate a definitive vision of a new state and a new era (Postero 2017). The results of the Indigenous mobilization in Ecuador, however, while profound and transformative, were less stark and characterized more by negotiation, calibration, and re-positioning as circumstances changed and opportunities ebbed and flowed.

The contemporary history of political change in Ecuador and that of the emergence and growth of the Indigenous movement go hand in hand because the Indigenous movement emerged as one of the prime protagonists to demand democratic transformation since the end of military rule in 1979. Taking advantage of newly found political space, Indigenous organizations began consolidating themselves into ever larger confederations. In the highlands, the Kichwa Organization *Ecuador Runakunapak Rikcharimuy* (Movement of the Indigenous People of Ecuador, ECUARUNARI) was founded in 1972, and by the 1980s it had become one of the most effective and powerful Indigenous organizations in the country. Amazonian Indigenous organizations formed the *Confederación de Nacionalidades Indígenas de la Amazonía Ecuatoriana* (Confederation of Indigenous Nationalities of the Ecuadorian Amazon, CONFENIAE) in 1980, in their efforts to resist the destruction wrought by oil exploration and extraction, and to better assert their territorial and human rights (Sawyer 2004). Historian Marc Becker (2011b, 5) notes that this was one of the first uses of the terms "nationalities" among the titles of Indigenous organizations, signaling a shift in the ways in which Indigenous activists perceived themselves and their relationships with dominant, Mestizo society. By employing the word nationality, Indigenous peoples were making claims beyond ethnicity or minority to now include notions of autonomy, territory, and a distinct identity. 1986 saw ECUARUNARI and CONFENIAE found CONAIE, which would serve to forge a common agenda and a centralized voice for the country's Indigenous peoples in their confrontation and negotiation with the Ecuadorian State.

Throughout the 1990s, CONAIE built and led broad-based movements that advocated sweeping changes in Ecuadorian society to address the inequality that often crossed economic and racial lines. CONAIE mobilized its base communities throughout the country to fight for Indigenous cultural and territorial rights, while it simultaneously sought out allies in broader social movements that were resisting the neoliberal agenda being imposed on the country. Instead of seeing economic and ethnic rights as competing or prioritized claims, CONAIE synthesized them as part of its intercultural strategy because breaking the colonial pattern of ethnic oppression and exploitation also meant resisting capitalist economic relations. The 1990s and the first years of the twenty-first century were particularly unstable political times for Ecuador as street protests, often organized by CONAIE, resulted in three presidents being removed from office before their terms expired. Furthermore, the near constant mobilization of Indigenous organizations and other social movements made it nearly impossible to impose neoliberal reforms and exposed the inability of traditional parties and political elites to effectively manage the country.

The turbulence and resilience of social movements laid the groundwork for the unlikely victory of Rafael Correa in 2006. Promising a "citizens' revolution," the self-proclaimed socialist ran as an independent, free from the trappings of the political parties. Once in office, he fulfilled his major campaign promise of calling for a Constituent Assembly to reorganize the Ecuadorian state along more horizontal, sustainable, and democratic principles. The broad calls for social, economic, and political change should have made Correa and CONAIE natural allies. Their partnership, however, was built on shaky ground from the beginning. CONAIE had spent years working through various organizations and social movements to articulate a radical vision of what Ecuador might be. Based on a foundation of intercultural knowledge and practice sharing, CONAIE leaders hoped to dismantle the colonial legacy of the country's political, economic, and cultural institutions to create democratic, horizontal, and participatory ones in which people could create more sustainable and secure lives. While their critical standpoint toward neoliberal economics, along with the inequalities associated with it, found an echo in Correa's campaign, the more profound questioning of modernity, development, and the need for local autonomy fell on deaf ears and precipitated increasingly acrimonious confrontations. Correa's vision of social change, although anti-neoliberal and associated with the more radical tendencies of Latin America's turn of the century "pink tide," was nevertheless firmly grounded in the post-Second World War consensus of development and did not question the notion of a unified national identity and purpose. He made important concessions toward understanding the country's ethnic minorities as contributors to the national character but resisted attempts to define plurality as something more than superficial difference, seeing it instead as a threat to national unity and to his authority.

Correa's autocratic tendencies became visible as he consolidated power into his office. By using the rhetoric of the Indigenous and other social movements, and by incorporating some of their demands into his agenda, he co-opted independent social movements and effectively neutralized their momentum and their drive for more profound change (Pachano 2010). This dynamic was particularly evident in his deteriorating relationship with Indigenous and environmental organizations. Instead, Correa accused Indigenous leaders of being "infantile" and environmentalists as being willing to sacrifice the poor for their cause. Activists who attempted to maintain their autonomy from the state soon found themselves the targets of repression, often being arrested and charged under draconian anti-terrorism laws for non-violent civil disobedience. This criminalization of protest came to define the relationship between autonomous social movements and a Correa administration intent on consolidating its "citizens' revolution" (Becker 2012). Although his policies included a more distributive form of capitalist development, the country's social movements continued to advocate for more profound change. In attempting to subsume the ethnic and cultural demands of the Indigenous movement to larger questions of economic justice, Correa embarked on a strategy of managing cultural difference, rather than incorporating the decolonial critiques inherent in the Indigenous movement's intercultural project (Martínez Novo 2014).

One of Correa's main promises as a candidate was to call for a Constituent Assembly, which would "re-found" the Ecuadorian state, decolonize public institutions, disempower neoliberal policies, provide a framework that was inclusive of the country's diversity, and orient the country toward the more just and sustainable relationships that the twenty-first century demanded. Although many Indigenous activists were pleased with this proposal, as it encompassed what they had been advocating over the previous twenty years, there was also concern that it was an attempt by Correa to co-opt their language and their proposals and to displace them as political players (Becker 2011a). The Constituent Assembly was a contentious process that reflected contemporary political dynamics embedded in the longer *intercultural* struggle being played out in Ecuadorian society over the past generation. While the final draft of the constitution did not resolve all of the long-standing problems posed by inequality and the vestiges of colonial power, it did frame new narratives of collective identity and common purpose upon which a more equitable society might continue to be built (Martínez Dalmau 2016). In a step toward decolonizing the institutions of liberal democracy, it proposed, among other innovations, an intercultural, plurinational state; recognized gender equality; purposed the state to actively facilitate citizens' pursuit of *Sumak Kawsay/Buen Vivir* (Living Well); recognized the rights of local communities' voice in the extraction of natural resources; and posited nature as a subject of rights. These were not small victories in the trajectory of Ecuadorian history and represented the efforts of traditionally marginalized groups to fully participate in the construction of public life. Many authors point to the innovations in the Ecuadorian constitution, including the central focus of the Indigenous concept of *Sumak Kawsay* as an organizing developmental and governing principle (Acosta 2012; Becker 2012; Gudynas 2011), the advancement of environmental rights as basic human rights (Barié 2014; Weston and Bollier 2014), and the ongoing process of institutionalizing Indigenous territorial rights (González 2015; Lupien 2011).

The implementation of those changes, however, proved difficult and even more contentious, with Indigenous and other popular organizations charging that the Correa administration paid only superficial heed to the intercultural, plurinational demands of the constitution. Perhaps the greatest level of conflict was over the use of natural resources. The Correa administration, along with other left-leaning governments in the region, implemented a development strategy based on what many critics labeled neo-extractivism or reprimarization of the economy in order to finance ambitious infrastructure and economic support programs for the country's poorest citizens. These critics charged that once "leftist" governments took power, they failed to pursue creative alternatives to capitalist development (Coryat and Lavinas Picq 2016; Gudynas 2013). Others argued that there was little alternative given the global hegemony of neoliberal capitalism. Rene Ramírez Gallegos (2012), Correa's former secretary of national planning and development insisted that the progressive state had a duty to meet the material needs of its people. Continuing extractive practices, but investing those resources more directly to the service of the population, was a type of "good capitalism" in a transition process toward a new economy and a new state of "well living" (*Buen Vivir/Sumak Kawsay*) rather than one of endless private accumulation. Since the immediate transformation of capitalism was unrealistic and counterproductive, the objective of Correa's development policy was to build the foundations for a more sustainable future by planning for an eventual post-extractive economy tomorrow. The country's comparative advantages in natural resources were to be put in the service of financing programs to end poverty today.

These policies, however, ran into staunch opposition from environmental and Indigenous activists who believed that extractive economies, rather than leading to long-term improvements in the human condition, accelerate the global climate catastrophe and undermine local autonomy. Despite short-term benefits of extracting and selling oil, minerals, and monocultural crops on the international market to finance poverty reduction and infrastructure improvement, critics of Correa's economic model rejected this sort of alternative development, calling instead for an alternative *to* development. They argued that large-scale mining and oil drilling flew in the face of both the letter and spirit of the 2008 constitution by overriding local (usually Indigenous) communities' wishes for their territories and by violating the rights of nature through irreversible and massive environmental destruction. Just as the supporters of the Correa administration pointed to their efforts as steps toward *Sumak Kawsay*, critics also argued that *Sumak Kawsay* demands an immediate and radical rethinking of what human development ought to be (Alaminos Chica and Penalva Verdú 2017; Acosta 2012; Gudynas 2015; Gudynas and Acosta 2011; Lalander 2014). Besides particular policy disagreements, these disputes highlighted substantial ideological differences and continuing intercultural conflicts. Correa's progressive government, despite at least some superficial recognition of other cultural approaches toward accumulation and defining the good life, was still locked into a framework dominated by a developmentalist discourse that measured progress based on capital accumulation and the ability to provide increasingly greater material prosperity, regardless of the long-term impacts of environmental destruction, the physical limitations of growth, or the impacts on local communities (Caria and Domínguez 2016).

These disagreements about development policies coupled with the limited representation of Indigenous organizations in institutional politics suggest that the role of Indigenous organizations in bringing about change in the country was not a simple, straightforward success story. Filled with missteps, poorly chosen allies, disastrous miscalculations, and often bitter infighting, the country's Indigenous organizations saw their influence rise and ebb in the years around the turn of the century (Becker 2011b, Ospina Peralta 2009, Resina de la Fuente 2012a). Even in areas of the country with a large Indigenous population, Pachakutik, the party most closely affiliated with CONAIE, was unable to consistently deliver victories, or even substantial numbers of votes, for party-endorsed candidates (Mijeski and Beck 2011). The reasons for this lack of success are complex, including the belief among many Indigenous voters that Pachakutik was, like other political parties, too willing to make compromises and directed by a top-down decision-making process. It also points to some of the weaknesses of ethnically oriented political initiatives, in general, and suggests that Indigenous voters looked to factors other than just ethnic identity when they went to the ballot box (Lalander 2010b; Ortiz Crespo 2012; Sánchez Parga 2013).

The contributions of the movement to the processes of restructuring the Ecuadorian state and society, however, cannot be underestimated. First and foremost, and despite lingering problems of racism and structural inequality, the recognition of ethnic plurality as a fact of public life in Ecuador was a generally accepted proposition. That does not mean that the meaning of that plurality or the construction of a truly plurinational state was beyond debate (Becker 2012) but in a generation's time, the country's minority populations were recognized as distinct and vital members of national society and not just folkloric remnants of the past. The national political process, although at times polarizing under the administration of Rafael Correa (2007–2017), was at least stabilized in comparison to the previous decade and Indigenous leaders sought new avenues for participation.

INTERCULTURALIZING LOCAL POLITICS AND COMMUNITIES

Within this national context of negotiating power and the meanings of interculturality and *Sumak Kawsay*, I turn to some of the experiences of individuals and organizations in Otavalo, Cotacachi, and their surrounding communities to develop a more detailed account of how intercultural thinking and practice intervened in people's lives. The area offers a unique set of political, cultural, and historic circumstances to elaborate intercultural analysis. Kichwa politicians governed municipal governments from 1996 until 2014; rural communities were undergoing rapid transformation and built complex ties with urban areas; craft and trade networks created dense transnational circuits of cultural exchange and appropriation; and, over the years, cultural activists in the area had invested substantial resources in initiatives to revitalize the Kichwa language and to strengthen and resignify annual festivals in attempts to construct and connect an increasingly far-flung community.

Located approximately one hundred kilometers north of Quito along the Pan American Highway, the city of Otavalo serves as the administrative center and market hub for the communities of the Lago San Pablo Valley[5]. Slightly more than half of the canton's combined urban and rural population of 115,000 people self identified as Indigenous (INEC 2014), and it was distinguished for its international crafts market, making it both an important tourist destination and a sending point for many Kichwa global travelers. A few kilometers further north is Cotacachi, a much smaller canton, with 43,000 people—about one-third of whom identified as Indigenous (AUC 2010; INEC 2014). The diversity of the area was obvious even on a superficial level. Sitting in the Parque Bolívar in front of Otavalo's city hall on any pleasant afternoon revealed the comings and goings of numerous kinds of people: an older Otavalo man who still wore the traditional blue wool poncho, felt fedora with a long braid falling out the back, white pants and white shirt; a younger Otavalo teenage boy, with a similar long braid, busy looking at his phone, wearing Nike shoes and a Hollister sweatshirt; Kayambi women, distinguishable by their pleated skirts and felt hats crossing through the park on their way to the market; a Mestizo man dressed in jacket and tie talking with his female Otavalo co-worker, in her traditional embroidered blouse, *anaco* (long skirt), and *alpargatas* (sandals) as they headed back to their offices in city hall; a Colombian puzzle maker, selling his twisted wire creations to school children; an Afro-Ecuadorian woman hawking yucca and coconuts; and two blond women speaking German while taking pictures of the park.

In addition to outwardly different groups of people in Otavalo and Cotacachi, the Kichwa community itself is highly heterogeneous. Otavalos, Kayambis, and Karankis all live in the area and although belonging to the same nationality (Kichwa), ethnic differences are important in terms of dress, traditions, and internal organization. One experienced Otavalo organizer from Peguche, Pacífico Fachamba, who worked extensively abroad and in Cotacachi, noted to me that, "I would have no idea how to organize on the other side of the lake. The Kayambis have their own way of doing things that is completely different than how we do things here in Peguche. Strange, isn't it? I mean, they live right next to us, but they are completely different" (Peguche, December 11, 2011). Social stratification brought about by uneven economic success further created internal cleavages, as did the differences between families who lived in the cities and those who lived in more traditional (although rapidly changing) rural settlements. Through the late twentieth century Evangelical Christianity made important inroads into Kichwa communities as well, creating tensions with more traditional Catholic followers.

Furthermore, Kichwa-Otavalos have a long history of economic success through weaving and other handicraft production and have established dense transnational trade and travel networks, which contribute to the region's cultural diversity. Travelers from abroad come frequently to Otavalo and many Otavalos take on the role of *mindalá*, or traveling merchant, and leave, usually temporarily, sometimes permanently, for faraway places. When they return for good or just to visit, they bring back new language competencies and the latest fashions, trends, and technologies from abroad. Despite, or perhaps because of, political and economic successes, there was also anxiety that instead of being forced to assimilate to White-Mestizo norms, younger generations of Kichwa people—who have grown up with Spanish schools, Mestizo friends, (at least a little) money in their pockets, and who continually update Facebook and Twitter accounts—might willingly surrender what their grandparents and parents built barricades to preserve. Although there might be a clear theoretical distinction between Western and Indigenous cosmologies and social practices, in the experiences of many area residents, the boundaries between those distinctions grew increasingly porous in the early years of the twenty-first century. That is not to say that differences had been erased, rather that dynamics between groups were ever more fluid, and in a continuing uneven playing field, there was always the danger that interaction with the dominant group could lead to loss of meaningful differences.

INTERCULTURALIZING POLITICS

Despite the setbacks that Indigenous political organizations experienced at the national level, one would expect that given those organizations' remarkable mobilizing capabilities and organic connections with many communities that they would consolidate their achievements through electoral success in areas with high concentrations of Indigenous peoples. And, indeed, Kichwa mayors represented Otavalo and Cotacachi from 2000 and 1996 respectively, until 2014, in what Rickard Lalander (2010b) referred to as the "return of the *Runakuna* (Indigenous people)" to positions of institutional authority. These electoral victories depended on politicians' abilities to build coalitions not only between different Indigenous organizations, but also across ethnic lines. Although Otavalo and Cotacachi have significant Kichwa populations, and winning coalitions clearly needed substantial Indigenous support, both municipal governments used the descriptor "intercultural" to characterize their worldviews and their policies. They both built on the organizational bases of the Indigenous movement and relied to greater and lesser degrees on ethnic solidarity with Kichwa communities. Neither government, however, would have been easily characterized as "Indigenous" in the sense of attempting to impose some sort of exclusionary Kichwa structure. Rather, they notably pursued pragmatic policies that successfully integrated various types of knowledge and organization, outreach and financing.

This broader approach, however, also cost them support from their Kichwa bases and exposed divisions within an increasingly heterogeneous Indigenous community. Differences in terms of class, work, formal education, religion, and urban/rural divides made political representation of a singular Indigenous voice or agenda impossible (Radcliffe 2015). Despite providing a more visible platform for Indigenous people and ideas, governments in both municipalities were also harshly criticized for not promoting even more radical reforms or paying enough attention to the needs of rural communities. These tensions demonstrated the difficulties of interculturalizing politics because interculturality itself is a political discourse often employed by particular actors to further their symbolic capital in a given situation. When politicians talked about "intercultural coalitions," the meaning of that phrase often just connoted an attempt to incorporate different communities for electoral purposes, but it did not necessarily mean the kind of profound rethinking many theorists of interculturality support. Otavalo and Cotacachi provide examples of different approaches that Indigenous politicians took toward interculturality and, ultimately, the many continuing challenges.

Mario Conejo, a sociologist by training, won election as mayor of Otavalo in 2000 and 2004 running on the Pachakutik slate. He ran on a platform to bring intercultural change to municipal politics and policies by providing a voice not just for historically marginalized Kichwa people, but also for all of the municipality's ethnic groups (Kowii 2006). He broke with Pachakutik shortly after his second election citing ideological differences with the party, which he believed had failed to adjust to the changing reality of Ecuador by continuing to fight battles it had largely won, such as land titling and an end to official discrimination. This split with Pachakutik caused irreparable harm with many of the Indigenous organizations affiliated with CONAIE, who saw it as a betrayal of their trust and of their cause. In 2009, he again won reelection running on President Correa's Alianza PAÍS slate, in large part through the support of the urban core (both Mestizo and Kichwa) (Lalander 2009). Besides proving that an Indigenous person was more than capable of leading the municipal government, he was also widely credited with making governance more transparent and soliciting participation in the planning process (Ortiz Crespo 2012). He was also criticized, however, for continuing with top-down implementation of projects once they were decided. In 2014 he lost his seat to Gustavo Pareja, the former Prefect of Imbabura Province. Despite being Mestizo, Pareja made substantial inroads in the largely Kichwa rural communities, many of whose inhabitants saw Conejo's policies as disproportionately favoring the urban center and neglecting their infrastructure and other development needs. The intercultural process, while certainly related to identity politics, also promoted a dialogue that moved beyond abstract notions of cultural identity to include material concerns, as suggested by Pareja's ability to win handily even in largely Kichwa districts.

Like Otavalo, Cotacachi is ethnically mixed and spreads out from the mountains to the subtropical Intag region. Cuban-trained economist Auki Tituaña was mayor from 1996 until 2009, and like Conejo, he constructed a broad coalition of local political organizations. The alliance that his CONAIE-affiliated party, Pachakutik, forged with UNORCAC, which affiliated with the *Federación Nacional de Organizaciones Campesinas, Indígenas y Negras* (National Federation of Peasant, Indigenous and Black Organizations–FENOCIN), was both essential to his success and somewhat surprising given the historic and ideological rivalries between CONAIE and FENOCIN. UNORCAC had organized most of the rural Kichwa communities in Cotacachi since the late 1970s and Pachakutik was particularly influential in the urban areas. Unlike Conejo in Otavalo, however, Tituaña and UNORCAC set about to substantially restructure the municipal government, founding the *Asamblea de Unidad del Cantón Cotacachi* (Unity Assembly for the Cotacachi Canton–AUC) as a means of gathering input on decisions about funding projects, implementing a participatory budget process, and experimenting with forms of direct democracy (Cameron 2010; Tituaña Males 2000; Stolle-McAllister 2013). Internationally recognized for its transparency and efficiency, Tituaña's administration also launched several educational and health-service initiatives that sought to cater to and strengthen the municipality's cultural diversity. By 2009 the tense relationship between UNORCAC and Tituaña broke down amidst personal disputes, arguments about urban versus rural priorities, and a disagreement over how closely to work with the Correa administration. UNORCAC founder Alberto Anrango, running on the Alianza País slate, won election that year and marginalized Pachakutik from municipal politics. Anrango, who was often criticized for his lack of vision and initiative, in turn lost his seat in 2014 to Jomar Cevallos, a Mestizo and a former technical adviser and leader of the AUC, who won easily, even in UNORCAC strongholds, promising transparent government, strong planning, and a dedication to the principles of intercultural governance.

Clearly, Indigenous people and organizations were able to occupy spaces of institutional power in order to advance particular agendas, which was itself an indication of the interculturalization of politics at the local level. The irony, however, was the inability of the historic organizations of the movement to control the political process. Groups affiliated with CONAIE found themselves unable to hold onto political power, despite continuing as important players in the political landscape, particularly through their work strengthening and networking rural organizations. The loss of Kichwa office holders to Mestizo candidates, who held similar ideological views, also suggested that while ethnic identity was important, Indigenous voters chose candidates based on who they thought best prepared and able to fulfill their promises and improve living conditions.

REARTICULATING KICHWA COMMUNITY AND CULTURE IN THE TWENTY-FIRST CENTURY

Despite the fact that the Indigenous movement of the late twentieth century built its organizational and ideological apparatus around the concept of community, these political divisions suggest the impossibility of pointing to a homogenous Indigenous community in the northern highlands. A combination of the flattening pressures of nationalism and globalization combined with the very success of the movement, which sought greater participation of Indigenous people in public life, contributed to the destabilization of those communities. A major cause of community change has been economic dislocation, which has taken its toll particularly on young people in rural communities, who increasingly found work in large agricultural industries like cut flowers or moved to the cities to work in construction or other professions. This physical exodus from the community was also compounded by a general unwillingness or inability to continue with traditional forms of shared labor (*mingas*), substituting instead economic relations mediated by money rather than face-to-face sharing of tasks.

This shift away from historic community relations, however, was not just the result of global economic structuring, but came from some of the gains of the Indigenous movement itself. One of the goals of the movement was greater social integration of Indigenous people. Access to formal education and to daily interactions with members of other cultural groups put pressure on what it meant to be an Indigenous community as individuals from those communities were drawn into other local and national social formations and adopted some of the cultural patterns of those other communities. Historically, the Kichwa language was one of the cultural markers of ethnicity in Kichwa communities. Many communities have been effectively bilingual for generations, but the past generation has witnessed a definitive shift toward Spanish, which is now the norm in many Kichwa communities. Educational and economic pressures, therefore, meant that being ethnically Kichwa did not necessarily mean speaking Kichwa (Sánchez Parga 2009).

Heterogeneity manifested itself within communities in many other ways as well, including uneven economic development and religious differences. Because there were always differences in power and economic resources, rural communities were never completely egalitarian. The relative success of some families, particularly those tied to handicraft production and commerce in and around Otavalo led to the rise of a class of producers that, at times, exploited other Indigenous families and branched out into other areas of economic production. These families were increasingly able to send their children to university, producing a new generation of professionals, whose interests and life horizons were very different than those living in rural areas. At the same time, the rise of evangelical Christianity, sometimes related to the individualistic attitude of commercial development, contributed to substantial changes within communities, and often led to bitter inter-community splits and debates about what it meant to be Indigenous (Colloredo-Mansfeld 2009).

These changes in and around Kichwa communities, however, did not necessarily mean the end of the communities, but rather their transformation through efforts to redefine community and to collectively construct new ways of being Kichwa. Otavalos, for instance, as a group, unlike many other Indigenous groups in the region, experienced greater economic mobility and invested some of that economic capital into a cultural revival demonstrated through an increasingly involved and elaborate calendar of festivals, and interest (by some) in revitalizing Kichwa language use. Local festivals such as *Inti Raymi* (in June) and Pawkar Raymi (in February) were reinvented over the past generation to emphasize community identity. Michelle Wibbelsman (2009) documented the internal negotiations and sophisticated outreach attempts among the organizers of Pawkar Raymi as a means to re-center a sometimes deterritorialized community, while at the same time inviting the outside world to participate in and recognize Kichwa cultural differences. It became a means of defining the community both to the local participants as well as to the wider world.

Adaptability characterized the attempts to construct community in the twenty-first century. Community members brought back knowledge from other places and adapted it to their community, given the larger contexts in which they were embedded. The intercultural challenge was to negotiate how to be uniquely Indigenous, while also being part of a globalized, cosmopolitan world (Ordóñez Charpentier 2014, Maldonado 2004). In many ways, this process was the interculturalizing of these communities. They were clearly changing, but they were not becoming "mestizo" or folkloric versions of themselves, rather they were dynamic and distinctly Kichwa communities. Some things, such as the traditional *mingas* may have been fading, but the communities themselves were transforming rather then being lost. As people spread out around the world, for instance, technology kept sometimes far-flung community members connected with home, through regular Skype or Whatsapp calls. Websites and Facebook pages developed by migrants allowed the sharing of videos of *Inti Raymi* in Chicago, Prague, Madrid, or New York.

Just as identities and cultural expressions are not forever fixed, but rather contingent on changing contexts, so are communities that make use of, negotiate with, and resist the influences of other cultural groups with whom they have contact.

These themes of intercultural change come together in the efforts of the predominantly Kichwa-Otavalo and Kichwa-Kayambi communities of the páramo (high grasslands) around the Mojanda lakes to manage their territories. Faced with declining water supplies, the communities decided in the late 1990s that they needed to better understand and manage the páramos. Working closely with local organizations, community elders, and technical experts from regional non-governmental organizations (NGO) leaders charted the degradation of water sources by deforestation, agriculture, overgrazing, and cyclical burning. After exhaustive consultations with all affected communities, careful measurement of water flows, and appropriate ceremonies to seek forgiveness and guidance from *Pachamama, mingas* (collective work parties) were organized every weekend for a year to replant the basins with native trees and shrubs. Years of debate and deliberation also led community members to difficult decisions about limiting high altitude land usage, the writing of legally binding language into internal governing documents, and the organization of agroecological cooperatives. Although only one example, the Mojanda projects provide insight into intercultural approaches to problem-solving that meets the needs of local communities, providing them with ways to adapt to and help shape the outside world without having to abandon who they are.

Intercultural approaches provide an engagement with different narratives about human relationships with nature, accumulation and distribution of capital and other resources, and what it means to live sustainably (Caria and Domínguez 2016). Community leaders expressed that they saw themselves as part of their natural surroundings and believed that attempts to secure their water supplies and to continue agricultural production were intimately tied not only to meeting certain technical requirements, but also in shoring up their reciprocal obligations with *Pachamama*. They saw the success of their efforts dependent not just on good advice from outside experts, but on the strong foundations of local knowledge and local organizations. The process itself contributed to the revitalization of those community organizations and helped families envision and enact different ways of staying on their lands and continuing to be a community. Beyond working together across cultural lines, these projects represented a deeper sort of interculturality because at their hearts is a critique of the developmentalist discourse that dominates discussions of resources and human-nature relationships. It was not a rejection of all things modern and Western, instead it was the articulation of an intercultural vision of the good life, which borrowed from the beliefs and practices of multiple cultural groups.

INTERCULTURAL DIALOGUE BEYOND THE MOUNTAINS OF ECUADOR

Like all ethnographies, the stories and voices in this book are a snapshot, an artificial freezing in time. I also think this book is a particularly blurry snapshot. It is blurry not only because it was taken over a long period of time, but also because everyone in it was always moving. Over the ten years that I conducted field work, people's life circumstances changed: children grew up and had their own children, babies became young adults, spouses died, people moved, opinions evolved. At the same time, however, I think it is valuable as a means to elaborate on what an intercultural society might be, and where intercultural theory is both helpful and lacking.

It became obvious in my interactions with people that no one was following a pre-determined and unified script about identity, belonging, change, and relating to cultural "others." What struck me, instead, was the profound heterogeneity of thought, belief, and practice among a wide variety of Kichwa people. That heterogeneity also led to ambiguous approaches to the intercultural reality in which they found themselves.

Some clearly articulated a refined political understanding of differentiated power relationships and possible paths to remedy them. Others, however, were more concerned with how to fit into the new normal and how to best make use of opportunities that previously did not exist. And yet others were most concerned with surviving and attempting to keep their communities together in a world that was rapidly changing around them.

If interculturality is the means that helps me understand the dynamics of the Otavalo Valley of the early twenty-first century, and even though activists, politicians, and others used that word and (some of) those ideas, it is not a top-down ideology that is driving change. A common mistake of many outside analysts is to force our vocabulary onto others' actions and motivations. Although I continue to use that vocabulary because it is helpful to me, I hope that this book demonstrates that an important part of intercultural analysis is to focus on a profoundly local perspective. The vocabulary of intellectuals and politicians is often not reflected in the way people talk. But, their words, their actions, and their constructions of community do give us insight into how people negotiate constraints and opportunities. Interculturality points us toward dialogue. That dialogue can only be meaningful if, despite the filters that we all have, we truly attempt to listen to the perspective and context of those with whom we are conversing. For interculturality to be decolonial, it also must take into account the ways in which coloniality has structured our relationships, meaning that we need to find ways to step back from the hierarchies, including epistemological ones, created by unequal relationships. One way to engage that process is to understand the "radical localness" (Altmann 2017), inherent in the ways in which people make sense of and create their worlds, even (especially) when they do not fit neatly into our frameworks.

Finally, in the globalized world in which we find ourselves, it is imperative that we not see interculturality, decolonization, or integrated rural development simply as things that other people are doing or experiencing. One of the many lessons that I learned from my years in

Otavalo is that we are ever more tightly connected. Superficially, of course, globalization has made us all part of a large system. Technology makes it increasingly easy to stay in touch with friends and colleagues all over the world, making distant people part of our local, everyday lives as well. At a more perhaps uncomfortable level, however, participating in that system also reinforces the inequalities that structure our lives. It is imperative therefore that as we try to understand the intercultural struggles of Kichwa people in Ecuador, that we do so from the perspective of those struggles playing out under their own logics and life circumstances, which will be different than mine or yours (unless you happen to be Kichwa person reading this book). More importantly, while respecting those differences, those of us not from the Otavalo Valley also need to reflect on how we fit into the structures of coloniality and work on decolonial strategies in our own intellectual, political, economic, and cultural work.

Notes

1. I use the non-standard capitalization for Indigenous and Mestizo as terms that indicate sub-national groups within Ecuador. I also refer to people by their recognized nationality, in this case predominantly Kichwa, and their particular ethnic group, Otavalo, Kayambi, or Karanki for people living in this area. Some political and cultural activists also refer to themselves as *Runa*, the Kichwa word for Indigenous person. I have tried to respect the titles that individuals assign themselves and have found that in conversation most people use the generic Indigenous to describe their ethnic identity.

2. *Anaco* is the traditional long skirt worn by Kichwa-Otavalo girls and women.

3. In 2007, I, from the so-called first world, did not have a cell phone.

4. Standard English does not recognize the plural of knowledge. I asked bilingual Indigenous and Mestizo friends in Ecuador and Mexico if I should translate it as "ways of knowing." They thought insisting on the plural "knowledges" better described the meaning and disrupted the dominant way of understanding knowledge, so I pluralize it.

5. Administratively, Ecuador is divided into provinces, cantons, parishes, and communities. Cantons generally consist of both rural and urban areas and function roughly as counties in the United States. In the case of this study, the cities of Otavalo and Cotacachi are the administrative seats of the cantons that bear the same name. The city of Tabacundo is the administrative seat of the canton of Pedro Moncayo. While the municipal governments of the cantons have primary responsibility for infrastructure, development projects, and record keeping, the Decentralized Autonomous Governments (*Gobiernos Autónomos Descentralizados*—GAD) of the parishes have increasing responsibilities for day-to-day activities and to coordinate requests from the various communities to the municipal government for projects requiring outside support.

CHAPTER 2

INTERCULTURAL THEORY
AND CIVILIZATIONAL CRISIS

Multicultural politics is affirmative action;
intercultural politics is transformative action
—Fidel Tubino (2013, 617)

Over the past three decades, the term intercultural has circulated widely
among educational reformers, social activists, academics, and, increasingly, bureaucrats in nation-states attempting to manage culturally
diverse populations. With so many uses, coming from such differentially
situated speakers, it often becomes a signifier with no clear referent.
Worse yet, as anthropologist and social activist Patricio Guerrero (2011)
argues, interculturality has

> been so instrumentalized by the academy, sectors connected to
> power and its institutions, the dis-in-formation media and even
> the actors that promote it, [that it] is telling us very little; to the
> contrary, it has been transforming itself according to the latest
> fashion, empty of the insurgent political meaning with which it
> emerged (73).

Indeed, interculturality is a malleable political discourse used to bolster any number of ideological positions, much the way multiculturalism is often deployed to suture over differences without addressing tensions between groups. As an insurgent discourse (to use Guerrero's term), however, intercultural practices and arguments are not based just on relationships between groups, or superficial differences, or state policies aimed at managing those differences, but rather they are grounded in material relationships of inequality, plurality, and epistemic difference. It takes as a starting point subjects' location in those webs of difference to take into account how power structures those differences into inequalities. The purpose of intercultural dialogue, therefore, is not necessarily a simple tolerance of the other, but rather an engagement with the other to fashion a framework through which a heterogeneous society can move forward based on the principles of conviviality, mutual learning, and profound respect for difference.

Indigenous activists and their supporters have been at the forefront of fundamentally transformative intercultural proposals that critique the asymmetrical social, economic, political, and cultural relationships that characterize our societies by envisioning more horizontal and sustainable relationships and practices. It is no coincidence that Indigenous and Afro-Ecuadorian activists have been the primary promoters of inter-culturality because they represent the sectors most marginalized by the last half millennium of colonial discourses and institutions. As the neoliberal experiments of the late twentieth century exacerbated the region's inequalities, the foundations of the colonial/modernist project have also been shaken. The intercultural project, therefore, ultimately aims to deconstruct the homogenizing discourses of nationality, rooted in colonial institutions, by forcing not only the recognition and inclusion of marginalized sectors, but, importantly, demanding that the structures that created their marginalization be transformed. In other words, trans-formative interculturality does not seek inclusion into asymmetrical relationships, but rather advocates a process of decolonization to restructure those relationships. Decolonization, however, also demands that both dominant and subaltern social sectors be included in dialogue and debate about how to create a new, different kind of society (de Sousa Santos 2016). It is not a process that only includes Indigenous, Afrodescendent, and other marginalized communities, but also necessarily insists on substantial change at the level of state institutions, public practices, and the attitudes of privileged sectors.

Need for structural change, although certainly not a new argument, particularly from the perspective of marginalized sectors, has become acute in recent decades. The underpinnings of the homogenizing project of modernity, particularly singular narratives of national unity and prosperity, have become less persuasive as models of governance, representation, and economic growth seem unable to sustainably and meaningfully incorporate disparate peoples. Ethnic minorities around the world, for instance, have resisted attempts by states to incorporate them into an imagined nationality, resulting in repeated conflicts of various degrees of severity. Similarly, even as the global reach of transnational capital appears to be at its zenith, the economic, social, cultural, and environmental limits of the continuous growth upon which development is predicated become increasingly apparent. Viable alternatives, however, are also few and far between. In Latin America the rise of the "pink tide" of center-left and left governments, while reorienting national priorities, still based their models of economic growth on extractive capitalism and, with perhaps the exception of Bolivia, on a unified national state[1].

It is in this context of ongoing, civilizational crisis, therefore, that proponents of Indigenous rights explicitly link their demands, not to inclusion in the system that has historically and systematically marginalized them, but rather to a more profound rethinking and restructuring of that system. Their marginalization from colonial administration, national construction, and capitalist development was not just an oversight, but rather was, and is, integral to the very fabric of those systems. Proponents of interculturality, therefore, reject the notion of a homogenous national identity, arguing instead for a plurality of identities as more reflective of actual populations and more productive in terms of finding solutions to collective problems. Similarly, they reject the label of multiculturalism arguing that multicultural practices are in essence attempts by states and international organizations to recognize and manage cultural differences by incorporating those differences into the neoliberal (or neopopulist) architecture of contemporary states.

Intercultural challenges to the basic terms of nation and belonging strike at the core of the colonial project by rejecting the terms upon which societies ought to be organized. Ethnic marginalization, for instance, goes hand-in-hand with the divide-and-conquer strategies of elites, economic oppression, and the construction of a national unity that obscures profound, structural inequalities. Therefore, in order to overcome those inequalities, with the goal of permitting a meaningful, productive, and respectful dialogue between the different social sectors that comprise the country, the structures themselves that have created and sustain those inequalities must also be challenged. Social transformation, and not just inclusion, is the ultimate goal of the intercultural processes being advocated in Ecuador and throughout the region.

This chapter is organized around four interrelated arguments. First, calls by Indigenous and other marginalized groups for recognition and participation do not necessarily equate to a desire for better inclusion into systems that exploit them. Proponents of interculturality have argued that policies of multicultural tolerance of others, as adopted by neoliberal states over the latter part of the twentieth century, while successfully highlighting superficial cultural differences, failed to address the inequalities that informed those differences. Systematically addressing inequality leads to my second point that intercultural policies lend themselves to rethinking the state. Indigenous activists throughout the region, but most successfully in Ecuador and Bolivia, have demanded a move away from the inextricable linkage between states and nations. Instead they envision states as plurinational entities that create the space for multiple cultural groups to develop along lines that conform to their worldviews and social practices as they negotiate a common way forward. This more radical approach to cultural difference leads to my third point. Intercultural demands are not responses simply to a passing political crisis but rather are symptomatic of a more profound civilizational crisis brought on both by the failure of dominant institutions to provide for the common good, and of a strained economic model predicated on the contradiction of infinite growth despite finite resources. The last section argues that because interculturality is a response to this civilizational crisis, it must be seen as a decolonial option for social reorganization. It is not just a call for Indigenous peoples to be engaged in dialogue about their participation in society. For that dialogue to be in any way meaningful, however, requires the more substantial project of dismantling what Anibal Quijano (2000) has called the colonial matrix of power. It is a fundamentally radical proposal that involves a broad re-conceptualization of the ways in which cultural groups interact with each other by removing Western norms and social structures from their places of privilege. It imagines, instead, a cultural system in which many ways of being in and understanding the world interact horizontally with each other.

UNDERSTANDING CULTURAL DIFFERENCE: IDENTITY AND INEQUALITY

States and societies throughout the region have struggled with various strategies to name and negotiate differences, with terms such as, *mestizaje,* pluricultural, multicultural, and intercultural surfacing most commonly[2]. Although these labels are often used interchangeably, they have different meanings and political implications.

After Independence from Spain, ruling elites throughout Latin America inherited colonial institutions, including identities defined by rigid racial and ethnic hierarchies. One of the challenges of new nation-states was to forge a unified national identity that differentiated them from their Spanish past while obscuring the social inequalities associated with the cultural diversity of the new countries. The discourse of *mestizaje*, which promoted an identity based on the combination of European and Indigenous cultural and biological traits, emerged as the ideological cornerstone to constructing new nations. Under the narrative of *mestizaje*, citizens of Ecuador (or Mexico, or Bolivia etc.) are mestizos: that is, people of mixed heritages. Although *mestizaje* tended to glorify and essentialize an Indigenous past as central to the construction of a new race, it also historically sought to erase cultural differences by inaccurately presenting the nation as an ethnically homogenous, modern, Euro-oriented whole. "Indians" as distinct and legitimate people, belonged in the past. Contemporary Indigenous people were easily marginalized, and *mestizaje* served to contain and normalize class and ethnic inequalities. It reified social, political, and cultural power by denying the existence of difference, proposing instead a new national sameness.

Recent struggles of the region's Indigenous and Afro-descendent populations have focused, therefore, on reclaiming ethnic differences within a cultural system dominated by an ideology of mixing. That is not to say that groups have not experienced a constant mixing of cultures. After five hundred years of contact it is impossible to point to an untouched "European," "Indigenous," or "African" culture that has remained uninfluenced by the others.[3] The fluid exchange and adaptation of information, discourses, practices, media, and commercial goods, have been well established and often referred to as the hybridization of Latin American cultures between multiple ethnic groups, epistemologies, and cultural systems. (García Canclini 1995, 2004; Telles and García 2013; Wade 2005; Wickstrom and Young 2014). While Indigenous and other marginalized groups often make strategic use of that *mestizaje* or hybridity as they attempt to position themselves in relationship to other groups, the critique of *mestizaje* concerns the ways in which states and elites deploy it as a discourse of power that obscures and reifies social inequalities.[4]

Throughout the nineteenth and twentieth centuries, as elites were extolling this combination of cultural legacies to construct a national identity, actually living Indigenous peoples were marginalized from participation in public life, and European-oriented practices and epistemologies dominated national development. After independence, Indigenous communities lost what little protection they had from the Spanish Crown, found their lands encroached upon, and their communities bonded in various sorts of debt peonage to increasingly large landholders as the white, European-descended *criollo* elite continued to occupy positions of economic, political, and cultural power. While recognizing and often glorifying the importance of past Indigenous peoples, the independent states relegated actually living Indigenous peoples to the role of savages and hyper-exploitable labor. *Mestizaje* developed as official state ideology through the twentieth century, as countries sought to overcome the many internal ethnic and class divisions that continually threatened the fabric of nationhood, by encouraging non-white and non-mestizo peoples to abandon their own cultural identities for a new, national *mixed* identity (Cervone 2010; Stolle-McAllister 2014). *Mestizaje*, therefore, became the means through which a singular national identity could be articulated in an environment of competing cultural frameworks, and like all totalizing discourses, it smoothed over and erased actually lived social and cultural heterogeneity.

Marilyn Grace Miller (2004) argues that *mestizaje* had "not solved problems of race and class in Latin America, but instead had compounded them by employing a rhetoric of inclusion that operated concurrently with a practice of exclusion" (4). Intercultural proposals challenge this misalignment of rhetoric and practice. Fidel Tubino (2002) summarizes:

> The exclusion of the original cultures from national projects was sidestepped through the theory of cultural mestizaje: national identity was presented as the result of the synthesis of Indigenous and Hispanic. It was, however, a synthesis that was never actually produced, but rather gave way to complex processes of superposition, hybridization, and linguistic and cultural diglossia.

> Because of that, a societal intercultural project necessarily implies reform of modern liberal democracies with the goal of making them *inclusive democracies*. Cultural democratization of national states does not imply their disappearance. Modern national states should reform themselves to be re-constituted in social spaces that practice tolerance and dialogue between cultures. That is, they ought to be pluralized (190).

Interculturalizing national states, therefore, represents a radical challenge in that modern states are fundamentally monocultural and uninational, and despite multicultural efforts at inclusion do not allow for other meaningful ways of being. Principally, they are founded on enlightenment notions of rationality, individualism, and capitalist development, to the meaningful exclusion of other symbolic systems, and have imposed themselves over a plurality of cultural systems that continue to exist within national territories. Tubino emphasizes that reformulating the state is neither an anti-modern project nor a nostalgic call for some idealized past that never existed. Rather, "what it rejects in modernization is its homogenizing Western bias. What is at stake, then, is the possibility of recreating modernity based on multiple traditions" (Tubino 2013, 618). Modernity and Western ideas, norms, and practices constitute part of the intercultural project, the object of which is to build new structures that allow for those cultural contributions to enter into a constructive dialogue with other cultural formations.

An important part of the struggle of the region's marginalized ethnic groups, therefore, has been to carve out a space in which cultural difference is extracted from mestizaje and recognized as an inherent part of national life. Naming and explaining cultural difference constitutes an important component of the struggle. The term pluricultural, for instance, is used to acknowledge that different cultural groups share the same national territory. It neither implies that states need do anything to accommodate minority groups, nor does it recognize any sort of imbalance between them. It is, however, an important first step in questioning the monocultural and universalizing discourses of modern states. In the case of Ecuador, the 1998 Constitution recognized the country as pluricultural. It was the first time in nearly two hundred years of independence that the state recognized the diversity of cultural groups in the country, thereby adding an implicit understanding that one did not need to be White-Mestizo to be fully Ecuadorian (Roitman 2009). While that recognition was important, it failed to meet the needs and desires of the country's Indigenous nationalities and Afro-descendent populations to be more equitably represented and integrated into a different kind of nation.

Multiculturalism seeks to push the process a bit further by fostering tolerance of other groups and, in liberal states, guaranteeing that individuals have the ability to express their rights as full members of society, regardless of ethnicity, gender, social class, sexual orientation, or membership in any other category through which people suffer discrimination (Kymlicka 2012). Fidel Tubino (2002, 181) argues that multiculturalism has its roots in North American disillusionment with the melting-pot model as a result of the civil rights struggles of the 1960s and 1970s. Despite changes in laws and social norms resulting from those movements, individuals continued to face discrimination and social exclusion based solely on their belonging to minority groups, and that real cultural, political, and power differences continued to exist between groups. US society did not form a singular, homogenous national culture even after the formal institutions of discrimination were dismantled. The primary discursive result of that process, therefore, was the elaboration of "tolerance" as the means through which different cultural groups ought to relate to one another. Tubino (2002, 181–182) distinguishes between negative tolerance, accepting people different than oneself in the interest of constructing a peaceful society, and positive tolerance attempting to understand the perspective of others from their viewpoint as two of the defining multicultural manifestations through which individuals navigate cultural diversity. Negative tolerance has generally prevailed in multicultural policies, resulting in attempts to eliminate discrimination of previously marginalized groups by providing (somewhat) preferential treatment, in the sense of affirmative action or quotas, to right past wrongs, and to encourage more complete integration into public life (Tubino 2002, 184).

Despite the normative improvement that multicultural tolerance brings to a situation of systematic discrimination, it has serious limitations. Although multicultural policies potentially improve the standard of living of victims of discrimination and promote better social relations, they often strengthen negative stereotypes even while they attempt to generate more opportunity for historically marginalized groups. By encouraging identification with one's group and tolerance of (but not necessarily true dialogue with) others, these policies tend to highlight barriers between groups. When combined with differential treatment for particular groups, these policies can lead to the creation of parallel societies rather than a society based on equal exchange. Peripheral groups, while being recognized by dominant institutions, remain peripheral and relate more to the center than to other peripheral groups, and often end up competing with each other for resources.

Multiculturalism, therefore, because it does not account for the power asymmetry of social relationships, also fails to create a viable framework for equality, mutual learning, and conviviality between groups (Herring and Henderson 2015). Edwin Cruz Rodriguez (2013, 26-30) notes that much multicultural theorizing comes from established liberal democracies and categorizes groups as majority and minority, based mostly on population numbers, and even further divides groups between immigrant groups and groups settled previous to European colonization. He argues, instead, that it is more helpful to analyze societies in terms of dominant and subaltern groups, which neither always correspond to relative population sizes, nor to time of arrival, nor to ancestral territorial claims. Liberal multicultural discourses, while providing space for cultural difference and paths to political power for "minority" groups, seek either the eventual assimilation, particularly of immigrant populations, to liberal norms, or the autonomy and *de facto* separation of native groups, unless and until individuals choose to abandon their cultural homes in favor of modern liberalism (Werbner 2012). There is no mechanism under multiculturalism for subaltern groups to engage dominant groups in an assessment and realignment of liberal values and culture, because liberal modernism *is* the end goal and the norm against which other worldviews must be judged.

Instead of challenging the power of the status quo, multiculturalism highlights and reifies social and cultural differences, often trivializing or folklorizing the cultural manifestations of subaltern cultural groups. Elite groups use multicultural discourse to incorporate and continue colonizing other ways of knowing and being rather than entering into meaningful dialogue with them because to do so would compromise their monopolization of epistemological, cultural, political, and economic power. Instead, nation-states generally have sought to recognize and assimilate cultural differences into existing systems of inequality through a series of multicultural initiatives that simultaneously recognize differences between cultural groups while ignoring the asymmetrical relationships between those groups. Multicultural policies often preach tolerance of difference and seek to highlight contributions of particular ethnic or cultural groups to the diversity of the nation, but they fall short of asking why some groups are more privileged than others in terms of access to economic, social, and cultural capital.

Because multicultural policies tend not to question the underlying power relationships between social groups, neoliberal policy makers have frequently relied on multicultural discourses as a means through which to implement their policies. By understanding exclusion to be mostly a product of ethnicity or other type of discrimination, multiculturalism attempts to incorporate those affected groups into the dominant political and economic system as individual citizens participating in the market. It is no coincidence that multiculturalism arrived in Latin America as part of the neoliberal restructuring of economic and political institutions in the 1980s. States and outside international organizations, like the World Bank or development NGOs, began recognizing cultural others and providing them with targeted development funds as a means to not only alleviate poverty but also to better incorporate them into the dominant economic model. These types of multicultural strategies could be lauded as inclusive as they recognize the particular situation of marginalized groups and attempt to assist them in overcoming material disadvantage through a certain amount of local control and input. These policies, however, as much as they might be a step in the right direction, do not address structural inequalities because they seek to incorporate marginalized groups *as distinct groups* into a system that is still based on inequality and exploitation of social differences. As money flows into projects and as groups compete for those funds, they often become demobilized from their efforts to create more profound change and transformation as the focus of development policies becomes competition within and between groups for resources.

Interculturality as a strategy of liberation and societal transformation, however, aims to transform the underlying inequalities so that different cultural groups can contribute to the ongoing processes of defining themselves and the social projects in which they wish to engage. Tubino (2013) characterizes these differences:

> Where multiculturalism aims to produce and produces parallel societies, interculturality seeks to produce integrated societies with symmetrical relations among different cultures. Multicultural policies avoid cultural confrontations (*desencuentros*). Intercultural policies promote the meeting (*encuentro*) of cultures. Multiculturalism promotes tolerance, interculturalism dialog. Multiculturalism does not eradicate prejudices and negative stereotypes that contaminate relations between different cultures. Interculturality seeks the eradication of the prejudices that are the basis of social stigmatization and cultural discrimination. Multicultural policies are affirmative action; intercultural policies are transformative action (617).

If multiculturalism hopes to generate respect for other groups and eventually incorporate them into the logic of dominant ones, interculturality seeks to find ways in which members of different cultural groups might engage in honest dialogue to create, from positions of equality and respect, new social, political, cultural, economic, and ecological structures.

The simplest definition of interculturality is a cultural exchange, not just the sharing of physical space of different cultural groups, but the free, equal, and open exchange of knowledge and practices between groups for their mutual benefit (Salazar Medina 2011, 116). Cruz Rodriguez (2013) similarly condenses the ideals of interculturality as "respect, conviviality, dialogue and mutual learning" (92).[5] Behind that simplicity, however, lays a complex web of historic inequalities and the conflation of culture and cultural group to produce the notion of unchanging social entities. As a process initiated by Indigenous and other marginalized groups, it has as a goal the reformulation of those structures of marginalization. Interculturality, therefore, becomes transformative in ways that multiculturalism cannot because, in seeking out truly mutual, dialogical relationships, groups and individuals must confront not only personal inequalities and prejudices, but also the social structures that construct and reproduce them (Aman 2014). Such a reflection requires both the repudiation of those structures and the creativity and insight garnered from conversation and debate between different cultural perspectives and experiences. This dialogue does not seek the fusion or mixture of cultures nor the incorporation of one into another, but rather is a creative process that allows for new visions, structures, and relationships that will ideally lead to the foundation of a new society.

Key to differentiating between these concepts is distinguishing between culture as a static thing, a set of inalterable, intrinsic components of individual and group identity, and that of culture as a dynamic process. Cultural groups do not exist as completely autonomous and unchanging entities. Interculturality, like the concept of culture itself, is a process through which meaning is created and social organizations constructed and reproduced, and as such it is not necessarily an achievable goal but rather a means to articulate concrete projects. Catherine Walsh

(2009) argues that rather than thinking of intercultural as an adjective to describe some definitive end, such as intercultural education or an intercultural state, it might be more effective to consider it a verb—to interculturalize education or to interculturalize the state. In fact, she warns that, "a danger arises when inclusion is simply assumed as the proposal or the goal...taking away its meaning as a project and process of continual negotiation and action. Interculturality is something to construct and not a goal to achieve" (C. Walsh 2009,142). Intercultural, therefore, is not just a descriptor of a diverse society nor is its aim the inclusion of marginalized groups into an otherwise asymmetrical system (C. Walsh 2009, 41). The goal of interculturality is to destabilize elite social constructs so as to break up the subordinate/dominant order that creates and enforces hierarchies among different ethnic groups (C. Walsh 2009, 55). This process, therefore, is not reducible to a mixture of cultures to provide for the best possible world, but rather is a dynamic process of creation that opens up new spaces and new projects aimed at decolonization and at creating numerous possible worlds.

Because interculturality challenges cultural hierarchies, it is not necessarily an easy or harmonious process. The ultimate goal might be a society in which decisions are made through dialogue rather than imposition, but because it is born from struggles over power and social inequality, the road to that goal is highly contentious. Unlike multiculturalism, intercultural critique recognizes the unequal distribution of power, and although it seeks ways to eliminate those inequalities, it must do so in conditions set by those already existing asymmetrical relationships. Intercultural dialogue, therefore, requires a continual confrontation of those social, economic, cultural, and personal inequalities.

These conflicts arise not just from disputes between cultural groups, but also from the difficulties associated with cultural change more generally. Since culture is a dynamic process, interculturality represents one of the ways in which cultures can change. One of the common misconceptions around interculturality is that it is an attempt of Indigenous people and others to somehow preserve or *save* their cultures. This attitude assumes that culture is a finite and definitive set of practices or beliefs that are unchanged through time. Of course, the opposite is true. Tubino (2013) reminds us that "cultures are conserved through change" (611), and that interculturality, therefore, is not about saving cultures, but about promoting a mutually respectful and beneficial dialogue between groups about transforming their social relations. Cultural identities are not autonomously constructed entities, but rather are "relational identities" (Tubino 2013, 612), always dependent on their relationship with and to other cultural groups. Noting that cultural exchange is a constant part of human interaction, Victor Hugo Torres (2011) argues that, "the concept of interculturality also alludes to the *meeting of cultures* that permits their mutual growth. In a certain way, interculturality always implies a loss and a gain, as there are many things that are both lost and gained in relationships between cultures" (29, emphasis in original). As such, because in pluricultural countries cultural groups are in constant contact with each other, there is an ongoing exchange of information and cultural discourses.

The dialogues and encounters of intercultural interactions, therefore, imply not only the manufacture of new projects, but also the transformation of those cultures that come into contact with each other. This process is certainly not new, as all cultures are constantly changing themselves and adapting to their interactions with others. What interculturality proposes, however, is to question and restructure the relationships of those interactions. Unlike multiculturalism, therefore, interculturality does not propose just the *inclusion* of minority groups, but rather the transformation of all cultural groups involved in that transaction. To propose that the recognition of difference or the inclusion of minority groups as the *goal* of interculturality (as multiculturalism often does) would be to misunderstand the processes of cultural change and ignore the power differential between groups. Such misunderstanding, while perhaps leading to somewhat more equitable opportunities, fails to promote profound change. Furthermore, by ignoring that cultural groups are effecting change on each other, multiculturalism facilitates the assimilation of the relatively weaker group into the more powerful one.

This need to better understand the ways in which cultural groups mutually influence each other leads Patricio Guerrero (2011, 78–79) to conclude that part of the intercultural process also involves an intracultural process in which members of cultural groups need to examine their own beliefs and practices as they evaluate how they are relatively positioned to other groups. Centuries of racialized hierarchies and systematic stigmatization of non-European languages, cultural practices, and social organizations have created deep mistrust between members of different cultural groups, as well as deeply entrenched internalized racism. In order for meaningful dialogue to occur, not only must individuals across cultures be able to see each other as equals, but also internalized beliefs about inferiority and superiority must be challenged and changed (De la Torre 2006). Because culture is always constructed relationally to others, ignoring the inequalities between groups and one's own position in those hierarchies of power serves only to perpetuate those inequalities and to subvert productive dialogue. Acceptance of others and the recognition of others' contributions to the construction of self allows for the foundations of equality that promote intercultural dialogue. Such dialogue among equals also means that all involved are aware and open to the changes and transformations that are necessary to create the kind of society that constantly seeks out equality among its members and an equitable distribution of material and cultural benefits. It requires understanding that no cultural group or tradition (majority or minority, dominant or subaltern) holds a monopoly on truth, and that devising solutions to the seemingly intractable problems that we mutually face requires the insights of all cultural traditions and the creative possibilities unleashed from that encounter.

Interculturality, therefore, is not an achievable goal (Altmann 2017; C. Walsh 2009). Not in the sense that a society based on mutual respect is impossible, but rather in the sense that interculturality itself is not the end but the means. It is the process through which as a human society we might tap into the wealth of knowledge and insight that can come from a mutually respectful exchange. That process itself may be at times painful as we recognize the physical and symbolic violence inflicted on groups and individuals in the name of civilization. It is also a difficult process not only because meaningful communication between different groups is often complicated, but also because that communication requires a constant challenge to the structures of inequality that govern our lives. Interculturality is contentious, therefore, because it provokes questions, discussion, debate, and doubts about the legitimacy of social relationships at both the personal and institutional level. However, by calling into question the ways in which we relate to each other it also opens up the possibility for fundamental transformation of those personal and institutional relationships.

CIVILIZATIONAL CRISIS

It is no coincidence that intercultural demands began appearing in Latin America (and elsewhere) in the latter part of the twentieth century. Although the term was first applied in the Andean region to bilingual educational programs for Indigenous children, it took on a decidedly political connotation in Ecuador, where the country's Indigenous organizations, led by CONAIE, placed their desire for an intercultural society plainly in the center of their calls for substantive reform in the country (Martínez Novo 2014). The timing and the geography of the articulation of interculturality as a political and epistemological discourse are indicative of a wider questioning of broader systems of accumulation, development, and division. The civilizational system, characterized by the historic and current marginalization of Indigenous and African-descendent populations, had itself entered into a series of related and seemingly unsolvable crises.

Speaking specifically of Bolivia, but applicable to the Andean region in general, Bolivian vice president and sociologist Alvaro García Linera

(2004) argues that the crises of the past generation represented the coinciding of both a short-term cycle rejecting the failings of the neoliberal state and a longer cycle witnessing the undermining of the colonial system in place for the last five hundred years. Anthropologist Arturo Escobar (2010a, 7–10) also describes a dual crisis of neoliberalism and modernity being expressed through the emergence of Indigenous and Afro-descendent organizing in the region during the late twentieth and early twenty-first centuries that resulted in two responses. The first, which he terms alternative modernizations, sought to end neoliberal hegemony but did not necessarily question the underlying logic of development. The second and more radical response was a decolonial one based on "different sets of practices (e.g. communal, indigenous, hybrid, and above all, pluriversal and intercultural), leading to a post-liberal society (an alternative to euro-modernity)" (Escobar, 2010a, 11). The faltering legitimacy of these systems and their apparent inability to reproduce themselves constituted a civilizational crisis that provided an opening through which different ideas and different ways of being might emerge.

The most immediate crisis has been that of neoliberalism. Proponents of neoliberalism sought to address the problems of economic stagnation and hyper-inflation taking root in the region in the late 1970s and early 1980s by integrating the region's economy more closely with the global market through the elimination of trade barriers, the reduction of state spending on social services, the weakening of labor rights, and the general subordination of public policy to private interests. Its focus on macro-economic growth and control of inflation resulted in certain successes, such as relative economic stability, increased foreign investment, and rapid growth in some segments of the economy, particularly those connected to export-oriented industries. Neoliberal political reforms also led to a certain decentralization of power and a rise in the acceptance of multicultural discourses, which opened up limited political space for historically subordinate groups. These relative successes, however, came at the cost of greater economic inequality, substantial decreases in public investment in infrastructure, public health, and education, the loss of national autonomy for internal markets, and the reprimarization[6] of much of the region's economy (Coryat and Lavinas Picq 2016). The dependence on mineral, petroleum, and monocultural agricultural extraction as the engines of economic growth exasperated social-environmental conflicts and continued the dislocation of historically marginalized communities. There have been lasting cultural repercussions also as neoliberal discourses repositioned people from citizens to consumers, from collectives to individuals, and subjected them to intense attempts at new articulations of identity, desire, and need.

Ecuador was no exception to this process. The round of economic crises that correspond most closely with the rise of the contemporary Indigenous movement and its calls for an intercultural reassessment of not just economic policies but more profound economic assumptions, can be traced to the collapse of the military-led petro-boom of the 1970s and subsequent neoliberal reforms of the 1980s. The flood of dollars into Ecuador in the 1970s, brought on by high oil prices, was also accompanied by an unsustainable rate of borrowing, generating real growth only in those sectors most closely linked to the oil industry (Gerlach 2003). The communities from whose lands the oil was being extracted were often left with environmental catastrophes, social conflicts, or cultural extinction (Acosta 2009; Sawyer 2004). In the highlands, Indigenous and other communities of small agricultural producers saw limited opportunities from two rounds of land reform and no real dividends from the country's oil boom. The return to civilian rule in 1979 was quickly followed by the collapse of world oil prices and the inability to make payments on the massive debt accumulated over the previous decade. Ecuador, like most of the rest of the continent, acquiesced to International Monetary Fund (IMF) mandates and undertook a series of reforms aimed at reducing the state, cutting social services, and reorienting its economy to large-scale export of not only oil, but also other natural resources and agricultural products. Although they temporarily stabilized the country's macroeconomic picture, these neoliberal reforms were most costly to the country's poorest sectors, which saw what little economic security they experienced fall quickly away. Over the next two decades, the neoliberal agenda exasperated the already large gulf of economic inequality as it forced ever-greater numbers of people into migration and wage relationships, resulting in an accelerated pace of individualization and atomization of communities (Sánchez Parga 2009).

As García Linera and Escobar suggest, however, the crisis of neoliberalism by the beginning of the twenty-first century was not only a turn in neoliberal economic policy, but also an existential crisis to the civilizational model imposed since the European Conquest. Despite adaptations over time, the model of economic development has been the colonial model of extraction of natural resources. Although neoliberal reforms sought to reinforce this model by extolling Ecuador's competitive advantages, the underlying logic remained the same since the Spanish began forcibly extracting gold from the Andes (Larrea 2006). As Pablo Ortiz-T (2011, 103) contends, this model has not only failed to address the problems of poverty globally, but also produced greater inequality and more poverty in areas heavily dependent on extraction. Development by means of exporting natural resources, whether it be oil, metals, or agricultural products, not only fails to substantially raise the standard of living of the communities producing those goods, but also forces them to enter into economic relationships based on wages and cedes control of their territories. These logics are in direct contradiction to the social relationships developed over generations based on reciprocity, complementarity, and solidarity. In this context, therefore, it is only logical that the country's Indigenous movement has been a clear and consistent voice against neoliberalism and economic imperialism because the models proposed by global and national elites were incapable of including them in meaningful ways.

The social and cultural resistance to neoliberalism/modernity is fueled not only by its failure to produce social equality, but also by the realization that the growth promised by capitalist development is predicated on endless exploitation of natural resources. The exploitation of those resources comes at increasing costs in terms of environmental destruction and social conflict (Acosta 2009). As those resources, particularly fossil fuels, rare earth minerals, and increasingly water become scarcer, the impossibility of endless accumulation becomes all the more evident. The list of environmental catastrophes in the making is virtually limitless, including mass extinctions and significant loss of biodiversity, rampant pollution of air and water sources, deforestation, global climate change, water and food scarcities, and the depletion of non-renewable resources. Just as with the inequalities highlighted by the seemingly perpetual economic crises, the expanding environmental crisis also has its most direct impact on the poor (Martínez-Alier 2003). Access to water supplies both for human consumption and crop irrigation becomes increasingly difficult to secure as aquifers are depleted, contaminated, and/or unequally captured by large agribusiness operations (Gaybor Secaira 2010, 54-56). Peasant farmers find themselves forced to push the agricultural frontier deeper into the forests and higher into the *páramos* (Coryat and Lavinas Picq 2016). The agenda of development and capital accumulation being advanced by dominant groups is both unsustainable and directly and immediately detrimental to the most marginalized social sectors.

The fields of contention, therefore, are not only economic, but also social, cultural, and epistemological. Eduardo Gudynas (2005) argues that Enlightenment thought, which forms the foundation of current dominant economic, social, and political practices, has constructed human beings as distinct from nature, with the latter viewed as a commodity to be dominated, controlled, and exploited for the advancement of human civilization. Nature, however, has limits, and industrial society is quickly approaching if not surpassing those limits of sustainability, raising the specter of our inability to reproduce current societies. This Enlightenment construction of nature, which is the foundation of modern political and economic power, is challenged not only by non-Western worldviews, but also by an increasing awareness throughout various social sectors that the present regime of resource extraction and human consumption is preventing ecosystems from replenishing themselves and creating an existential threat to human civilization (Gudynas 2016). Environmental and Indigenous groups, however, are engaged in an ongoing process of articulating oppositional discourses that place human beings as part of a complex natural system and that sees nature as a living entity and not something to be commercialized (Le Quang and Vercoutere 2013). These groups take aim not only at neoliberal regimes, but also increasingly at progressive governments as well, which continue to function under a developmentalist logic (Gudynas 2015; Moreno 2013; Oviedo Freire 2013; Stolle-McAllister 2015). They advocate not only a change in political leadership, but also a reshaping of the underlying symbolic systems that we use to make sense of the world.

This challenge to the dominant views of nature and development highlights a more general cultural crisis throughout our societies, but particularly in Latin America and Ecuador: namely, a challenge to the hegemony of a homogenizing, Eurocentric modernity. Escobar (2010a) understands modernity to be

> the kinds of coherence and crystallization of forms (discourses, practices, structures, institutions) that have arisen over the last few hundred years out of certain cultural and ontological commitments of European societies. [...] With the modern ontology, certain constructs and practices, such as the primacy of humans over non-humans (separation of nature and culture) and of some humans over others (the colonial divide between us and them); the idea of the autonomous individual separated from community; the belief in objective knowledge, reason, and science as the only valid modes of knowing; and the cultural construction of "the economy" as an independent realm of social practice, with 'the market' as a self-regulating entity outside of social relations (7).

The modern nation-state, steeped in this hegemony, as a product of European expansion and global domination, developed around the idea of a singular nation, internal heterogeneity notwithstanding, repressing other ontological systems. The political and cultural manifestation of modernity in Latin America became *mestizaje* through which elites were able to build political, economic, and cultural systems that, while recognizing superficial cultural differences, conformed to the underlying logics of modern, capitalist development, through the exclusion of other epistemological and organizational systems (Polo Blanco 2018). Development became normalized, as the economy and markets became reified entities around which human activity seemingly revolved. This process necessarily marginalized other ways of understanding and organizing human relationships with nature and with other human beings.

Indigenous and Afro-descendent movements pushed back against these homogenizing dynamics and demanded that their cultural practices and forms of social organization be respected and valued. Although there have always been different forms of resistance to and negotiation with assimilationist projects, the clear articulation of calls for local autonomy, and for dialogue between cultural groups as an alternative to acquiescence, points to a profound anxiety about the cultural premises of modern states. The proposals for plurinational states in Ecuador and Bolivia, for instance, strike at the heart of the homogeneity and universality espoused by modernity (Acosta 2015). Rather than accepting the racialized hierarchies upon which modern states are built, the defense of other types of organization, knowledge, and sociability signal instead a shift to horizontality and plurality as the basis for larger social constructions.

Finally, as would be expected, this constellation of crises is also intertwined with a profound political crisis. With the return of formal democracy to the region after the military dictatorships of the 1960s and 1970s (the military governments themselves, of course, indicated a serious political problem to begin with), traditional parties throughout the region slowly lost their legitimacy, resulting in various levels of political instability as the norm. In response, around the turn of the century a heterogeneous new left, populated to varying degrees by social-movement activists and disaffected professional politicians, democratically took power in most countries of the region (Barrett, Chavez, and Rodríguez Garavito 2008; Ellner 2014; Webber and Carr 2012)[7]. Ecuador was no exception to this trend. Since the return to democracy in 1979, the country's traditional political parties proved to be incompetent, as government changed hands between right-wing and center-left parties. Beginning in the 1990s political instability increased, as three consecutive elected presidents were forced out of office by popular protest, leading to ten different heads of state between 1995 and 2007, as well as the rewriting of the country's constitution in 1998 and 2008. This crisis in institutional continuity reflected the failure of elites to effectively represent the majority of the country's population, particularly in terms of cultural heterogeneity and economic inequality.

These interrelated crises can be viewed as an overall civilizational crisis in which the foundations of dominant society were being questioned as its basic institutions and premises lost legitimacy. Even progressive governments espousing decidedly anti-neoliberal rhetoric found themselves trapped in this web of civilizational crisis. Issues of representation are still murky with struggles between national plurality and unity, economies are still dependent on the export of natural resources, political legitimacy is always tentative, and environmental pressures continue to grow (Canelón Silva 2017; Coryat and Lavinas Picq 2016; Conaghan 2017; Postero 2017). Ultimately, these crises, individually and collectively, do not have a foreseeable, long-term solution because the economic, social, and political model of development predicated on unlimited growth and global hierarchies has not been substantially or meaningfully challenged. That is not to say that subaltern groups have (or ought to have) the answers or a coherent, comprehensive vision of what a different society might look like. Obviously, these communities themselves have also been formed in relationship to the same conditions and under the same dominant modes of control. Nevertheless, their calls for meaningful dialogue based on equality and on negotiation between different assumptions, perspectives, and epistemologies find an opening as the old models fail to produce the progress that they espouse.

At the same time, to be clear, crisis and alternatives do not mean that neoliberalism or Eurocentric modernity is simply disappearing or being wholly replaced by other models or other ways of living (Mignolo 2017). The intercultural challenge of subaltern groups, who are of course also products of coloniality and modernity, instead, is to decenter those dominant discourses. They propose different horizons, which may include parts of neoliberal and modern discourses and practices, but they place those discourses among a constellation of possibilities, rather than the preferable or even only end product of human civilization. The experiences, for instance, of even the most radical of Latin America's left governments of the early twenty-first century (Venezuela, Bolivia and Ecuador) suggest that reforms were often more radical in rhetoric than in practice. Post-neoliberal policies, for instance, might have sought to better distribute resources, but even the most socially committed governments were unable to break with neoliberal reprimarization, as they continued to be dependent on extractive practices and commercialization of natural resources on the world market in order to finance ambitious social programs (Estay 2018). They were contradictory and uneven responses, to be certain, but they also pointed to the weakening of dominant hegemonies in place since European expansion and conquest.

CHALLENGING THE COLONIAL MATRIX OF POWER

By proposing a genuine dialogue among cultural groups positioned as equals, based on acceptance of difference, respect, willingness to live with the other and open to mutual learning, proponents of interculturality also advocate a decolonial process. Interculturality represents a challenge to what Aníbal Quijano (2000) has dubbed the coloniality of power and corresponds to Escobar's (2010a) contention that, beyond post-neoliberal governments, some Latin American political actors are formulating post-development and post-capitalist projects. Intercultural propositions on equality between groups and competing world visions decenter Western modernity, opening the possibility of imagining different articulations

of what living well could and ought to be. Modernity posits one historically specific cultural formation (itself) as universal and as the natural
end product of human evolution, while subordinating, co-opting, or
attempting to erase other possibilities. By insisting on the rights of all
cultural groups to exist according to their own norms and participate as
equals in discussions and debates about a common future, interculturalists
seek to chart new forms of sociability that reject the hierarchies created
by colonialism and modernity.

Colonialism and modernity are inextricably linked. Without European
expansion into and control of the Americas, Africa, and Asia, European
modernity would have been very different. The historic circumstances that
gave rise to modern European states and the consolidation of capitalism
as the dominant mode of production and accumulation included the
appropriation of wealth from the Americas. This original accumulation
of modern capitalism not only financed European economic growth, but
also (combined with Europe's control over the (forced) labor market in
the Americas) allowed it to form a truly world economic system that
beat out all other competing models of production and accumulation.
Although history is replete with empires imposing their economic, social,
and cultural models on vanquished territories, for the first time, European
elites were able to create a truly worldwide system and constructed its
colonial/modern hegemony as the natural outcome of human history
(Quijano 2000, 533). It became a totalizing discourse that posited itself as
the logical and only pinnacle of human civilization.

This outward expansion was also accompanied by the consolidation
of the European states around the notion of a singular nationality.
Internal minorities were suppressed and alternative modes of production
eventually subordinated to capitalist production throughout the continent.
This internal homogenization accompanied these same states' expansion
into America (and then the rest of the world), where they enacted similar
strategies of delegitimizing cultural others and incorporating them into
a world economic and political system that they controlled. Although

European elites depicted modernity as inevitable, their ascendency was the direct result of particular historic circumstances and their ability to marginalize other ways of knowing and being in the world. Quijano (2000) insists that,

> modernity becomes divorced from the specific historic sequences that made it possible. In other words European modernity, which would only be possible with the colonization first of what is now Latin America, is seen as the norm and the only possible outcome of human history. This of course ignores other possible modernities, understood as innovation, scientific knowledge, etc. that could exist and does exist outside Europe (543).

The exclusionary ontology of European superiority and universality is the heart of the intercultural critique being promoted by Indigenous organizations.

Although colonialism, understood as the Spanish Crown's control over its Latin American territories, came to an end at the beginning of the nineteenth century (Cuba and Puerto Rico being exceptions to this time frame), formal independence did not bring an end to coloniality. Quijano describes coloniality as "the social classification of the world's population around the idea of race, a mental construction that expresses the basic experience of colonial domination and pervades the more important dimensions of global power, including its specific rationality: Eurocentrism" (2000, 533). Despite outlasting formal colonialism, these classifications form the foundation upon which hegemonic discourses function in the modern world. Following Quijano, Mignolo (2011, 8) elaborates that modern societies, despite presenting a face of progress and advancement, operate through a colonial matrix of power, which consists of control of the economy, political authority, gender/sexuality, and knowledge and subjectivity. Although the colonial matrix of power alters itself through time and contexts, it nevertheless continues to promote the centrality of European history and culture as the inevitable and natural culmination of human civilization, to the exclusion of all others.

The rise of capitalism and the world system was not just the imposition of economic domination; it also created forms of subjectivity and social categories. A key element in the consolidation of this power matrix was the fusion of economic exploitation and the worldwide classification of "races" of people. Colonial processes labeled people and positioned them within hierarchies of labor and power. In a similar process to the internal homogenizing processes going on in European states, colonial powers flattened out internal heterogeneity within the peoples they conquered. The diverse peoples of what was to become the Americas, for instance, became "Indians," even though they had very little in common with each other, except occupying space on the continent. Similarly, Africans captured from different cultural groups throughout that continent and sent as slaves to the Americas were simply "blacks." They were simultaneously stripped of their unique identities and repositioned as a different race of people. These differences, however, were also infused with inequality. Racial categories of labor were established and naturalized, with Europeans at the top as the natural beneficiaries of the work of the lesser races. "The Eurocentric version is based on two principal founding myths: first, the idea of the history of human civilization as a trajectory that departed from a state of nature and culminated in Europe; second, a view of the differences between Europe and non-Europe as natural (racial) differences and not consequences" (Quijano 2000, 542).

The superiority of Europe in terms of race, liberal values, and economic organization are posited as the cause of European superiority rather than the result of its imposition on others, and thus the legitimating reason to marginalize, exclude, and exploit those others. Positioning European and North American civilization as the end point of a universal historic trajectory leads over time to the notion furthered by modernization and development theories that the rest of the world, by imitating their more advanced counterparts, will someday catch up to them. This progression, of course, ignores that relative superiority in terms of economic advances are predicated on the continued exploitation of the global south. Relative impoverishment and prosperity are mutually constitutive and simultaneous processes, rather than simply lineal points on a universal trajectory.

The colonial matrix of power, therefore, although adapted over time and contexts, operates under the assumption, and strengthens the proposition, that European modernity is "naturally" superior to other forms of economic, social, and cultural organization, while obscuring the actual relationships between differently positioned groups in local and global hierarchies. Even the radical anti-neoliberal governments of early twenty-first century South America, for instance, framed their arguments and policies around a discourse of modernization and integration into the capitalist world market, believing that providing natural resources to meet the industrial needs of the capitalist machine would lead to "development." Although these governments sought to more equitably distribute the capital derived from extractive practices, the underlying logic was that improving the population's living standard was dependent upon adherence to developmentalist practices. A central part of that strategy is the exclusion of other ways of knowing and being in the world, which necessarily degrades local autonomy, excludes non-Western conceptions of the relationships between humans and nature, and marginalizes other conceptions of living well (Acosta 2012; Gudynas and Acosta 2011). Finally, multicultural discourse, as discussed earlier, while recognizing that certain groups have been excluded from the relative prosperity of modernity, seeks ways of integrating those groups into a system that still promotes European modernity, without reflecting "critically on the fact that those who are welcomed to be included may not necessarily want to play the game generously offered by those who open their arms to the inclusion of difference" (Mignolo 2011, 250).

Proposed by people on the margins of the colonial/modern system, transformative interculturality represents a challenge to the colonial matrix of power, by insisting first and foremost that all sectors of society have a right to engage in discussions as equals. Since inequality between groups in terms of power, economics, prestige, and acceptance of epistemological traditions is the founding point of coloniality, subjects speaking from the margins and insisting on equality represent a rejection of that foundation. The Indigenous movements have not only been historic leaders in the fight against neoliberalism, but also have a long history of resisting capitalism and other forms of colonial exploitation, often aligning themselves with the region's socialist and communist parties throughout the twentieth century (Becker 2008; Becker and Tutillo, 2009; Grey Postero and Zamosc 2005).[8] A demand for equality, therefore, necessarily must address the economic system that creates and enforces inequality. The second related sphere of the colonial matrix of power challenged by interculturality is that of authority. Proponents of interculturality look not only to state structures imposed and transformed over the centuries for the service of elites and the promotion of capitalist development, but also insist that local and ancestral authorities be recognized (Esteva 2015). There is a constant tension between liberal representative democracy and direct, communal democracy, and between individual rights and collective rights, which intercultural dialogue hopes to negotiate. Indigenous organizations have long advocated a plurinational approach to state construction as a means to decentralize authority by recognizing that diverse communities also have diverse forms of governance. Although not always foregrounded, the third sphere of the colonial matrix of power, definitions of gender roles and sexuality, also become points of debate under intercultural discussions. The systematic subordination of women, for instance, not only through colonial institutions, but also within Indigenous communities, is challenged not just by including women in discussions historically monopolized by men, but also by making visible the ways in which excluding women's concerns and identities form part of the overall system of control and oppression. Finally, interculturality challenges colonial/modernity's monopoly on epistemic production by insisting that Western ways of knowing are some of many, and that no single cultural system has all of the answers to society's problems.

Interculturality becomes a decolonial process because it proposes an open-ended dialogue involving all cultural groups. Proponents seek to decenter dominant groups by making visible the racial, class, and gender hierarchies that they employ to maintain power. It is this more radical critique of the mechanisms of power that distinguishes the intercultural project from the multicultural one, as it challenges not just the exclusion of certain groups, but more importantly the logic behind their exclusion. Mignolo defines decoloniality as "both the analytic task of unveiling the logic of coloniality and the prospective task of contributing to build a world in which many worlds will coexist" (2011, 54). Interculturality, therefore, is decolonial precisely because of its insistence on negotiating between cultural groups, which it repositions as equal and mutually constitutive. Indigenous knowledge systems and cultural practices, therefore, are not somehow lagging Western ideas, practices, and knowledge on some universal, evolutionary scale, but exist alongside them.

Involvement in intercultural dialogue recognizes that initiatives do not come from any one particular social group, but from the interaction among all groups. The dominant logic that created systems of inequality will not solve the problems of inequality. Likewise, although Indigenous, Afro-descendent, mestizo-peasant and worker, women's and other systematically oppressed groups offer insightful critiques to the systems that oppress them, the solutions to those problems do not necessarily come only from subaltern groups. Catherine Walsh (2009) argues instead that interculturality could nourish and orient a new reality that seeks out "relationality and complementarity" between the various subaltern and dominant groups, rather than looking for the predominance of any one particular tradition (18). As a process of social construction, interculturality seeks to include all social sectors in a diverse and plural project, rather than a multitude of parallel (or contradictory) projects and processes. Guerrero (2011) imagines this new social project as

> constructing an intercultural justice, an intercultural university, an intercultural education. This process starts from an intracultural affirmation, of a revitalization of their own cultures, of their cosmos of differentiated meaning, but that nevertheless has the

capacity to dialogue with difference, to seek out which aspects of justice and education will mutually enrich us and contribute to peaceful conviviality with this difference (83).

Since no cultural group possesses answers to all social problems, looking only inward in attempts to find those answers only serves to fall into the dominant, colonial pattern of racial and ethnic division. Rather, Guerrero suggests that from a standpoint of intracultural self-knowledge and confidence, all members of society have a right and responsibility to participate in dialogue toward creating more equitable and sustainable relationships.

This discussion, importantly, must also include the contribution of dominant social sectors if it is to advance. All too often, interculturality is seen as an Indigenous or Afro-descendent project, but that implies neither a critique of dominant cultural assumptions nor the recognition of the privilege that "universal" knowledge and "natural" social hierarchies confer on particular groups at the expense of others. By insisting on the broad need for participation, proponents of interculturality expose the ideological and epistemological power structures that reproduce the still-existing social inequalities founded in European colonization of the continent. Furthermore, it holds out that Western modernity also has important contributions to make to an intercultural society. Because it makes visible the logics of coloniality and the universalizing of a particular type of modernity, interculturality hopes to decenter Western modernity, locating it, instead, as one of many different ways of approaching the world. It opens up what Arturo Escobar (2010a) classifies as "alternatives to modernity" that might de-naturalize the hegemonic tropes of economic, social and cultural domination (47).

Institutionalizing Interculturality and Radical Localness

What role should interculturality play in institutionalizing social change? Corresponding to social movement pressure and the interest of political actors, the constitutions of both Bolivia (2006) and Ecuador (2008) explicitly describe their societies as intercultural and seek to define the common good along those lines by recognizing the historic exclusion of Indigenous and other cultural groups and providing them with means to participate in a restructured state. While this recognition is an important step toward creating the groundwork for a more equitable society, articulating interculturality as part of an official ideology raises questions about the ability for marginalized groups to continue advocating for different relationships or their "alternative modernities." As minority groups increasingly interact with the modern state, how do they maintain their autonomy? Modernity writ large is adept at assimilating other cultural and political formations without conceding its overall logic and its support of capitalist/developmentalist discourses and practices (Mignolo 2011). While institutional space is opened, however, it is important to continue to pay attention to what Philipp Altmann (2017) refers to as "radical localness:" the meanings and practices that comport to local logics and experiences. This localness, of course, is composed also of national and global discourses with which people interact but, by keeping discussions of interculturality grounded in what people want and understand based on their position within various webs of meaning, the ability of dominant discourses to assimilate others is reduced. Interculturality demands this balancing of institutionalization without losing sight of variability of local experiences.

The decolonial horizons pointed to by intercultural theory and practice raise two critical questions about the possibility and potential problems of institutionalizing interculturality. The first set of questions stems from the almost utopian vision of a decolonial society. How does it serve as a guide for people to implement concrete change? How do groups and individuals negotiate the aspirations of a more equal society with the structural impediments beyond their control? How (or do) individuals from subaltern groups avoid assimilation into dominant ways of life as they interact with and begin to occupy positions within modernity's institutions? The second set of questions has to do with the state's attempt to institutionalize interculturality. What are the dangers of having a critical discourse become part of the state's ideological apparatus? Even in the hands of a progressive government, does it lose its transformative potential? The implications of having national states adopt an intercultural discourse without necessarily fundamentally changing the dominant logics of capital accumulation and development are problematic, as some of the contradictory and controversial development policies carried out by the governments of Rafael Correa and Evo Morales would suggest (Acosta 2015; Conaghan 2017; Postero 2017).

Outside of perhaps fringe fundamentalists, no one is advocating an impossible return to a mythical past, untouched by change and innovation. Indeed, intercultural aspirations call for using elements of all cultural groups, including those of Western modernity, to forge a different way of understanding and being in the world. The challenge is in creating alternative modernities that allow individuals and groups to participate fully in the contemporary world without having to sacrifice their own unique identities and practices. These alternatives are based on the multiple traditions that comprise the actually lived experiences of pluricultural societies and represent significant challenges. Being Kichwa in the early twenty-first century, for instance, is not the same as being an Indian in the early twentieth century. But, full participation in the twenty-first century does not necessarily mean having to forgo being Kichwa. It is possible, as one young transnational traveller from Otavalo noted, to be "a *runa, a wambra* and a *reggaenotero* at the same time" (Runakuna 2007, 34)[9]. Identities and communities are always relational and not pre-determined, static entities; therefore the type of modernity that interculturality promotes would be fluid.

As intercultural theorists point out, however, cultural groups are not on a level playing field and therefore need to work toward equality. In the meantime, however, those powerful global discourses of development and consumerism, which create desires for goods and a particular way of being, influence Indigenous communities as well, making the dialogue between cultures ever more complicated. The continued reality of diglossic language and cultural arrangements that exist in Ecuador and throughout the region highlight that, despite the substantial gains of Indigenous and Afro-descendent movements, the struggle for equality is still very much an unfinished project. Tubino (2013), however, argues that "cultures are not what they are, but rather what they become; they do not posses a timeless essence that must be 'saved' from external influences. They are temporal, changing realities in process; change is their essence" (611). As change occurs, therefore, the intercultural process is not necessarily the preservation of Indigenous culture, which like all cultures is in a constant state of change. Rather, it calls for the repositioning of subjects in asymmetrical relationships, so that those from subordinate positions are able to defend themselves from "passive assimilation" (Tubino 2013, 611), to be active participants in the co-creation of their worlds.

The current situation provides two substantial challenges, then. First, there is an internal struggle of some marginalized people in relationship to hegemonic discourses, and the danger of being "willingly" assimilated or colonized into the dominant worldview and practices. This dynamic represents a very different threat than the forced assimilation of earlier generations, where institutions obligated people to change names, dress, language, and social organization as a means of enforcing hierarchical differences. Today, as individuals willingly participate in social spaces demarcated by national and transnational discourses and express desire for consumer goods and ideas from around the world, it becomes difficult to point to that which makes groups different. The homogenizing effect of transnational capitalism and culture is seductive, and its effects on local cultures are not always clear.

The second challenge continues to come from without, from the state adopting and co-opting the discursive space that interculturality carves out for subaltern participation. Once a state officially adopts intercultural, plurinational discourses as official policy and guiding principles, do those discourses lose their critical edge? If state officials, as they did in Ecuador and Bolivia, use the language of social movements and purport to promote interculturality, are they actually agents for the kinds of radical change that activists are demanding or do they simply occupy those discursive spaces and resignify those concepts with meanings and practices more akin to neoliberal's deployment of multiculturalism? Do they become new methods to manage cultural diversity and to promote capitalist development? Are they, in a sense, managing diversity?

Ecuador's 2008 Constitution represented a sea change in conceptualizing the state (Acosta 2015; Barié 2014; Becker 2011b). Among other important contributions, the constitution recognizes Ecuador as intercultural and plurinational and names the Andean philosophical framework of *Sumak Kawsay* as a means of rejecting developmentalist ideologies and of founding a different way of conceptualizing the common good (Gudynas 2011; Radcliffe 2012; Weston and Bollier 2014). Furthermore, the constitution makes explicit mention of Indigenous collective rights, territory, governance, education, and justice (González 2015; Lupien 2011). The implementation of that agenda, however, was uneven as the state continued to depend on extractive and export-driven models of development. At the same time, social movements, particularly the Indigenous and environmental movements, found it increasingly difficult to organize as the state appropriated many of their discourses and arguments, and the Correa administration increasingly suppressed dissent of organizations that it did not control.

From a theoretical perspective, incorporating a contentious discourse like interculturality into state institutions ought to give pause. Intercultural theorists are clear that, in order to create an intercultural society, state structures need to be drastically reorganized. The political and economic systems left by colonialism and liberalism are simply incompatible with the sustenance of diversity and the open dialogue needed to create more equitable relationships. Along those lines, the Indigenous movement in Ecuador (and elsewhere) has argued consistently for the creation of a plurinational state in order to allow them to participate as full citizens without having to abandon their own cultural heritages (Becker 2012; Salazar Medina 2011). With the 2008 Constitution, it would appear that the movement won an important victory in that effort. However, unfulfilled promises left the movement in a difficult position in terms of how to best frame their arguments, when at a superficial level they have already won the debate. The risk, therefore, is that the state appropriates the discourse of interculturality without actually promoting the processes of fundamental change needed to carry out the difficult and at times conflictive dialogue between and among cultures (Martínez Novo 2014). Does declaring one's government or state "intercultural" become a way of avoiding conflicts and governing from the perspective that equality already exists (when, of course, it does not)?

This strategy would vacate interculturality of its contentious potential and its ability to critique state and economic structures. Like all cultural discourses, interculturality is vulnerable to appropriation by groups in power to demobilize dissent and to justify continued oppression and inequality. Shortly after the implementation of the 2008 Constitution, Guerrero (2011) pointedly argued that interculturality

> as an expression of struggle for the life of people subjected to domination is now usurped by power [] with the goal of depoliticizing the political, liberating, insurgent and decolonizing meaning that interculturality has, and transform it into an instrumental concept, necessary to manage the difference of the other and include it in its civilizational project (77).

From a symbolic perspective, therefore, tying the concept of interculturality to a state project runs the risk of the state appropriating the argument of interculturality without actually committing itself to the fundamental and difficult processes of change that its proponents promote. Rather, while leaving some spaces of debate open, declaring a state to be intercultural closes many other spaces of dialogue as it asserts that interculturality has already been achieved, leaving the debate at the formal recognition of difference, the encouragement of respect, and incorporation into a system that is still based on profound inequalities (Ramón 2011). It becomes another manifestation of liberal multiculturalism, while obscuring the term and discourse from those advocating more radical change.

Intercultural processes bring to the fore tensions about adapting cultural change in the face of assimilationist pressures. Through their struggle for rights and recognition and their articulation of a different kind of society, Indigenous activists have provided a foundation upon which broader discussions about not just inter-group relationships, but also a potentially new civilizational project might be built. This project is also very much dependent not only on just subaltern groups adjusting to dominant ones, but also on dominant groups questioning their own common-sense understanding of their culture and their relationships to power. Interculturality—that is the process of seeking out equality, coexistence, and mutual learning in the service of creating a more just and sustainable society—is a project that ultimately requires the interrogation of both individual attitudes and the systems that created and depend on the domination of some groups over others.

It also suggests that the point of entry into inquiries of interculturality ought to be at the level of local experience. There is no singular cultural experience of any group. The multiplicity of the ways in which Indigenous people engage with and create their modernities and their worlds is essential toward understanding the intercultural process. It is not just an attempt to transform social and political institutions but part of the complicated ways in which people engage the heterogeneous and unequal cultural terrains in which they find themselves. To (partially) avoid the colonial logic that flattens out difference and conforms knowledge to the parameters of modernist thought, it is essential to try to build knowledge from the non-conforming perspectives of the margins.

NOTES

1. See Nancy Postero's *The Indigenous State: Race, Politics, and Performance in Plurinational Bolivia* (2017) for an in-depth account of how this process developed in Bolivia.
2. These terms, and variations of them, are used differently in different academic traditions. My usages are derived from US and Latin American terminology. Many European scholars for instance use the term "interculturalism" in a similar manner as I use the word "pluriculturalism" and/or superficial multiculturalism.
3. The possible exception to this would be, of course, the very few remaining uncontacted peoples of the Amazon.
4. See Stolle-McAllister (2005) for a critique of theories of hybridity and a discussion of the contingent ways in which social movements construct their own *mestizajes* and hybridities in their struggles with states and other powerful interest groups.
5. See Cruz Rodriguez (2013) for an in-depth critique of liberal multiculturalism, particularly as conceived by Canadian political philosopher Will Kymlicka, as a creation of Northern, liberal democracies with difficult translation to the Latin American context. In particular, Cruz Rodriguez takes exception to Kymlicka's assertion that "minorities," while maintaining their rights to cultural difference, must ultimately accept the ground rules of liberalism.
6. Reprimarization refers to a country returning to the export of primary materials as a main source of foreign revenue, reversing trends toward diversification and industrialization.
7. By 2015, that trend had largely shifted back to the right throughout the region.
8. They broke with the Marxist parties in the mid- to late-twentieth century when those parties began to insist too much on the class orientation of Indigenous communities at the expense of their cultural distinctiveness.
9. *Runa* is Indigenous person and *wambra* is young man in Kichwa.

CHAPTER 3

INTERCULTURAL POLITICS IN OTAVALO AND COTACACHI

Together with the right to elect goes the right to be elected.
—Santiago Ortiz (2012, 205)

Auki Tituaña, the first Kichwa mayor of the northern town of Cotacachi (1996–2009), explained that part of being Indigenous in the twenty-first century means "to have the responsibility of having survived 500 years of genocide, to preserve and use our ancestral knowledge to make the present and the future more fair and free for everyone" (Interview, Cotacachi, May 29, 2007). This observation highlighted an important discourse of contemporary Indigenous activists: namely, that because of their historic marginality, they were uniquely positioned to contribute to wider debates about democracy, rights, development, and sustainability not *just* for Indigenous peoples but for *all* Ecuadorians. Indigenous communities, leaders, and intellectuals have been protagonists in the politics of Cotacachi and Otavalo, over the course of the latter half of the twentieth century into the twenty-first. Employing the tactics first of everyday resistance, then to open rebellion against discrimination and marginalization, and finally to winning, democratizing and modernizing local state institutions, their struggle simultaneously constructed political subjectivity for Indigenous peoples and transformed the political culture of the wider society. At its heart, the political process headed by Indigenous people in the region has been an intercultural endeavor. Alliances with Mestizo allies, intra-ethnic heterogeneity, and negotiations with the national state over resources and decision-making procedures all characterized the era of Indigenous municipal leadership of the turn of the century.

The cantons of Otavalo and Cotacachi, located in the southern part of Imbabura Province and headed by eponymous cities, consist of highly heterogeneous populations of both rural and urban, Mestizo and Indigenous inhabitants. Otavalo's 2014 population was approximately 115,700 people of which about 55% were Indigenous, and 57,000 lived in the city. Cotacachi had approximately 42,800 people, of which 37% were Indigenous and 7,500 resided in the city (AUC 2010; INEC 2014). The Indigenous population primarily occupied the countryside and consisted mostly of Kichwa-Otavalos in both Otavalo and Cotacachi. Several Kichwa-Kayambi communities, however, also lived in the southern part of Otavalo, and Kichwa-Natabuelas and Kichwa-Karankis resided to the north in Antonio Ante and Ibarra. Both cities experienced an influx of Indigenous people, and Kichwas represented a majority of the urban population of Otavalo. One third of the rural territory was in the hands of small landholders, who owned on average 2.9 hectares in Cotacachi and 1.7 hectares in Otavalo. Most of these lands were in private hands, and titled to individuals and families (Ortiz Crespo 2012, 112).

Although Otavalo and Cotacachi represent a core area of the national Indigenous movement, are located next to each other, and share many common characteristics, they also have very different histories and different paths towards Indigenous empowerment and intercultural policies. The canton of Otavalo revolves around its famous market city, which has become a hub of activity for local agricultural and artisan producers who bring their goods to market for both local consumption and for the important tourist market. Over the past several generations, Otavalos have built up effective textile, handicraft, music, and tourist industries, enriching some families, employing many more, and creating a network of merchants and community members spread throughout the country and around the world (Atienza de Frutos 2009; Colloredo-Mansfeld 1999; Kyle 2000; Maldonado 2004; Sobczyk and Soriano Miras 2015a). Although this process contributed to social stratification among community members, wealthier families also effectively used some of their profits to improve standards of living and invested in the revitalization of local cultural events. Some Kichwa families also "re-took" the city of Otavalo by systematically purchasing land and businesses in the city and in the process became the dominant economic force, as well as the demographic majority. While Cotacachi also profited somewhat from its neighbor's successes in textile production and tourism, its economy continued to be based primarily in subsistence campesino agriculture, leather production, and, increasingly, agribusiness in the form of flower *haciendas*, which employed large numbers of day-laborers. There was some Kichwa migration to the city of Cotacachi, but Mestizo families still dominated the urban areas. Like their rural counterparts in Otavalo, declining plot size made subsistence agriculture precarious as a means of maintaining a family and most families were also dependent on wage labor from the flower plantations, commerce, and construction work in nearby cities.

Despite these differences, Kichwa political activists and intellectuals held the office of mayor of Otavalo from 2000–2014 and Cotacachi from 1996–2014. This era represents an important step in the Indigenous movement's struggle for inclusion and participation, as it broke with the exclusion of the colonial and republican eras that explicitly subordinated Indigenous communities to Mestizo political leadership. It was also a logical step in the organizing history of both areas as the movement transitioned from demands for land, recognition, and an end to discrimination toward making concrete proposals about inclusive development, modernization, and sustainability. Symbolically and institutionally, therefore, governing these municipalities represented the Indigenous incursion into the heretofore Mestizo urban strongholds to institute policies geared toward the benefit of greater numbers of the region's inhabitants. Taking power and governing in both cantons depended on cross-ethnic and cross-class alliances, and the challenges of governing, while building and maintaining those multicultural coalitions, also brought to the fore historic and ideological differences within the regional Indigenous movement.

Mayors Mario Conejo, in Otavalo, and Auki Tituaña and Alberto Anrango, in Cotacachi, did not win their respective elections based only on smart campaigns, but rather as part of the local trajectory of political contention. They all had long activist histories defending the rights of local Kichwa people and promoting alternative spaces for Kichwa voices. Conejo and Tituaña, in particular, also brought academic experience and reputations for efficiency and transparency. Certainly their victories and successes were based, at least in part, on ethnic affinity and the desire of Indigenous organizations and networks to see their representatives in office. They were also very much dependent on their abilities to persuade not only Indigenous but also Mestizo voters that they would oversee the implementation of development projects that met the needs and desires of the electorate.

HISTORIC NETWORKS OF LOCAL POWER

National and local states are not monolithic, a-historic constructions, but rather are historically situated and multi-layered networks of individuals and organizations with both complimentary and competing agendas. The multiethnic, although predominantly Kichwa, region of Otavalo and Cotacachi is no different. Although certainly transformed and adapted over time, until the end of the twentieth century the local power structure was fundamentally colonial, built on the city's racialized domination of the countryside. Indigenous abilities to resist and challenge that order ebbed and flowed over years, but it was not until the late 1990s that they were able to effectively challenge Mestizo control of their communities. Neoliberal decentralization, coupled with the fortification of the Indigenous organizations and networks founded in the 1960s, provided the opportunity for Kichwa activists and politicians to mount effective electoral campaigns. As the national movement challenged the legitimacy and effectiveness of traditional political parties, local politicians built inter-ethnic alliances with progressive Mestizos and won municipal-wide elections. These victories served not only as an effective channel to help meet material demands of Kichwa communities, but also an important symbolic victory against the colonial legacy of governing institutions.

The history of local power in the region is one of constant negotiation and imposition between Indigenous communities, the state (both colonial and republican), and local White and Mestizo elites. Tanya Korovkin (2001, 44) explains that colonial authorities ruled in part through traditional Indigenous leaders, *curacas*, by exchanging limited territorial control and political prestige for submission to the Crown. Since this arrangement meant that Indigenous leaders depended on the colonial state, they had little autonomy. With Independence, the new republican leaders constructed a liberal state built on private property and individual rights, which, of course, were extremely limited in the case of Indigenous people, who at best were viewed paternalistically and at worst as savages needing to be properly civilized. The new state eliminated colonial Indian tribute but attempted to consolidate power by curtailing the vestiges of semi-autonomous Indigenous jurisdictions, subordinating their authority to the national state, and making communally-held land available to private interests.

As in colonial times, power emanated from the urban strongholds. White-mestizo voters elected provincial, canton, and parish leaders. Governors, appointed by the central government, named political bosses (*jefes políticos*) in the cantons, who appointed their representatives (*tenientes políticos*), always Mestizos, to maintain law and order, collect taxes, and oversee compulsory and unpaid Indigenous labor for public projects in the surrounding rural areas. Because literacy in Spanish was a requirement to vote until the late 1970s, Indigenous communities were effectively excluded from any formal representation. Korovkin (2001) argues that during the nineteenth and early twentieth centuries, Indigenous communities, despite being able to "preserve and reconstruct many of their local cultural practices, ... effectively lost the right to manage their affairs within the communal boundaries without obtaining in return a right to participate in national politics" (45). Local communities were politically controlled by outside powers, but Indigenous individuals were not conferred with rights of citizenship or representation in the national arena.

The Otavalo Valley was little different from the rest of Ecuador. Politically connected Mestizo families, based in the cities of Otavalo and Cotacachi, controlled the institutions of power and used them to extract wealth from Indigenous communities through both institutional and extra-institutional coercion. The *jefes* and *tenientes* collected taxes and fines, compelled free labor for public works projects, and assisted the Church in collecting its tithe from the communities' harvests. They also dealt harshly with dissent by imposing fines and employing violence where necessary to ensure compliance. Because Indigenous communities had little recourse to national state institutions, and no effective way of pressuring local governing structures, they were marginalized from power with scant recourses to enact meaningful change.

Two interventions into the lives and livelihoods of rural, Indigenous peoples by the populist-nationalist state in the twentieth century began to weaken, perhaps inadvertently, these local power structures. The first, the 1937 *Ley de Comunas* (Law of Communes), recognized community institutions and established the legal framework for the *cabildos* (community council) and assemblies through which communities could govern themselves. Communal assemblies, composed of all members of the community, became the ultimate authority and selected a *cabildos* with a president, vice-president, treasurer, secretary, and other officers who organized mingas and other projects. These positions, or charges, were democratically selected and rotated between community members although, historically, more powerful families often dominated them. Besides organizing local work projects, the *cabildos* and community presidents also mediated inter-communal disputes and represented the community to other communities and to outside entities like government agencies and NGOs. This structure also established direct links between communities and the central government, creating channels around the local bosses to demand redress for various grievances, particularly protection of their lands from expansion-minded *haciendas* (Guerrero and Ospina 2003). The *Ley de Comunas*, of course, did not end oppression in the countryside, nor were its protections uniformly enforced, but what was intended to be a mechanism through which the state would assimilate the Indigenous population ironically became a means through which Indigenous communities strengthened their identities and constructed the organizational building blocks that would later help them assert more of their rights.

Over the years, Indigenous people organized increasingly dense networks through the *comunas, cabildos, juntas de agua* (water governing boards), and *organizaciones de segundo grado* (second degree organizations, OSG). These entities brought together various local and regional organizations around cultural celebrations, production cooperatives, education initiatives, and other aspects of everyday life in a process that Rudi Colloredo-Mansfeld (2007) has characterized as "vernacular statecraft," a replication of state functions without direct control of the state. These types of organizations became the means through which communities sought to protect themselves and advance their agendas: particularly, to increase their access to land, to end discrimination, to win recognition of their cultural distinctiveness, and eventually to exercise their rights as full citizens. By mediating between the state and local concerns as well as creating networks between communities, the *comunas* became the foundation of the movement for rights that gathered steam beginning in the 1960s and formed an integral part of the national movement of the 1990s.

The second "modernizing" effort of the state were the two rounds of land reform (1964 and 1973) aimed at breaking up large, inefficient landholdings by pressuring landowners to either make their lands more productive or face their expropriation and devolution to Indigenous people living and working on the *haciendas*. Ortiz Crespo (2012, 109–110) reports that, in the Otavalo/Cotacachi area, sixteen *haciendas* were "intervened" as a result of land reform while others were parceled out or modernized. Despite these reforms, however, by the early twenty-first century there were still high levels of inequality in the region, with only one-third of the land and ten percent of the water resources in the hands of small landholders (less than 20 hectares) (Ortiz Crespo 2012). Even if the land reforms were minimally effective in actually redistributing land, the struggle for claims and titling became key points of contention for the Indigenous movement through the 1980s and 1990s.

Prior to land reform, Indigenous communities for the most part had one of two types of relationships with the *haciendas* that dominated rural life. One was *huasipungo*, under which community members received a plot of land, along with use of water and firewood, in exchange for working on the owner's land. In theory, workers were to be compelled to work no more than four days a week and were to be financially compensated for other work; in practice, workers had few rights and were for all intents and purposes eternally indebted to the landowner. Indigenous workers were unable to accumulate their own capital, which meant they could not leave and had scant prospects of improving their material lives. The second kind of relationship to the *hacienda* was *yanapa*. Under *yanapa*, families owned their own plots of land and worked a certain number of days for the local *hacienda* in return for the use of water, forest products, and pasturelands (Ibarra 2010, 420–421). Just as with the *huasipungeros*, the *yanaperos* also shared a paternalistic relationship with the *hacendado*, who was sought out for loans, offered gifts at festival time, and was asked to be godfather and sponsor of children, weddings, and other important life events. As David Kyle (1999, 434) notes, the relationship was as much ideological as it was economic because it established and reinforced the hierarchies between Indigenous peasants and wealthy White-Mestizo landholders.

Although an exploitative relationship, the *yapaneros* at least had the possibility of developing skills beyond subsistence agriculture and of accumulating capital through the manufacture and sale, particularly in Otavalo, of textiles and handicrafts. These Indigenous campesinos were also able to buy lands from Mestizo landlords when they became available from the land reform or from pressure by Indigenous communities from within the *hacienda*. They were also able to acquire lands from other Indigenous small landholders as the opportunities arose. This difference between these community-*hacienda* relationships would play a substantial role in how the communal organizations and politics of Otavalo and Cotacachi developed, as most of the Indigenous communities around Otavalo were characterized by *yanapa*, while those around Cotacachi were *huasipungo*. As the political boss and the *hacienda* system slowly began to break down beginning in the 1960s, the former *yapaneros* were in a position to take advantage of their increasing capital accumulation to buy land and to invest in the textile, tourist, and handicraft industries. This social stratification would lead to some cleavages within the movement but also helps to account for the different trajectories developed by the movements in Otavalo and Cotacachi.

Land disputes were perhaps the most tangible and pressing aspect of the struggle in both locales, but they were also seamlessly intertwined with more widespread calls for the recognition of civil, political, social, and cultural rights of the area's Kichwa communities. In her classic study of Otavalo of the late 1960s and early 1970s, for instance, Gladys Villavicencio (1973) observed that the Indigenous communities remained tied to their land even as they were beginning to occupy spaces in the urban sector and economy, and that they "want integration into national life, but as a differentiated ethnicity, with equal rights and obligations, with a recognition of the values of their own culture and a desire and consciousness of the freedom decide their own future" (284). The connections between land disputes and the right to own land, with all of the economic, social, and cultural implications that entailed, were never far from calls for recognition of difference and the right to participate in national society as equals to, but at the same time different from, the national Mestizo norm. As individuals moved into the cities, Otavalo in particular, they did not sever their ties to their rural communities, keeping land disputes intimately connected with struggles for political participation and cultural rights. These skirmishes for rights and recognition took place in the markets, demanding fair prices for Indigenous producers; on the buses, where Indigenous riders refused to ride in the back; in public spaces, where Indigenous people demanded the right to wear their native attire and to not defer to Mestizos by stepping off the sidewalk; and in the schools, where demands for bilingual education and the right to full participation became increasingly vocal. Although at times the struggle adopted different postures depending on the political contexts and the immediate actors, land and culture, economic opportunity and political equality were always interconnected.

Otavalo's Cultural Activists: Campesinos and Intellectuals

In Otavalo, as elsewhere in Ecuador, Kichwa networks of political power developed around resistance to discrimination and demands for a more equitable distribution of, and access to, land. With their roots deep in rural communities, Otavalo's Kichwa politics were also shaped by the predominant *yanapa* relationship that many communities had with the *haciendas*, particularly in the areas immediately adjacent to the city of Otavalo and to the north, such as Peguche, which granted them some limited autonomy. In these communities, over time, families developed artisan, weaving, and marketing skills, which allowed them to create and accumulate financial capital. This capital increased their standard of living, which was used to purchase both rural and urban properties and provide for the formal education for their children. They developed closer, although still often contentious, relationships with the majority Mestizo population and were able to articulate their rights not only in terms of their community cultures, but also in the language of national society as well.

The *hacienda* and political boss systems were at the heart of maintaining the colonial order that stole land and labor from Indigenous people, that either ignored or tried to assimilate them, that belittled cultural difference, and that denied their rights to participation. In the mid-twentieth century, therefore, organized rural communities used various strategies to pressure *haciendas*. Common everyday resistance methods included work slow-downs and using *hacienda* resources such as water and pasturelands without permission and without compensating the owners. Festivals became a time to question and mock authority. As communities became more self confident, their protests became more pointed and confrontational, aimed squarely at breaking local authorities' mechanisms of control. In the 1950s, for example, communities around Lake San Pablo opposed the development of a tourist project, resulting in the death of three of their members. In open letters to the Bishop in Quito, they complained about the abuses of tithing in an attempt to halt that practice, which created economic hardship for many families. Organized communities refused to participate in the *faenas*, the obligatory, unpaid work projects organized by the local and provincial governments (Korovkin 2001; Ortiz Crespo 2012, 141–143). These types of protests challenged both the ideological and economic foundations of the local matrices of power.

As they continued to demand rights to the value of their labor and to exercise increasing, although still limited, autonomy within community structures, Kichwa activists also engaged in a two-pronged strategy to win land rights. On the ground, communities occupied the *haciendas* on which they worked and carried out strikes and other protests to pressure *hacendados* to give them their plots of land by making the *haciendas* unworkable. A parallel strategy was to appeal to the *Instituto de la Reforma Agraria y Colonización* (Institute for Agrarian Reform and Colonization, IERAC) to intervene on their behalf and dissolve the *hacienda* by proving that they exceeded the allowed size and had not modernized their operations in accordance with the law. While it was a slow process, these efforts did change landownership in the region. Santiago Ortiz (2012) observed that,

> by the end of the twentieth century, the canton's landscape had changed. About half of the lands were in the hands of the communities and the rest in modern *haciendas* connected with floriculture, horticulture, tourism, and ranching in the hands of businesses. That is, the great *haciendas* of the 1940s were distributed in the 1970s between community members and *hacendados* connected with agribusiness (148).[1]

Land disputes, however, were not just between Kichwa communities and White-Mestizo *haciendas*; they also sometimes caused conflict between communities as well. In order to acquire land, some better-off families, those that came from *yanapa* communities and who had made money through the textiles and handicraft industries, were inclined to buy lands from *haciendas* that other Indigenous families were pressuring to dissolve. From their perspective, buying land outright was easier and faster than the direct actions and appeals through the IERAC. The communities, usually former *huasipungeros*, which were in the process of occupying *haciendas* and appealing to the government to award them land, however, felt betrayed by these members of other Kichwa communities.[2] Increasingly, *yapanero* families accumulated capital in both the countryside and in the city of Otavalo itself, creating different perspectives and priorities within the movement.

By the late 1960s and early 1970s, a new kind of social activist was emerging in Otavalo from the struggles around rights. Urbanization and social stratification, while changing the dynamic of community relationships, also produced activists with different perspectives on the struggle.

The *Federación Indígena Campesina de Imbabura* (Indigenous Campesino Federation of Imbabura, FICI), the region's umbrella organization for Indigenous organizations, was founded in 1974 and immediately became a site of contention between urban and rural based organizations. Although they shared many common agendas, they often came to the struggle with competing goals and interests. At times these tensions proved creative and made use of a variety of talents and resources, while other moments found them conflictive, pitting communities against one another, because of class differences and competing interests. Based in Otavalo, artisan and merchant families were increasingly exposed to outside cultures and were able to provide for formal education for their children, who began attending university (often with the help of progressive tendencies within the Catholic Church, the Cuban government, and progressive NGOs). Economic success also created greater self-esteem and appreciation of their own culture. Interactions with people from other parts of the country and throughout the world, who appreciated the work of the Otavalos, fed into a sense that their culture was unique and valuable (Meisch 2002). The central government even held up Otavalos (artisan, merchant Otavalos) as exemplary, a pride of Ecuador and a model for other Indigenous people to follow.

A group of young intellectuals and political activists, primarily from relatively prosperous families in Peguche, found themselves caught between the rural, Indigenous world of their parents to which they maintained substantial ties, and the urban, Mestizo world in which they operated. They formed a study group, the *Taller Cultural Causanachunic,* in which they read about class struggle but also developed a distinct ethnic perspective, being skeptical of orthodox Marxist perspectives on culture as a straightforward superstructure to the economic system (Huarcaya 2010, 311). Part of their struggle, therefore, was clearly to fight for social justice for Indigenous people. A young Mario Conejo, for instance, was arrested trying to stop the practice known as "*arranchar,*" in which Mestizo market vendors would stop Indigenous producers from entering into town and force them to sell them their goods for much less than their actual value (Ortiz Crespo 2012, 161). At the same time, however, they moved the discussion of rights beyond the class prism that their allies in the leftist parties insisted on using. By the 1980s they were engaged in a concerted effort to define their culture as different but equal to Mestizo culture and, using their training as linguists, anthropologists, and sociologists, outlined a new, intercultural vision of regional and national life. They sought to resignify racist language and practices and, from positions of relative prestige, reclaimed their cultural heritage. Bilingual education and access to ancestral medicine became focal points of their projects. They also were leaders of the national movement, helping to articulate CONAIE's vision as it became the public face of Indigenous rights after the 1990 Uprising.

Regionally, they also affiliated themselves with, and helped to build, the FICI as a means not only to broaden their own nascent power base, but also to maintain an organic connection with the struggles of the rural communities. From the beginning, there was tension in the organization. The original leadership came from economically more secure families and was particularly interested in the cultural aspects of the struggle. Many activists from the base communities, although also interested in cultural problems, were also in the midst of contentious land disputes. The organization, however, with the technical expertise of a cadre of young, university-educated advisors, fought for both land rights and to end Mestizo discrimination and exploitation. The FICI became the most important Indigenous organization in the province, affiliating over one hundred communities and developing sections to organize for cultural events, land rights, development projects, environmental protection, women's rights (both within the communities and in the wider society), and effective political rights for Indigenous people. Furthermore, the federation acted as an intermediary between communities and development agencies and NGOs on various projects. Its ability to mobilize support for direct actions and for articulating a vision of social and political change made it a key actor in local, and later national, politics.

By the mid 1980s, FICI had successfully supported communities in their struggles for land and led the efforts at abolishing Mestizo collection of tithes for the church and forced labor for public projects. Building on its initial successes, the FICI leadership decided that it could pressure the state into providing better services (Korovkin 2001, 48). In 1988, working in an alliance with the *Partido Socialista Ecuatoriano* (Socialist Party of Ecuador--PSE), FICI leaders were elected to the Municipal Council in Otavalo and the Provincial Council of Imbabura, from where they were able to advocate for public projects and more direct support for Kichwa communities (Ortiz Crespo 2012, 152). Whether or not to participate in elections was a contentious issue within the Indigenous movement. With the return of democracy, Indigenous individuals in Otavalo were courted by political parties to run for office as a means of attracting Indigenous votes. After the formation of Pachakutik in 1996, however, Indigenous candidates also began running for office representing their own party. The FICI leadership backed Pachakutik candidate Mario Conejo for mayor in 1996. Although he lost that election, it set the stage for his eventual win in 2000 and demonstrated the clout of the Indigenous organizations and their deep roots and networks throughout rural communities and the city of Otavalo.

Cotacachi and UNORCAC

Like Otavalo, Cotacachi is ethnically diverse, with a Mestizo-dominated urban center, a Kichwa-majority Andean region, and (unlike Otavalo) a mixture of ethnicities in the subtropical Intag region. If the political and social networks that Kichwa communities constructed in Otavalo were often characterized by a certain tension between rural and urban, campesino and intellectual, class and ethnic tendencies, the Indigenous communities of Cotacachi were, to a certain degree, more homogeneous than their Otavalan counterparts. In pre-land reform times, most Indige-nous campesinos lived under the *huasipungo* system, which meant that they were more directly bound to and dependent upon the *haciendas* on which they lived. This dependence made it virtually impossible to achieve meaningful economic, social, or political autonomy. Under these conditions, the tensions between urban and rural communities that took hold in Otavalo's Indigenous networks did not manifest themselves in Cotacachi. Instead, the canton's communities allied themselves with the *Unión de Organizaciones Campesinas de Cotacachi* (Union of Campesino Organizations of Cotacachi, UNORCAC), to create a powerful and effective force for economic and political change.

Land tenancy issues in Cotacachi were even more extreme than in Otavalo. In 1974, before the second phase of land reform, 1.1 percent of the population controlled over 60 percent of the land, while 92 percent of the campesino population controlled only 23 percent of the land (Guerrero and Ospina 2003, 96). Most Kichwa campesinos eked out a precarious existence, having to perform generally unpaid labor for the *haciendas* and the church, which continued to collect its tithe well into the 1970s. For example, the largest *hacienda, Hospital,* is estimated to have owned between 15,000–30,000 hectares. The *hacienda* system maintained its power through the *gamonal* (boss) system, under which the local priests, the *tenientes politicos,* and the municipal authorities, managed all aspects of public life, excluding Indigenous communities from the foundations of power (Ortiz Crespo 2004, 61). In addition to the crushing poverty imposed on them by this arrangement, the Cotacachi police and local authorities also subjected Indigenous people to systematic abuses. Arbitrary arrests, torture, and the occasional killing were not only a means to keep the population fearful and powerless but also another means to extract economic resources from them, in the form of fines, bribes, and unpaid labor.

The land reform of the 1960s and 1970s resulted in a minimum impact on land tenancy in Cotacachi. Santiago Ortiz reports that only 3.5 percent of the land was redistributed, as most of the large *haciendas* avoided expropriation by modernizing their operations (2004, 63). By the early twenty-first century, Indigenous families owned on average one-half hectare, which made subsistence farming impossible without supplementing it with work in the cities or local agribusiness operations. This arrangement often led to men being absent during the week as they sought work elsewhere, leaving women in charge of households and family farming operations (Interview, HC, Cotacachi, October 31, 2011). What did change, however, with land reform was the abolishment of *huasipungo*. Indigenous families were no longer bound to particular *haciendas* through debt and were no longer obligated to provide free labor to *hacienda* owners, the church, or the municipal authorities.

These changes in legal and land ownership structures were accompanied and pushed further by Indigenous organizing efforts, which found their focus in the UNORCAC, whose leaders broke from the FICI over disagreements in priorities. Many Cotacachi activists felt that the FICI leadership, based in Otavalo, was too focused on cultural issues, whereas they were advocating a more militant struggle against economic and social exploitation and for land rights (UNORCAC 2008, 23). Founded in April 1977 as a federation of twelve communities, UNORCAC dedicated itself to advocating for the rights of Indigenous communities which, at the time, were not only subject to racial discrimination but also systematically excluded from such social rights such as potable water and education. In November of that year, local police arrested, tortured, and murdered activist Rafael Perugachi, which galvanized Indigenous support for change and quickly swelled UNORCAC's ranks to include 43 communities in Cotacachi. By the turn of the century, all forty-five Kichwa communities affiliated with UNORCAC. Unlike FICI in Otavalo, however, there were few internal tensions between cultural and class issues as the Cotacachi communities saw the defense of their cultural heritage and cultural rights as being intimately connected to their class position as campesinos. UNORCAC saw the liberation of rural, Indigenous communities from dominant institutions as coming from communities' traditions of self-organization, reciprocity, and ancestral knowledge of local ecosystems, agriculture, and medicine. To further these efforts, UNORCAC affiliated itself with the *Federación Nacional de Organizaciones Campesinas, Indígenas y Negras* (National Federation of Peasant, Indigenous and Black Organizations, FENOCIN)[3], with its strong orientation toward leftist economic justice and political action. The relationship between UNORCAC and FENOCIN proved to be fruitful, as local leaders drew on the resources and experiences of the national organization. Furthermore, because of their success organizing along both class and ethnic lines in Cotacachi, many UNORCAC activists also became influential leaders in the national organization.

The organization eventually became what some participants characterized as a "shadow municipality," in the sense that it positioned itself as the intermediary between communities, NGOs, and the state, particularly in the area of development projects. The 1970s witnessed efforts within the communities to give identity and direction to the organization, which was officially recognized by the Ministry of Agriculture and Ranching in 1980. Through the 1980s, UNORCAC supported communities in their disputes against *haciendas* for land and brought an end to the Church's collection of tithing in 1984. The organization also advocated for improved social services by negotiating with a variety of NGOs and state agencies. It sought to promote literacy through bilingual and other education programs and improve electric and water services, roads, recreational spaces, and health. By the 1990s, UNORCAC described its work as "development with identity."[4] Making connections between ancestral knowledge, local organization, and effective, transparent execution of NGO-funded projects, it consolidated its local, regional, and national leadership. By the turn of the century, in its own words, it had

> broadened its actions to include economic development, tourism; protection and management of natural resources; promotion of agroecological production to guarantee nutritional sovereignty; Indigenous health and the revitalization of ancestral medicine; organization building; cultural identity; and the strong encouragement of Indigenous women's participation throughout its programs and projects (UNORCAC 2008, 25).

Its capacity to organize communities, to cooperatively deliver services, and to promote sustainable development projects to increase income for families besieged by lack of land and economic opportunity also made UNORCAC an important player in local politics. Taking advantage of the country's return to democracy and the elimination of Spanish literacy tests, UNORCAC, in an alliance with the *Frente Amplio de la Izquierda* (Broad Left Front, FADI) ran one of its founders, Alberto Anrango for a seat on the Municipal Council. With his victory in 1979, he became the first Kichwa elected official to the Cotacachi municipal government. Since then there has been at least one UNORCAC-affiliated Kichwa member of the municipal government, including the first woman, Magdalena Fuérez in 2000. Through the 1980s and 1990s, UNORCAC partnered with FADI and the PSE to promote Indigenous candidates in their continued efforts to increase democratic participation in municipal politics (AUC 2010; Lalander and Gustafasson 2008; Ortiz Crespo 2012; Ospina 2006). In 1996, UNORCAC allied itself with Pachakutik and its candidate, Auki Tituaña, who won the election for mayor with 30 percent of the vote in a multiple candidate contest.

From self-defense and advocacy group, to "shadow municipality," to major partner in actually taking over the municipal government, UNORCAC demonstrated that the canton's Kichwa communities could organize themselves, build both regional and national intercultural alliances, and become the major political player in the region. The roots of the organization's power could be found in its dual message of local organizing traditions coupled with differentiated integration with national society.

CONSTRUCTING INTERCULTURAL POLITICS: 1996-2014

The process of taking municipal power at the end of the twentieth century by Kichwa politicians in both Otavalo and Cotacachi required creating intercultural politics from the ashes of the *hacienda* power system that had dictated social and political relations since colonial times.

Pressuring simultaneously from outside and inside institutional channels, the region's Kichwa leaders weakened the inefficient Mestizo networks that operated on patronage and allegiance to discredited political parties and ideologies, thereby positioning themselves to replace those networks. Taking power, however, required the building of viable coalitions that would reach out not only to Kichwa voters and organizations, but also to Mestizos (Lalander 2010a, 2010b). In an area characterized by high levels of heterogeneity, between and within ethnic groups, it was not a simple matter of nominating a charismatic Indigenous candidate but rather a need to articulate an intercultural vision and concrete plan that would speak to the economic, social, and cultural concerns of a wide group of citizens.

Otavalo: Intercultural Struggles

The political terrain in Otavalo at the beginning of the twenty-first century was fraught with the intercultural tensions highlighted by the Indigenous uprisings of the 1990s. The traditional White-Mestizo power blocks in Otavalo were losing their grip on local institutions due to the withdrawal of the neoliberal state, which led to the simultaneous decentralization of authority and the limiting of patronage capabilities of traditional elites. At the same time, the national Indigenous movement made limited, but important, political gains through the late 1990s, changing the overall debate about Indigenous institutional capacity and participation. In the context of Otavalo, Pachakutik hoped to improve on its near miss in 1996 and capture the municipality in 2000. The other tension came from within the Kichwa community itself, as debates over identity, cooperation with Mestizo groups, and development priorities, which had been visible since the land reform process, became ever more acute.

The competing tensions between the more urban-based, intellectual activists and the rural-based tendencies, rooted in community activists' struggles for land that characterized FICI throughout its existence, became a central issue in nominating a candidate for mayor. The two primary candidates starkly represented the differences running through regional Kichwa communities. The first candidate, Mario Conejo, (who was from a prominent artisan-merchant family, a university trained sociologist, part of FICI's technical team, and one of the leaders of Otavalo's "cultural activists") had run unsuccessfully for mayor in 1996 and advocated an intercultural approach to governing the canton. The other major candidate was Carmelina Yamberla, from the parish of Ilumán. A tireless advocate for equitable land distribution, women's participation, and development in the rural sectors, she emphasized the need for the municipal government to prioritize the development and infrastructure claims of poorer communities (Ortiz Crespo 2012, 200). Although local and national Pachakutik officials eventually settled on Conejo, the decision-making process was bitter. In the end, Yamberla decided to form her own political organization to run against Conejo in the general election, which set up a political rivalry that informed local politics throughout Conejo's fourteen-year administration.

Conejo won the 2000 elections with 46 percent of the vote, beating Yamberla by more than twenty points, and promised to modernize the municipal government by implementing intercultural initiatives to democratize decision-making processes by being more inclusive of all of Otavalo's citizens. After winning, he began working with a multiethnic team of technical advisors oriented toward long-term results, which set out an ambitious program of urban renewal through strategic and detailed planning. The primary channel for collecting information and prioritizing projects was the office of *Participación Ciudadana y Diálogo Intercultural* (Citizen Participation and Intercultural Dialogue). Through this office, Conejo's administration solicited concerns and proposals from the various ethnic and geographic communities of the canton by holding assemblies in both urban and rural neighborhoods. Once the information was collected, the municipal government, through the council and various other technical agencies, prioritized the work, budgeted projects, and transparently implemented them.

His approach was effective. He gradually won over more Mestizo voters who became convinced that his administration was interested in promoting the canton and the city of Otavalo, in particular, through tourism and economic development, rather than following an agenda built exclusively around rural Indigenous grievances. His presence as a Kichwa activist, who continually pushed for greater participation and visibility of Kichwa people, helped him remain popular among most Kichwa sectors, particularly those connected with the urban, merchant, and middle class groups, which constituted his base of support. Although he handily won re-election in 2004, he continued to run into conflicts with many Kichwa organizations, especially rural groups and FICI. These groups believed that his intercultural policies came at their expense, and they become an increasingly powerful opposition. In 2006, two years after winning re-election on the Pachakutik slate, he publicly broke with the national party, of which he had been a founding member. He constructed his own political movement, *Minga Intercultural*, which won seats for the municipal council in 2006. In the 2009 elections, Conejo won a third term, this time running on President Correa's *Alianza PAIS* (AP) slate, which allowed him to overcome the entrenched opposition of many Kichwa organizations (Lalander 2010b; Stolle-McAllister 2013). In many ways the 2009 elections were a referendum on Rafael Correa, who managed to transfer his popularity across the entire electoral slate in Imbabura. Conejo, however, faced a serious challenge from former Prefect, Gustavo Pareja, who put together a coalition headed by long time Kichwa rival, Carmelina Yamberla. Conejo won the election 43 percent to Pareja's 41 percent (with Pachakutik candidate José Quimbo picking up 12 percent), but his support in predominantly Kichwa parishes was weak and analyst Rickard Lalander argued that his victory was due more to the "Correa effect" than to his own popularity in these areas (2010a).

Gustavo Pareja and his coalition finally beat Conejo in the 2014 elections, 47 percent to 34 percent. Importantly, Pareja won soundly in all of Otavalo's jurisdictions, including predominantly Kichwa parishes (CNE 2014). Furthermore, AP candidates overall did better than Conejo in the races for municipal and parish councils, indicating that some voters split their votes to oppose Conejo, while supporting Correa's party. Although Pareja's victory was part of a wave of losses for Correa nationally that year, it was also due to a sense in Otavalo's rural Kichwa communities that their needs had gone unattended for too many years, as Conejo had focused much of the municipal development projects on infrastructure for the city at the expense of the rural communities. It was part of the ongoing tension within Otavalo's Kichwa communities that characterized Indigenous networks of power since the mid-twentieth century. While paying attention to ethnic issues in Otavalo, Conejo ran primarily on his effectiveness in completing infrastructure projects, promoting local development, and contributing to intercultural dialogue. By 2014, however, Otavalo voters had lost faith in his ability to adequately and effectively meet their needs and opted for a change, even if it meant voting for a Mestizo candidate over a Kichwa one.

Mario Conejo's administration was framed around the question of interculturality. Otavalo was declared the "Intercultural Capital" of the country, and its multiethnic and socioeconomically diverse population made interculturality an indispensible discourse to governing. Defining and implementing intercultural policies, however, was a matter of constant negotiation and conflict. On the one hand, Conejo saw himself as the mayor of all Otavaleños, which meant representing not only Kichwa people (themselves divided by geography, class, and religion), but also white-mestizos and Afro-Ecuadorians (Interview, Otavalo, March 3, 2007). While defending the cultural rights of everyone to participate, therefore, he framed his policies around what he saw as good for the municipality and not one or another particular group. He tried to artic-ulate a wide agenda based on economic development and inclusion of cultural diversity, without necessarily invoking a particular kind of iden-tity politics. Interculturality, therefore, became the policies and practices that his administration believed would benefit the population as a whole. This process was, of course, contentious, with much disagreement not only over particular initiatives, but also over questions of representation.

The city of Otavalo became the object of much of the municipal government's efforts to improve and revitalize the local economy as it was the motor of commerce and the tourist industry. Streets were repaved and made more accessible to pedestrians; the Parque Bolívar was renovated; markets reorganized, with food merchants moved to a new municipal market; a municipal library was built; a municipal school developed, originally outside of the national public school system with the mission of providing an innovative education for the city's children; the city's water infrastructure was modernized with multiple treatment plants reducing pollution into Lake San Pablo and local rivers; and solid waste pick-up was divided into compostable and non-compostable schedules, reducing landfill pressures and encouraging recycling. Public works in Otavalo, as in the country as a whole, were one of the currencies of political success—a visible demonstration of taxes being used to improve the standard of living. Funding these projects came from municipal operating expenses, national government support (which increased dramatically after 2007), international NGOs, and government grants (which the mayor often directly nurtured), as well as a system of mutual payment from neighborhoods.[5]

Interculturality, however, is not simply the mutual tolerance of multiple ethnic communities; it is often a contentious process between and within those groups as they compete, negotiate, and debate the best policies to advance their vision of the common good. Along those lines, given the history of intra-ethnic tensions, many Kichwa activists and organizations opposed Conejo and saw his actions as a betrayal of his roots. In particular, they resented that more resources were spent on improving urban infrastructure rather than assisting Kichwa communities and organizations directly. While the city's water infrastructure was improved, for instance, many rural communities were still dependent on their own labor to build and maintain their water systems (Armijos Burneo 2012). Similarly, city sidewalks were widened and beautified with colored tiles, yet roads within rural communities were left unattended and in poor condition. José Antonio Lema, President of the artisan's market union (UNAIMCO) complained that,

> The municipal government does not give us anything in terms of resources. There was a lot for long-term planning; they have a lot of well-paid advisors, but they don't have any immediate solutions for us. Mario Conejo has betrayed us. We put him in office twice and he has not given us anything. We even put up our own resources, money and time to elect him, but then he broke with us and formed his own party. This has helped out the political groups, the Mestizo groups that want to divide the movement. Those groups always want to show that the Indigenous are divided, but the Kichwa peoples here—urban and rural—are united behind Pachakutik (Interview, Otavalo, October 2, 2006).

Although Otavalo's Kichwa communities were not in fact united behind Pachakutik, which lost badly throughout the province and the country in the 2006 elections, Lema's position represented the discourse that Kichwa people *ought* to back what was seen as the Indigenous party and political arm of CONAIE, implying that Conejo was being disloyal not just to local organizations but to the notion of Kichwa nationality as well. Secondly, his argument underlines the notion that as a Kichwa mayor, put into power by the social and political networks of Kichwa communities, he owed it to those communities to prioritize their needs.

Conejo's approach, therefore, aggravated friction and contention within the municipality's Kichwa organizations, on display at least since the end of land reform. Many of those organizations, with their roots in poorer rural communities rather than the relatively more prosperous urban ones, had a different perspective on how to best advance their constituents' interests. They charged that Conejo, under the guise of interculturality, was willing neither to take the bolder steps needed to more fully undo the legacies of colonialism and racism, nor to provide the material support needed to overcome poverty. One particularly angry citizen charged that Conejo "was as bad if not worse than any of the White-Mestizo mayors that we have had," (Interview, Otavalo, November

2, 2013) in terms of corruption and paying attention to moneyed interests. Another long-time Otavalo activist and intellectual noted, "It's a shame. He has immense talent and vision, but in the end, he really has not done anything differently than a Mestizo mayor would have done" (Interview, LT, Atuntaqui, September 3, 2013). An environmental activist with the evangelical party *Amauta Jatari*, which had originally backed Conejo, noted that perhaps it was not so much co-optation by Mestizo interests as it was that Conejo's administration, while certainly including Kichwa individuals, "is not really an Indigenous structure. I mean, he has not changed the ways that the government operates or makes decisions, but rather he uses the same procedures and channels as before" (Interview, Otavalo, February 20, 2007). Conejo sought to include Otavalo's diverse population in the local government, without necessarily challenging the state institutions and structures of power, relying instead on his political and technical team to prioritize information gathered from throughout the municipality to carry out projects.

His decision to work within the system, while challenging racist practices and encouraging citizen participation, revealed Conejo's some-times controversial approach to interculturality and pointed to some of the limitations of implementing intercultural policies at the local level. Throughout his political career, he built a strong base of support particularly among Otavalo's urban Kichwa organizations, while at the same time reaching out to the White-Mestizo community. He joked that some of his critics, "say I am Indian-Mestizo" (Interview, Otavalo, March 1, 2007), because of his marriage to a White-Mestiza woman and his ability to move between both Kichwa and White-Mestizo environments. In many ways this adaptability could be seen as a goal of an intercul-tural society, where individuals transverse different cultural groups, borrowing and adapting from each as new projects and coalitions are created and brought to fruition. Furthermore, Conejo demonstrated that being Kichwa was neither a uniform nor a static identity, but rather a dynamic process of adaptation to changing circumstances. Despite some of his critics' charges that he was not really Indigenous anymore, he repeatedly defined himself as "an urban Indian," every much as Indigenous as his rural counterparts, albeit with a different perspective, and a different way of working.

His disputes with other Indigenous organizations highlighted the impossibility of defining a singular Indigenous ideology or political program; instead it showed that within this broad category were complex, sometimes competing, identities and discourses. Rather than falling under an umbrella "Indian" identity, Conejo insisted that Indigenous people come from different backgrounds and, although they have commonalities, they should not be beholden to particular definitions of Indigenous that neither reflected their real world circumstances nor their self perceptions. He argued that his disputes with CONAIE, Pachakutik, and FICI came from an inability of those organizations to adapt to new realities.

> The leadership has lost its compass. They have won the rights they were looking for, but they continue with the same argument. Many of the leaders come from a campesino background. Their struggles come from the fights for agrarian reform, but they continue with a paternalistic mentality—before with the boss and now with the state. [...] Why should we consider Pachakutik to be the only Indian voice? How can they represent everyone just because they are Indian? We are all different and have different ideas. Blanca Chancoso [one of CONAIE's historic leaders] says that to be Indian means to have dirt under your fingernails. Does that mean that those of us who are not campesino are not really Indians? Here, there are people with political ambitions. I have political ambitions. A lot of people want to be councilor, mayor, prefect, whatever. So, they should go with the party or the movement that works best for them, or one that they agree with ideologically. Why should they have to go with a party that is corrupt, that they don't believe in, and that doesn't represent them anymore? (Interview, Otavalo March 1, 2007).

This public break with CONAIE and Pachakutik raised questions about the difference between an *Indigenous* politics and an *intercultural* politics because Conejo simultaneously pointed to his right to represent himself as Indigenous *and* to participate as an active and equal partner with other cultural groups. He resisted, however, being subordinated to the interests of the national Indigenous organizations or to the local rural networks embedded in the FICI.

This argument also highlighted the ambiguity and tension not only in articulating an intercultural discourse, but also in attempting to implement concrete intercultural policies. Conejo positioned himself between an Indigenous discourse that called to a historic, collective identity and a more individualistic, modern, Western discourse that also allowed him to access the Mestizo world. For Conejo, and many Kichwa people, it was not an either/or binary situation; rather, one could employ both Indigenous and Western discourses simultaneously, as both constructed their lives. He rejected CONAIE and Pachakutik attempts to represent *all* Indigenous people, contending that the changing real-life circumstances in which people lived, rather than preconceived notions of identity, were the means through which groups and individuals shaped their political projects and their coalitions. Rather than falling under a monolithic Indian identity, Conejo insisted that because Indigenous people come from different backgrounds, notwithstanding shared commonalities, they should be free to construct identities and pursue dreams and projects that make sense to them individually.

Ariruma Kowii (2006), the mayor's brother and former subsecretary of education for intercultural dialogue, argued that Conejo was not a *Kichwa* mayor, but rather the mayor of what was truly a multiethnic community and that decolonizing the community meant that the government must work with all groups, not just the majority Kichwa ones. In his view, Otavalo represented a unique experiment in interculturality because, although Kichwa people represented the majority, they still only constituted part of the population, making more radical calls for Kichwaization of the municipality's institutions and territory impossible. Furthermore, imposing traditional Kichwa institutions and practices on the municipal government, he argued, would constitute a reverse kind of colonization

(2006, 170–172). Instead, the municipal government under Conejo worked toward finding mechanisms that coincided with national institutions, but which, at the same time, sought to incorporate the multiplicity of ways of living, traditions, ideas, and institutions of the municipality's multiethnic communities.

Without giving up a Kichwa identity, as mayor, Conejo opted for what he saw as a pragmatic and efficient way of moving Otavalo forward. He rejected seeking Kichwa autonomy because, in part, such a project would be impossible in the multiethnic environment of Otavalo, in which all ethnic communities had interrelated interests. He wondered why Indigenous people would pursue autonomy when as a majority they could exert their rights and simply elect officials to represent them, "and the question of nationalities. Go ask people in the communities and most of them won't know what you are talking about. They are not interested. They want solutions to their problems—land, fair prices, water, education, development, and an end to discrimination. That is what we are doing." (Interview, Otavalo, March 1, 2007). Interculturality, in his approach, meant finding solutions by encouraging participation as citizens, equal but different. In his view, the Indigenous movement had dismantled the official obstructions to citizenship, and now it was time to move forward by building out networks of power that permitted everyone's advancement.

His loss to Gustavo Pareja in 2014 would seem to indicate that ethnic solidarity and identity politics were only valuable to a certain point. Perhaps the fact that a Mestizo man, in alliance with certain Kichwa sectors and actors, convinced the majority of both Mestizo and Indigenous communities that he would better attend their needs is an indication that the intercultural dialogue was moving into a new phase. Pareja's ideology and development ideas were not that different than Conejo's, and sentiment seemed to be that a new administration would be able to respond better to the needs of the poorest sectors. It would not appear to be a return to pre-Conejo politics of ethnic exclusion, as the local state had been fundamentally transformed, and Pareja's success was clearly contingent on his Kichwa allies, much like Conejo needed Mestizo sectors to back him.

Cotacachi: Development with Identity

Much like Mario Conejo's victory in Otavalo, Auki Tituaña's 1996 successful campaign for mayor also depended on a multi-ethnic coalition that hoped to stamp out the vestiges of *gamonal* (political boss) power and replace it with a more democratic, modern, and inclusive system of local governance. Unlike Otavalo, however, Cotacachi's Indigenous organization, UNORCAC, had fewer internal divisions and had effectively built a network of community organizations that allowed it to speak for Kichwa communities and to efficiently deliver votes for endorsed candidates. Since the 1970s, UNORCAC had negotiated with FADI and the PSE to have one of its members represent the party in municipal council elections and held at least one seat since 1979. By 1996 UNORCAC leadership decided to run a candidate for mayor on its own platform. Because Pachakutik was formed as an explicitly intercultural political movement for the 1996 elections and seen as the party for the Indigenous movement, it was a logical choice to run a candidate through that party.

Party leaders sought out Pachakutik's Auki Tituaña, in an unusual but strategic alliance (Lalander and Gustafasson 2008). Tituaña was considered an "urban Indian" with family roots in Peguche, was educated in economics at a Cuban university, and had a successful career as a CONAIE development official. CONAIE and UNORCAC-affiliated FENOCIN, however, were often national rivals for support of Indigenous communities and were engaged in ideological debates over the balance that ethnicity, nationality, and social class ought to play in the struggle. Tituaña was often associated with the more ethnic tendencies in CONAIE. Those tensions, particularly over urban-rural priorities, would manifest themselves throughout Tituaña's three terms as mayor. At the same time, however, Tituaña and UNORCAC formed a balanced alliance aimed at ousting the entrenched conservative Mestizo interests in the municipality.

On the one hand, given Tituaña's limited experience with rural organizing and being an outsider to Cotacachi's communities, he would probably have made little headway without the support of UNORCAC. On the other hand, Tituaña's history of interacting with the Mestizo community in urban environments, his extensive international contacts, economics degree, and success in dealing with funding agencies made him an acceptable candidate to the urban Mestizo population that also wanted to modernize and democratize the municipality's institutions.

After coming to office, Tituaña and his allies in UNORCAC forged not only a new administration, but also a new way of governing. Because of their experience in development and governance issues, both Tituaña and UNORCAC officials stressed the importance of municipal planning throughout the 1996 campaign. However, because the municipal government had always governed in a top-down fashion in the interests of political and economic elites, there was neither a history nor institutional mechanisms for consulting the population for medium and long-term planning (Ortiz Crespo 2004, 121). Projects had generally been carried out through patronage and the whims of the mayor and his allies, rather than a rational plan aimed at maximum benefit for area residents. Within a month of taking office, therefore, Tituaña called for a general assembly of the canton's population, which would come to be known as Cantonal Unity Assembly of Cotacachi (*Asamblea de Unidad Cantonal de Cotacachi–AUC*). Rather than be a one-time or occasional consultation body, the AUC would constitute itself as a permanent institution, with an executive board and various commissions to work directly with municipal officials to determine budget priorities and to ensure that projects were efficiently and transparently completed (Bonilla and Ramos 2009; Santillana Ortiz 2006; Torres-Dávila 2003).

The AUC became an institution that gave life to the Indigenous movement's horizontal, intercultural aspirations. To both empower citizens and ensure that municipal authorities prioritized its desired initiatives, the AUC divided its work to assure adequate representation of the canton's population and its organizations. Representation in the assembly was organized through neighborhood, village, trade, or other types of organization. While the Andean (Kichwa) region was already effectively organized by community and accustomed to working in a multi-organizational format through UNROCAC and communities in Intag had successfully organized against large-scale mining operations, Mestizos in the urban area did not have similar organizations or a history of collective representation. The *Confederación de Barrios* (Federation of Barrios) was organized shortly before the first AUC general assembly, and it joined the various rural community/territorial organizations, along with producer, artisan, transportation, people with disabilities, women's, and youth organizations to begin establishing the needs and direction of the municipality. The way in which the AUC organized itself mirrored in some ways the UNORCAC's structure, with an annual assembly as the ultimate authority, an executive committee consisting of a president, vice-president, and secretary drawn from a larger twenty-five-member board of development and management. Membership was drawn from previously defined sectors as well as representatives from the municipal government and municipal employees. Furthermore, the AUC paid careful attention to balancing commissions by geographic regions and gender. The designing of proposals and overseeing of projects was divided into six commissions, again with representation from the various sectors to oversee work in tourism, agricultural production, health, environmental management, education, and artisan work (Cameron 2010; Ospina 2006; Santillana Ortiz 2006).

One of the most important features of the AUC was devising a partic-ipatory budget process. A mixture of ideas borrowed in part from Porto Alegre's experience in Brazil in the 1990s and in part from local experi-ence, the budget process became a concrete way to implement planning and to ensure that funds were distributed transparently. By making citizens co-responsible for the administration of funds, it also made plain the kinds of decisions, compromises, and prioritizing that goes into budgeting. Rather than backroom deals made between the mayor and close allies or paternalistic handouts from a benevolent government, the participatory budget process allowed various organizations to debate the allocation of funds. At the same time, the balancing of geographic representation on the various committees helped to ensure the political viability of the process. In some ways residents of the city center were given disproportionate representation in relationship to their population but, as Cameron (2005, 381) asserts, without their cooperation the process would not have survived. Although public investments, therefore, were not perhaps as dedicated to the most marginalized sectors or even allocated proportionately to the population, the process reflected the political realities of the canton.

Working with the AUC, UNORCAC, and other organizations, Tituaña implemented successful programs under the slogan of "development with identity." One of the key demands of the national Indigenous movement had been to provide economic opportunity for the most marginalized sectors of Ecuadorian society, while respecting cultural and organizational differences. Recognizing that subsistence agriculture was no longer a viable enterprise for most people, Tituaña and UNORCAC prioritized the transition to more diverse and integrated development. Development, of course, is a problematic discourse that has historically been used as part of a modernizing, colonizing project of transnational capital. As a result, Cotacachi's municipal government and autonomous organizations attempted to break from past development models by not forsaking their Kichwa identity and practices as the price for development. Instead, they embraced a variety of ways to develop and enact multiple modernities.

This openness to multiplicity manifested itself in the ways in which opportunities and services were provided to historically marginalized sectors. The first ten years of Tituaña's administration took place under Ecuador's neoliberal governments, which proved both a constraint on what they could do but also an opportunity to take advantage of the vacuum left by the retreating central state. After 1990, the central state devolved many governance issues to the municipalities and parishes, creating financial and political opportunities for local governments, even as it withdrew support for basic social spending such as health, education, and infrastructure. In the relative absence of the national state, Tituaña, along with the UNORCAC, successfully sought funding from international NGOs, which provided a certain financial autonomy from the state. They were able to contextualize their grant requests around the democratic, intercultural reforms underway in Cotacachi and gain the interest in many NGOs to support projects from Indigenous sectors (Almeida, Arrobo Rodas, and Ojeda Segovia 2005; Bonilla and Ramos 2009; Nazarea and Guitarra 2004; Torres-Dávila 2003). Furthermore, a committee of the AUC worked with local organizations to help them secure funding from international agencies by writing clear proposals with verifiable outcomes for their projects. In addition to program outcomes, they also encouraged people to participate, organize, and advocate for their collective needs and develop autonomous solutions.

In that context, Tituaña's administration and the AUC embarked on a mixed economy model committing outside aid of numerous NGOs, local community investment, and state funds to a variety of infrastructure, production, tourism, and health care projects (Rhoades 2006). The municipal government, for instance, maintained a controlling interest in the tourist services (restaurant, boats, hotel) at Cuicocha Lake but sold local communities shares in the project to raise money for improvements. Similarly, UNORCAC owned the *Runa Tupari* tourist agency that promoted community tourism throughout the region. Both projects earned money and allowed nearby communities to maintain control over the content of those projects, avoiding some of the exploitative and environmentally degrading practices of outside operators. Similarly, working primarily with women's organizations within UNORCAC, the AUC and the Tituaña administration identified problems of access and effectiveness of the state-run health clinics. Building on the insights and suggestions of these groups, they negotiated with the national government to reorganize the clinics in Cotacachi and founded *Jambi Mascaric* (Searching for Health) (Arboleda 2006). Under this system, residents could receive care from a physician trained in Western medicine, a practitioner trained in ancestral medicine, or a combination of the two. Furthermore, traditional midwives participated in efforts to systematize their knowledge and train other women to assist in pregnancy and childbirth, reducing complications. Part of the development strategies undertaken by the municipality since 1996 was fundamentally intercultural by not only engaging different cultural groups in decisions that affected them, but also by using ancestral knowledge in those processes and encouraging communities to take pride in their cultural traditions as a source of potential wealth, rather than something that was holding them back.

It was also effective. This experiment in participatory democracy and development with identity led to numerous national and international recognitions for the municipality and strengthened its well-established history of community organizing. In 2000, Tituaña, with the support of UNORCAC, AUC leaders, and the Federation of Barrios, won re-election with 70 percent of the vote, which was a testament to his transparent leadership and being an effective intercultural bridge. He won a third term in the 2004 elections, following the same path and deepening the participatory reforms begun in 1996.

That is not to say that the political relationships between the main actors in Cotacachi were smooth and without their tensions. In fact, the relationship between Tituaña and the UNORCAC was always fraught with tension (Lalander 2010b). As in Otavalo, class differences between Tituaña and *campesino* organizations shaped disagreements about priorities. Many UNORCAC officials, for instance, complained that Tituaña emphasized urban infrastructure projects, such as paving roads and renovating the principal plaza rather than ensuring that rural communities had functioning water systems, leaving it, instead, up to the communities to build and maintain their own systems. Disputes also arose over control of the Cuicocha Lake installations and access to lands in the national park, with communities wanting a more direct interest in running the tourist attractions there. Part of Tituaña's strategy had been to court middle-class Mestizo support in the city center, which while effectively boosting his base of support, also resulted in growing distrust of Tituaña among some Kichwa sectors and what was seen as a disproportionate amount of money spent on already relatively well-off (urban) sectors.

In 2008, the underlying tensions and differences over the new Constitution unraveled the coalition. Tituaña opposed the Constitution, claiming that it did not go far enough in recognizing Indigenous rights and that it concentrated too much power in the executive. UNORCAC and AUC leaders, however, worked actively for its approval, resulting in Tituaña shutting them out of municipal decision-making. This fallout also showed one of the institutional weaknesses of the AUC: since it lacked legal recognition, the municipal government was ultimately responsible for allocating budgets and executing projects. To a certain degree, the AUC was dependent on the goodwill of the mayor (Cameron 2010, 110). Of course, as it turned out, the mayor was also dependent on good relations with the AUC to get reelected. As a result of these disputes and long-simmering policy differences, UNORCAC nominated founder Alberto Anrango to President Correa's AP slate in 2009, and he won the municipal elections by a decisive margin (45.95 percent to 27.89 percent) (Lalander 2010b, 117–126). Anrango, despite his importance in Cotacachi's history and his impeccable credentials as a leader for Indigenous rights, was widely seen as a fairly ineffective mayor and lost his reelection bid in 2014 to Jomar Cevallos, who ran on a new political slate, *"Bien Vivir."* A long-time AUC advisor with development and planning experience throughout the country, Cevallos was seen as a well-prepared, serious candidate with deep roots in the community. Furthermore, the 2014 elections were the first election in over twenty-five years for which the UNORCAC leadership was unable to deliver even rural votes to its preferred candidate. One former community president and UNORCAC member noted before the election, "UNORCAC is in trouble. The leadership is weak and has not done anything new. People are upset that it has become too involved in politics and not enough in defending us or helping us with projects" (Interview, Cotacachi, January 6, 2014).

Political coalition-building in Cotacachi, therefore, was neither just a matter of ethnic identity nor class identity, but was also dependent on personalities, power dynamics, intercultural processes, the ability to deliver on promises, and national debates.

The experience in Cotacachi represented some similarities but also important differences with Otavalo in terms of constructing an intercultural alternative to governance. While mayor, Tituaña argued that part of the responsibility of being Indigenous involved using ancestral ways of knowing and organizing to propose and enact new social and political modalities. These new systems come about not from idealizing the past, but rather from combining things that work from the multiple societies and cultures:

> We could continue with the same as always—representative democracy—or a new model—participatory democracy, with wide participation, transparency and planning. It is not just infrastructure and the material, but it is also spiritual, of living well, of incorporating values, traditions, and ecology. We have had 500 years of purely material development: now it is time to combine the material and the spiritual (Interview, Cotacachi, May 29, 2007).

Tituaña's administration was recognized both for the symbolic importance of representing historically marginalized groups and for being an example of effective, inclusive, transparent, and democratic processes (Lalander 2010b; Ospina 2006; Ortiz Crespo 2012). These democratic and development processes represented a tentative step toward a more profoundly intercultural society. Participation in the AUC, for instance, was based on sectorial representation. Individuals were not elected, but rather were represented by the heads of organizations—neighborhood, production cooperatives, women's groups, young people's organizations, and so on. While there was clearly a danger that this structure could lead to the sort of corporatist behavior that has challenged democratic processes throughout the region (Cameron 2010, 100-101), it also represented part of Indigenous communities' organizational processes and communal sensibilities. Furthermore, it promoted dialogue and debate between different sectors of the larger municipal community over collective issues about resource allocation and policy priorities, which is at the heart of an intercultural vision.

There were clearly limitations to these processes related to both structural issues as well as relationship dynamics of the main players. The project in Cotacachi began under the neoliberal policies of the Ecuadorian governments of the 1990s and took advantage of some of the newly-opened political space provided by the decentralization of the state. However, there were no firmly established intercultural structures to encourage local autonomy and the kinds of social and economic transformations needed to create a more equitable society. Auki Tituaña explained, for instance,

there is only so much we can do here at the municipal level. We cannot change the system of land tenure, for instance. A lot of *campesinos* need land, but we cannot simply take it away from the larger *haciendas*; a solution to that would have to come from the state (Interview, Cotacachi, May 29, 2007).

Cameron (2005, 374) reported that large landholders involved in various agribusiness pursuits resisted attempts to tax them or to regulate their water or pesticide use, arguing that although these interests did not block democratization efforts, they did effectively demonstrate the practical limits of municipal jurisdiction. Even beyond the transformational limitations of local governments, the breakup of the Tituaña/UNORCAC/AUC alliance also indicated that even at the local level the process was never completely institutionalized.

Nevertheless, the willingness to understand the value and mutual influence of various cultural and epistemological traditions highlighted the success of Auki Tituaña and the UNORCAC in governance efforts in Cotacachi. Like their counterparts in Otavalo, they recognized that being Kichwa meant living in a mixed population, from which they could draw multiple ways of defining and resolving problems. Although they clearly participated in and with dominant White-Mestizo groups and institutions, neither project resulted in the assimilation into those larger groups because they insisted that their ancestral cultures, ways of knowing, and forms of organizing were not only valid but also made important contributions to larger regional, national, and global initiatives. Their development and political projects were fueled not only by a vision of how their world could be, but also by the concrete and changing realities in which their communities lived.

INTERCULTURALITY AS CHALLENGE TO THE COLONIAL MATRIX OF POWER

Although the concept of interculturality is often ambiguously applied to the uneven participation of minority groups with national societies, the political projects in Otavalo and Cotacachi provide some examples of how intercultural processes can be used by historically marginalized sectors. Specifically, these governing projects were part of a process that took aim at the colonial matrix of power, which consists of control of political authority, the economy, gender, knowledge, and subjectivity articulated around historically defined ethnic categories (Mignolo 2011; Quijano 2000). By moving beyond a straightforward agenda of identity politics or the redress of long-held grievances of Indigenous communities, the citizenship and governance efforts spearheaded by Kichwa groups and individuals sought instead to challenge the colonial structures of oppression and control. To be certain, the processes that led Mario Conejo, Auki Tituaña, and Alberto Anrango to the mayors' offices were conflictive and contradictory with false starts, moments of clarity, successes, and failures. These efforts, however, were, and would always have to be, partial, because interculturalizing institutions is not the same as creating utopian intercultural ones. Racism, for instance, does not magically disappear. Despite success in politics and business, many Kichwa professionals talked about slights, others' assumptions that they were hired as part of a quota fulfillment or political favor rather than ability (Interview, SR, Otavalo, September 14, 2013), or unflattering insinuations (in the form of a compliment?) such as "you are smart for an Indian woman" (Interview, CY, Otavalo, April 3, 2007). Despite enormous efforts put into equalizing the economic playing field, Western notions of development still frame discussions about what constitutes success; Kichwa people in the northern Andes are still the poorest sector, and land tenancy is still quite unequal.

But, the reconstitution of local politics under intercultural discourses and practices represented important steps in the never-ending process of creating a different, more just society. The importance of Conejo, Tituaña, and Anrango identifying themselves as Kichwa and coming from long personal and community histories of struggle for rights cannot be understated. A generation previous, their presence in the mayor's office would have been unthinkable. They were agents and products of a sustained and ultimately successful struggle against racist institutions. Their history of oppositional politics was also relevant. Although every political party in the area, regardless of ideology, promoted Indigenous candidates in elections, these three emerged from movements dedicated to empowering Indigenous people by laying siege to the remnants of the colonial power system. They won election and then re-election not by appealing to ethnic resentment, but by building on their bases of support and reaching out to progressive sectors of Mestizo society. They won over many other Mestizo voters by proving that they could enact efficient government. They did not, in other words, seek to build separatist or even ethnically autonomous enclaves, but rather sought, won, and changed the very political institutions that historically had oppressed them. It is telling that it was the Kichwa officeholders who transformed, democratized, and modernized those institutions, making them a more transparent and efficient means through which the citizenry in general could influence the direction of public projects, thereby breaking the power of traditional elites (Ortiz Crespo 2012, 227). They transformed those institutions so that different cultural traditions could concretize their interactions into tangible projects.

Ironically, by strengthening the municipal and parish governments, they also contributed to weakening their own organizations. Participating and being successful in institutional politics, while clearly important both in terms of symbolic power and the actual ability to make change, shifted the center of political power away from the Kichwa OSGs and toward government institutions (Ortiz Crespo 2012). The municipalities could provide services and resolve problems more efficiently than local organizations, making the municipal governments the main channel to achieve their goals rather than autonomous organizations. In Otavalo, FICI, which found itself as the opposition to Mario Conejo, saw its influence and its organizational capacity diminish after 2000. While part of that decline had to do with internal problems, it also was related to the municipality having more resources to respond to the needs of rural communities. Many rural community leaders saw the FICI's role primarily as organization-building but did not look to them for leadership in terms of projects (Interview RT, Gonzalez Suarez, October 10, 2013; LT, Atuntaqui, 4 June 2014). Politically, the organization was unable to deliver votes, decreasing its importance to political parties and contributing to its institutional marginalization. In Cotacachi, while UNORCAC was clearly the area's most important organization and maintained an active role in designing community-development projects by connecting communities to outside funding and representing them politically, there was some disquiet that it had become too focused on projects and institutional politics and lost some of its oppositional edge, becoming too much a part of the system (Interview, MC, Cotacachi, January 6, 2014). Participating in these experiments in intercultural governance, while greatly advancing much of the agenda of Kichwa activists in terms of recognition, participation, and equality, also cost them a certain level of militancy.

In terms of challenging the economic base of the ruling elite, the record is decidedly more mixed, as development continued to be the driving discourse behind the region's Indigenous organizations and municipal governments. Cotacachi offered the stronger critique of capitalist development. Recognizing that subsistence agriculture was insufficient to support families, first UNORCAC and later the municipal government worked on various projects to increase food sovereignty while maintaining and deepening local identities and practices. They encouraged families, and women in particular, who were often left to work the land during the week, to take advantage of and preserve the high density of agro-biodiversity by exchanging seeds, to use water wisely, and to develop and market native products to international, fair trade, and organic buyers (Interview, HC, Cotacachi, October 27, 2011). Artisan groups, working through the AUC, developed cooperative marketing organizations and pushed the municipal government to promote tourism and make infrastructure improvements to the town center. The AUC, through its Natural Resource Management commission, encouraged the municipal government to declare itself an "Ecological Canton" and then used that designation to pressure the municipality to support communities and organizations fighting large- scale mining in Intag, clearly a deviation from the logic of colonial/modernist development.

Alternatives to dominant models of development were not as obvious in Otavalo, whose economy was more dependent on its insertion into transnational commercial and tourist networks. The predominance of Kichwa families in important sectors of the local economy, however, in itself represented a substantial change. "As Indigenous families started buying businesses in town, they displaced the former Mestizo owners. Some of them were quite surprised to find an Indian now their boss, and were resentful. A lot of them left, but others stayed and got used to it" (Interview, CC, Otavalo, April 3, 2014). While it might not be the best example of an intercultural dialogue, the ascension of Kichwa families to control large sectors of the economic field represented an important transformation of control of this sphere of the colonial matrix of power. At the same time, however, just because the means of production were owned by Kichwa individuals did not mean that exploitation ended; in some cases it was carried out by rich Kichwa families against poorer ones (Colloredo-Mansfeld 2009).

Gender is the third leg of Quijano's colonial matrix of power, and the process of dealing with gender was a complicated one. On the one hand, FICI and UNORCAC both had women's sections and paid attention to the particular needs of women. But, with a few exceptions, notably Carmelina Yamberla who was president of FICI and ran for mayor in Otavalo in 2000, the public leadership of those organizations was predominantly male. Yamberla claims this was in part due to sexism on the part of her colleagues, although she personally was "always respected in the organization." She also argued that Western and Kichwa constructions of gender were different and that "complementarity in our culture between men and women, which means equality but difference, and Western culture which seeks a sameness between men and women often causes problems with Western feminists" (Interview, Otavalo, May 5, 2007). In Cotacachi, women's issues were an important part of UNORCAC's projects in terms of healthcare, where Kichwa women were often mistreated in Mestizo clinics; economic production, where women had an increasingly important role in providing family incomes; in ancestral knowledge, where women were often the keepers of knowledge about medicinal plants; and identity issues, where women were more often the protectors of traditional dress, Kichwa language, and other ancestral knowledge. By design and internal statute, women were represented on all bodies of the AUC and several served as president, which not only ensured that women's needs and opinions were considered in all initiatives, but also that women developed leadership skills. Although sexism and violence against women continued to be serious problems and enforced the dominant social hierarchy, the Cotacachi authorities attempted to empower women to protect themselves. Bonilla and Ramos (2009, 136–139) reported on municipal legislation to protect women from violence, and, also on efforts by the AUC and UNORCAC to spread word through their networks of community leaders to discuss ways in which violence could be avoided, and where it could not, to make women aware of the legal protections to defend themselves against abusive partners. This intercultural process (institutional legislation and community discussion) represented an attempt to change traditionally exploitative gender roles in ways that might be more effective than simply imposing laws.

One of the mechanisms of wielding colonial power, besides politically and economically controlling colonized ethnic groups and enforcing gendered relations of power, is the symbolic violence of homogenizing subaltern groups. "Indians," after all, did not exist as such in the Americas before the European invasion. As the political processes unfolded in both Otavalo and Cotacachi, the heterogeneity of the Kichwa population became increasingly apparent. Even, perhaps ironically, the defeat of Indigenous candidates in Indigenous communities suggested that questions of representation went deeper than ethnic identity. While Indigenous communities were more likely to vote for Indigenous candidates, they also voted for the candidates they found to be most effective in terms of experience, educational background, and proven ability to carry out their promises. The 2014 election of Gustavo Pareja and Jomar Cevallos, (who ran with Kichwa candidates on their slates) suggested the willingness of Kichwa voters to cross ethnic lines to support whom they perceived to be the better candidate.

This deconstruction of an ethnic homogeneity went hand-in-hand with the assertion of Indigenous people as full citizens of the Ecuadorian state. The colonial and republican state, until the late 1970s, functioned by ruling over essentially two distinct populations in the Sierra: Mestizos and Indians. Even after the state abolished this legal distinction and allowed Indigenous people to vote, paternalism and intimidation continued to characterize Mestizo attitudes toward Indigenous people. The political successes of Kichwa organizations and individuals and their effective exercise of power were steps in the process of achieving full citizenship. Shortly after he left the party, Mario Conejo argued that, despite the successes of the movement, CONAIE and Pachakutik remained overly tied to their roots in land struggles and

have not fomented Indigenous citizenship—with rights AND
responsibilities. We are equal with everyone else now, but they
keep fighting the same old battles [...] We are full citizens now,
but the process is still not complete. We have all the same rights
as everyone else, but we also have responsibilities, and many
Indigenous organizations do not understand that they have to
take responsibility for themselves, and not wait for the state to
give them something (Interview, Otavalo, March 1, 2007).

Another young professional Kichwa from Peguche, and a supporter of
Conejo and Correa, was even more sharp,

CONAIE, FICI, they're dead. They don't represent anyone anymore.
They are living in the past and haven't evolved. They still go
up to their daddy-government with their hands out, hoping for
something. It doesn't work that way. We go out, organize, get
the votes and make the changes we want to see. We have power
and don't depend on anyone (Interview, SR, Otavalo, September
14, 2013).

By asserting their rights as citizens, Kichwa activists shifted from being
objects of control to being the subjects of political debate. This transformation marked a particularly important discourse within the movement
as it evolved away from the forms of organization founded first in the
haciendas, and then in the rural-based movements against them, into a
more diversified set of organizations and demands.

At the same time, however, even these more individualistic perceptions
of citizenship did not completely negate the collective identities and
practices of these politicians and their organizations. In his analysis
of politics in Otavalo and Cotacachi, Santiago Ortiz (2012) argued that
Kichwa actors developed a differentiated type of citizenship, one that
found expression in both individual and collective identities, and political
participation based in a regime of human rights that is simultaneously
universal (applicable to all citizens in terms of participation and protection)
and particular (in terms of rights to self determination and cultural

difference). Similarly, in her study of the functioning of the *junta de agua* (water governing board) in the Otavalo community of Mojandita, María Teresa Armijos (2012) discovered a comparable differentiation in citizenship among that community's primarily Kichwa members. While they participated in universal political activities and enjoyed the rights of all Ecuadorian citizens, they were also engaged in intense self-governing practices around water distribution, which at times required different responsibilities from them than from urban citizens. Rural communities, in both Otavalo and Cotacachi, for instance, maintained their own water systems, including building and cleaning collection tanks, piping systems, and administering user fees. While this might help foster democratic citizenship based on mutual rights and responsibilities, it was also different than the rights and responsibilities for urban residents, who were not expected to contribute labor to the water system nor attend regular meetings about its operation. They just paid their monthly bill. The intercultural process demonstrated by not just the election of Kichwa people as political authorities, but also the differential participation of Kichwa communities and individuals as citizens dramatically altered the local political landscape and opened up new, as yet unmet, horizons for a more just political system.

The participation in, and winning of, institutional political space by Kichwa organizations represented not only a challenge to traditional politics, but also, perhaps ironically, a challenge to Indigenous calls for a plurinational society. The decision by Kichwa activists to pursue elected office (always a problematic endeavor for social movements) to a certain extent meant accepting as legitimate state structures and authority, which would seemingly preclude CONAIE's calls for a different kind of relationship between Indigenous communities and the state. Clearly people like Conejo (and most FENOCIN activists), while accepting and promoting ethnic differences, rejected the notion of nationalities as counterproductive and unworkable. Indeed, the Indigenous and Mestizo populations in Otavalo and Cotacachi were so interdependent, and in the case of the city of Otavalo intermingled, that the notion of autonomy was not clear at all. At the same time, the participatory and inclusive policies of both municipal governments and their willingness to oversee a dialogue and negotiation between different cultural traditions and practices suggested another type of plurinationalism. Conejo, Tituaña, and Anrango may have been the mayors of multi-ethnic jurisdictions, but they were also the proudly *Kichwa* mayors of those jurisdictions. The networks of political power that put them in office and ultimately removed them from office operated on the basis of this differentiated citizenship, simultaneously individual and collective, Western and Kichwa. This ability to be both things at the same time and to provide an institutional space under which citizens could debate, discuss, and fight for their vision of progress and living well were important contributions to the interculturalization of Ecuadorian politics, particularly at this local level.

These experiments in intercultural governance not only provided a platform and voice for Indigenous activists, but also were clear demonstrations of how previously marginalized sectors could contribute to creating a better overall living situation for everyone. Between 1996 and 2006, Ecuador suffered through a period of extreme instability as traditional political parties proved incapable of ruling, neoliberal economic policies created hardship and chaos, and people adjusted to a new public reality as a multi-ethnic, pluricultural society. At the same time, however, the cantons of Otavalo and Cotacachi experienced remarkable political stability through experiments in inclusive decision-making. A steady improvement in socio-economic indicators was achieved as municipal governments were realigned to support long-term planning based on the needs of its populations.

This relative success did not come from nowhere, but was the result of generations of struggle and the consolidation of social and political networks, originating in rural Kichwa communities, but gradually spreading through the urban sectors as well. Despite the importance of politicized ethnic identities, in the end, intercultural politics was not the same as identity politics. Although a Kichwa identity and Kichwa constituents were clearly the foundation for these projects, they were not the ultimate goals. In the cases of Otavalo and Cotacachi, successful politicians, while not forgetting ethnic difference, sought out common ground with other groups in order to devise pragmatic solutions to concrete problems. By using their historic ties to other social movements, these Kichwa organizations built cross-ethnic alliances while recasting the meanings and practices of dominant cultural discourses such as development and democracy. Internal divisions based on class, religion, geography, educational level, and political ideology within Kichwa communities were also an important element in this intercultural process as it demonstrated that there was no singular Kichwa position, but rather those positions were continually constructed in relationship to all the other groups.

Notes

1. For a more detailed analysis of twentieth-century land reform and land disputes in Otavalo, see Ortiz (2012, 144-150).
2. Andrés Guerrero (2001) provides a history of these types of land disputes, particularly around the Quinchuquí *hacienda* between *comuneros* in Peguche, who were attempting to buy lands and other Kichwa communities that were involved in direct pressure and attempting to win favorable judgments from the central government.
3. At the time, the organization was known as the *Federación Nacional de Organizaciones Campesinas* (Federation of Campesino Organizations—FENOC). It would later change its name to reflect the cultural diversity and intercultural objectives of the country's rural sectors.
4. See the collection in Rhoades (2006) for a more detailed description of the environmental, agricultural, and cultural projects undertaken by UNOR-CAC through the early twenty-first century.
5. Funds for neighborhood improvements, for instance, were raised using a 60/40 formula under which the municipality provided 40 percent of the funds for a given project and homeowners were billed for 60 percent of the cost, either through surcharges to water bills or in-kind donations of labor (Lalander 2010a, 510).

CHAPTER 4

KICHWA COMMUNITY IN THE RURAL AND URBAN CROSSROADS

We go back to the community every Sunday.

Many people have explained to me the Kichwa conception of time as being a spiral. It is cyclical; one can see that in the calendar of ancestral, religious, and civic festivals, planting and harvesting times, school years for children. At the same time, things do not simply repeat themselves. Each year, *Inti Raymi* or Pawkar Raymi is slightly different: family members and other companions come and go; a different family is *prioste*; different bands perform; Kichwa words are mixed with *reggaetón* beats. Some planting seasons are better than others; the rains are changing, coming later and less frequently; it is hotter; a tractor is hired this year to plow. Children go back to school every year, but in different grades, different teachers, new challenges. My patient Kichwa teacher told me,

> The thing about spiral-time is that you can also see where you have come from because we understand the past to be literally in front of us, something you can see. We walk along the spiral with

our backs to the future (we can't see it) and know that things are
both the same, but different (Otavalo, March 13, 2007).

I find this metaphor of time, as it reflects the experience of Andean
people, useful in puzzling out the question of community. Andean
communities, like all communities, have changed over time, but they
continue to exist. One can look at today's communities and see how
they are similar to, but different from, the communities of the past.
The spiral image is also helpful because over time, especially since the
latter half of the twentieth century, Kichwa communities also expanded
outward. From small rural villages tied by kinship and territory, to
regional, urban-dwelling residents, to transnational migrants, the circle
of Kichwa community continued to expand to include increasingly
abstract and imagined communities of Kichwa nationality. But, despite its
changes and challenges, it continued to be a multifaceted and increasingly
complex Kichwa community, with ties to spaces, people, and history in
the northern Andes. Living in the city, be it Otavalo, Quito, or Barcelona,
meant neither losing a Kichwa-Otavalo identity, nor severing ties to
communities of origin. These passages through time and space were
interconnected and interactive parts of an ever-evolving construction
of community.

Community, and the identities and practices associated with it, do not
necessarily move in a unidirectional, linear fashion. If Western, modern
thought posits time and development as a singular process with newer
forms replacing older ones in an inexorable march toward development,
the production and circulation of Kichwa community in northern Ecuador
suggests a process open to plurality and adaptation rather than replacement. Despite repeated attempts by the Ecuadorian state to assimilate
Indigenous communities into national institutions, they maintained a
more ambiguous relationship. They used political space opened by the
state (often forced by Indigenous mobilization) to define local and ethnic
difference, while also participating in broader national conversations. The
legal recognition of communal governance, land reform, the abolition

of *huasipungo,* the right to vote, and the universalization of primary education all contributed to change, but did not result in the whole-scale abandonment of community and its replacement of ethnically undifferentiated Ecuadorian citizens. At the same time, even as some community structures and identities were strengthened, those communities themselves were altered and transformed by their involvement, willingly or otherwise, with neoliberal capitalism, the central state, and an increasingly globalized cultural matrix.

Community has served as both the organizational and ideological foundation of Indigenous organizing and continues to serve as a referent point, yet the communities of the 1970s are not the communities of the 2010s, and as Colloredo-Mansfeld (2009) observed, Kichwa people "are at a particularly unsettled moment of their history. Sameness is in ever shorter supply" (13). As a trope, "the communities," whether used by Indigenous or Mestizo speakers in the area almost always referred to the rural Kichwa communities. While these communities were often idealized or essentialized as being unchanging, stoic bearers of ancestral values, unity, poverty, and "culture," they were of course highly dynamic entities subject to all manner of internal heterogeneity, conflicts, and social stratification. At the same time, the Indigenous movement itself widened the meaning of community to include a national Kichwa community. This new imagined community transcended historic territorial boundaries and created a broader identity, with its own sets of meaning and socio-political organizations. Migration also greatly altered what community meant. Otavalo merchants and other far-flung members both recreated community structures where they found themselves and appropriated and brought back outside cultural practices, capital, and artifacts, which were incorporated into local communities. Finally, the movement's very success in creating opportunities for Indigenous participation in national public life, through education, work, and politics, softened the boundaries between Indigenous and Mestizo, rural and urban, which historically characterized these groups, leading to an intercultural reformulation of the production, circulation, and meaning of community. These intercultural processes, while to a certain degree destabilizing traditional meanings and practices of community, were also the standpoint from which Kichwa people engaged their wider national and global audiences.

Community represents a thorny question for two primary reasons. Concretely, Kichwa (and other) people use it to describe the geographically-bounded rural settlements in which many of them live. They share struggles, hardships, celebrations, and history together. In a sense, the community is quite tangible. On a more abstract level, community is also an invented discourse that differentiates groups, which easily becomes a romantic projection of the past. Gerald Creed (2006) argues that modernity's idealization of the rural community "came to represent what was apparently lost" (25), and originates in "the dominance of the urban gaze and subject position—the degree to which the urban condition has come to define and filter interpretations of the contemporary global situation" (23). The *idea* of community comes to stand for shared values, collective efforts, and direct democracy imagined to have existed in the past but extinguished by the dislocations and discontinuities of modern, capitalist development. This idea is easier to sustain and empower with greater spatial and temporal distance because "it is the separation that allows the romantic elements that can't persist in face-to-face groups to flourish. The uniformity is actually increased by separation and difference, which allows for more selectivity and more denial of the anticommunity sentiments of conflict, tension and even contempt" (Creed 2006, 39). Some of the strongest proponents of community, therefore, are often those that no longer live in the physical community, but who seek to use an idealized past to construct an ideal of how their particular group ought to be.

Throughout the twentieth century, the actual lived communities of the Ecuadorian highlands experienced tremendous change and pressures due to being increasingly drawn into circuits of modernity. The desire to resist that assimilation found an expression in the reaffirmation and recreation of an idealized rural community as the antithesis of modern, capitalist, Eurocentric, Ecuadorian national society. This latest complex articulation of community, however, was not *just* a romantic gesture toward the past but rather an ongoing attempt to define and maintain difference, while interacting with broader sectors of national and global society. Miranda Joseph (2002) argues that community ought to be understood as a productive discourse in that "communal subjectivity is constituted not by identity but rather through practices of production and consumption" (viii). Community is not something that always simply existed (the romantic version of community) but rather something that was, and is, always created. What should be of interest, therefore, is not the static depictions of community, which are produced not only by the state but also sometimes by activists themselves, but rather the processes through which community is produced, circulated, and consumed. Creating community is social labor, which creates value and provides a meaningful framework through which people identify themselves and ultimately act. Community defines the particular ways in which people interact with each other in relationship (but not necessarily opposition) to the abstraction of society (Joseph 2002, 17).

Kichwa organizations were involved in this type of social production. They constructed, circulated, and consumed discourses of community in their attempts to negotiate with the discourses, practices, and sectors of dominant Ecuadorian society. While they often employed romanticized tropes of community, they were not looking to avoid the rest of the world and retreat into pastoral isolation. Rather, they actively engaged in intercultural processes of negotiation that constructed new types of community. This community production wove together discourses and practices of the past and representations of that past, with shifting internal and external social relationships. Historic continuity and collectivity were key elements in Kichwa constructions of community. State narratives, anthropologists, and Kichwa people themselves commonly characterized Andean communities by sameness—subsistence agriculture, Kichwa language, relative isolation, and reciprocal relationships of work and exchange. Ecuadorian anthropologist José Sánchez Parga (2009), for instance, noted that Andean relationships traditionally were governed by the communal sensibilities of the *ayllu*, "where the prominence of the common over the private makes participation and sharing a fundamental principle regulating all social behavior in general and where the collective personality incorporates individual personalities" (16). Collective work (*minga*) and collective decision-making played important roles in the reproduction of rural Kichwa communities, and these values and practices served as means through which activists mobilized support for their movements. Mary Weismantel (2006) contends that while *ayllus* were real constructions, their contemporary importance relates more to the ways in which they were upheld as *ideal* versions of community and collectivity, rather than the actually inherited collective practices throughout the Andes. They were, in other words, some of the tools employed to produce community.

The reality, of course, is that those communities were neither completely isolated nor completely egalitarian. In many cases, their very existence as a physical community was due to colonial and national administrative assignment. There was always some connection, albeit marginal and exploitative, between national society and rural communities. Furthermore, activists and sympathetic intellectuals, while noting the collective nature of much community interaction, also tended to posit egalitarian and democratic values to those communities. There were, however, always differences of opinion and social hierarchies within communities. Leaders employed various coercive mechanisms to police dissent and ensure compliance, such as imposing fines or withholding resources for failure to participate. Communities were not created in a historic void, and the changing circumstances of the twenty-first century also changed the ways in which they sought to produce and circulate community. The success of the country's Indigenous movement since 1990, combined with the economic integration fostered by neoliberal reforms, drastically altered the ways in which Kichwa people interacted with each other and with the larger nation, seriously challenging predominant narratives about community. As isolation and marginality, gradually and incompletely, gave way to acceptance and integration,

Kichwa people faced a series of issues, including class differentiation, social mobility, educational opportunities, and contact with other cultural groups that challenged traditional community and opened up the possibility of new community configurations, which Sánchez Parga called "the metamorphosis of the *ayllu*" (2009, 138). This metamorphosis, however, was not a natural process but rather part of the social and political project of Indigenous peoples to claim their places in and transform their worlds.

In chapter 2, I noted that Fidel Tubino (2013) argues that "cultures are not what they are, but rather what they become; ... change is their essence" (611). The same can be said for communities and the identities and practices that comprise them. As the differences between them and us, Indigenous and Mestizo, rural and urban, became increasingly blurred, there were struggles to ground community identity in traditional markers of Kichwa culture even while recognizing the inevitability of change. New identities and new forms of community that fit into the globalized world of the twenty-first century were negotiated in such a way that Kichwa communities were not completely assimilated into dominant Mestizo society. While there a number of interrelated areas could be examined to analyze the intercultural negotiation of change within Indigenous communities, in this chapter I focus on two primary manifestations of contemporary Kichwa community in the northern highlands. First, I discuss rural communities, which were the foundation of both traditional Kichwa society and served as an idealized discourse about what the larger community ought to be. The reality, however, was that even so-called traditional communities were highly dynamic, internally heterogeneous organizations that sought to adapt to their new realities. Secondly, Kichwa communities also transformed themselves through the processes of urbanization, migration, and globalization, which pulled Kichwa people into new relationships with each other and with the world around them, challenging values, cultural practices, and identities. While in both cases, community members expressed a sense of loss over some aspects of their collective lives, they also demonstrated efforts to revitalize and resignify practices, relationships, and rituals in their new contexts.

"These old Communities, I would say, have everything"

In his book, *Fighting Like A Community,* Rudi Colloredo-Mansfeld (2009) argues that with transformations of social life in the countryside precipitated by the dissolution of the *hacienda* system, "old racial markers did not so much disappear as metastasize. The polarities that once defined the Indian/White boundary—rural vs. urban, Kichwa vs. Spanish, illiterate vs. educated, peasant vs. professional—have become acknowledged internal differences of native communities" (13). These changes and differences within the community challenged preconceived notions of sameness often found in writing about Indigenous communities and identities, thereby necessitating a more dynamic means to analyze and understand community formation. Because of what Colloredo-Mansfeld characterizes as the Indigenous population's "deep pluralism" (88)—seen in the increasing differences in rural/urban living, educational levels, occupations, class, religion, political ideology, and other factors—leaders, activists, and other members were compelled to actively and constantly negotiate the meaning of community. Rather than seeing community, therefore, as an immutable and an *a priori* institution, he likens the process of community to Anderson's (1991) imagined communities built on idealized ties of horizontal solidarity. He emphasizes, however, that these ties are constantly tested, disputed, and negotiated and are not automatically or forever accepted, thus pointing to community as being a dialogic process among increasingly diverse groups of people. The communities were the bearers of ancestral knowledge and practices but were also confronted by how to balance that knowledge and those traditions with the pressures of modernization and the challenges of broader participation in national and global society.

In the Andes, communities were generally territorially defined groups oriented around sets of families. Traditionally these groups worked in agriculture and served as the basis for mutual economic support, resource management, and cultural reproduction. Over time, they also formed the basis of internal self-government and became the conduit through which local concerns were mediated with the state and other outside groups. The communities were not only the building blocks of the Indigenous movement, but also developed local leadership, defined their territories, and articulated issues. Although there has been a great deal of debate about the relative importance of cultural versus class-identity production as a function of rural communities, the area's Kichwa-Otavalo and Kichwa-Kayambi communities intimately connected these issues. As community organizations advocated for their economic wellbeing, they also connected those issues to being ethnically, and therefore organizationally and legally, distinct from their Mestizo neighbors.

The communities began their legal existence through the 1937 *Ley de Comunas*, which named the community assembly as the maximum local authority, with routine matters delegated to a community council (*cablido*) and various officers. Over time, other communal institutions, such as the *juntas de agua* were created to manage particular issues and resources. In a 2008 survey, Santiago Ortiz (2012, 121) found that Indigenous Otavalo and Cotacachi leaders saw their responsibilities, in order of importance, as maintaining community infrastructure, domestic water use, conflict mediation, application of justice, control of land transactions, control of communal lands, education, and water for irrigation. Furthermore, over half of the *comunas* in Imbabura were formed after the country's return to democracy in 1979, mostly from splits from other communities (117–118). Recognition as a *comuna* gives the community a legal identity and allows its members to make internal decisions and carry out certain policies while making requests from state agencies. The timing of community creation is important because it is linked not only to democratic reform of the state, but also to the increase in Indigenous suffrage and, of course, the Indigenous movement's calls for local autonomy. Although some community institutions were weakened by divisions over religion and partisan politics or the proletarianization of rural labor, the *comunas* played important roles in resolving internal conflicts, disputes with other communities over territory and resources, regulating land sales within their territories, and representing their people to outside agencies.

One leader of the Kichwa-Kayambi community of Inti-Culuquí, which belongs to the González Suarez parish of Otavalo, explained his role:

> My name is Roberto Tocagón, and I am leader of this community. I have worked for the benefit of the community since I was 15 years old. For 20 years I have been in the leadership: president, secretary, treasurer ... At least some of the communities are old ones that have survived since 1720: this community, the Angla community, and that of Tocagón and Pijar, although some other communities have more recently formed. Those old communities I would say have everything, are full of information. In other words, those are communities that have their history and much knowledge. For us, we could say they are libraries of learning, and that our elders held an enormous amount of knowledge, and today all this knowledge has been disappearing. I have known several elders here in my community who were well listened to: my grandparents, for instance. I am a descendant of the leaders after leaders after leaders, right? So maybe that's why my sons are also on the same path I followed by working hard and training themselves. I hope that not only my children, but the whole community of the San Pablo Basin, are leaders, because the problem is population growth. And this causes many problems in terms of agricultural productivity, especially in terms of natural resources. Because they [young people] go out, go out to work outside of the community, and this is causing their acculturation, the loss of knowledge...of our elders. Some young people today do not even know, where their communities' boundaries are. So we are working on this, focusing on these problems (Interview, Inti Culuquí, October 10, 2013).

In introducing himself to me, for an interview ostensibly about his distinguished conservation work in the *páramos* (high grasslands) in which he lives (see chapter 6), it was clearly important for him to establish some things about himself and his community, so that I would be able to better understand his work. First, that as a community leader, he has held a number of formal positions. Although these are elected positions, or "charges," appointed through the community assemblies, Don Roberto's family has been an influential one, and he assumes that this influence will carry on through his sons. Secondly, he points out that he is from one of the older communities in the area. Some communities, such as his, can trace their origin back to colonial documents, through their legal constitution under the twentieth-century *Ley de Comunas*. This pedigree distinguishes them from more recent communities that may not have the same deep history. Being an older community cements its legitimacy even further by being able to make broader claims about ancestral knowledge and territorial rights.

From this brief introduction to himself and his community, he also noted that his community was changing and not necessarily for the better. He pivoted from his son's education and training to describing some of the anxieties of rural communities: populations outgrowing agricultural productivity, making it impossible for people to support themselves; young people working elsewhere and acquiring other (and negative) cultural influences; and loss of ancestral knowledge, to the point that many young people do not even recognize their territorial boundaries. Although he was not afraid of change and did not eschew the outside world, the growing lack of local knowledge was obviously problematic. With a university degree in forestry, Don Roberto worked closely with a number of international NGOs and was the proud president of a cooperative of local organic producers, which directly provided to markets in Quito and Otavalo. Rather, his concern with the intercultural processes with which he and his community were involved was that they would lead to the loss of those elements—ancestral knowledge and territorial control in particular—that provided both cultural difference and economic survival.

Community leaders played an important role in terms of the functioning of the communities and also as an indication of how communities adapted to changing times. Community presidents were looked up to and entrusted with a great deal of responsibility for managing community affairs. Besides attending innumerable meetings with government officials, various community members, and organizations, they also mediated intra- and inter-community disputes, organized *mingas* for infrastructure maintenance, and served, at times, as spiritual confidantes. Roberto Tocagón explained that:

> I have also been a community mediator, well known in the Lake San Pablo Basin, with the people and with communities. We have resolved family problems, marriage problems, which now with the question of the flowers [flower plantations], parents are leaving and abandoning their children. Sometimes they find another partner in the company. The children are with grandparents, with aunts and uncles. It's not the same as being with their own father and mother, because of their special love and affection. This situation is a concern. So these are some of the problems I have helped solve. There have also been inter-community problems about territories, water. There have been criminal cases at the level of leaders, and that I avoided further problems. I have facilitated an agreement between the two parties to keep them from getting lawyers or involving the *teniente político....* I have helped resolve 130 problems; more than a lawyer. And I have helped people avoid losing money, in buying the lawyers, the authorities, although there are still problems everyday. Now I am just an advisor. Other colleagues are leaders who assume these responsibilities (Interview, Inti Culuquí, October 10, 2013).

In his recounting of some of the ways that he has helped his community, he indicates the importance of his role as a mediator, as someone who was trusted by others and was willing to try to resolve problems. He worked at all levels, from family disputes to inter-community conflicts around water and boundaries, to helping people avoid using lawyers and the courts to resolve disagreements. Community leaders, like Don Roberto, therefore, did not just execute state functions of office but were also involved in the everyday lives of their members.

Tocagón is in many ways quite representative of community leaders. First, he came from a well-known and trusted family with a history of leadership and personal success. Second, his formal education contributed to his attractiveness as a leader because communities often saw educational success as an important qualification that demonstrated knowledge accumulation, understanding of the technical side of various projects, and the ability to negotiate with the Mestizo world. At the same time, like much else in the rural world, the profile of community presidents and other leaders was changing. Long dominated by older, more experienced men, the desire for somebody who is "well-prepared" gave the edge to a cadre of younger leaders who finished school, and who, like their older counterparts such as Tocagón, understood how to negotiate both Mestizo officialdom and Indigenous discourse. Importantly, women began to assume important leadership roles and represented approximately one-third of the positions on community councils in the region (Ortiz Crespo 2012, 120).

That is not to say that community members worked things out peaceably all of the time. Life in the communities, as Roberto Tocagón insinuated, was often conflictive, fueled particularly by the anxiety about change. Colloredo-Mansfeld (2007) argues, "members of indigenous communities must work out problems beyond discourse, identity, and communication. They pursue conflicting interests, make and unmake relationships, and reproduce shared bases of economic life" (103). Doña Sarita, for example, was the first woman elected as president of her Kichwa-Otavalo community. Like many other leaders, she was a native Kichwa speaker, but bilingual in Spanish, and came from a relatively successful local family. Additionally, she had worked professionally in Quito, had good working relationships with many people in the municipal and provincial governments, and became an active member in the Alianza País political movement, playing an important role in AP's local victories. She was well liked and had a reputation for helping out anyone who asked. She found her initial widespread support and popularity eroded over the two years of her presidency, however, by community rivals and by rumors that her parents had acquired their lands years ago by stealing or tricking desperate families into selling them. She helped families displaced by expansion of the Pan-American Highway in 2009 gain better settlements from the government, promoted the community's *Inti Raymi* festival, and helped to organize a community tourism project. Nevertheless, she left office under a cloud of mistrust and acrimony. Although the rumors about her seemed, in the end, unfounded, the dynamic pointed to the divisions and difficulties that exist within communities. The reality of Indigenous community relationships, as with most human organizations, was marked by inequalities, rivalries, and unsettled differences of opinion.

Indigenous organizations and other radical political reformers often held up the communities as models of participatory democracy. All community members were invited and expected to participate in general assemblies and to serve in various positions if called upon. Issues affecting the community including development projects, water distribution, and political actions were collectively discussed and debated. The consensus-building processes of many communities helped solidify support for militant actions like blocking highways during the time of the uprisings because people collectively agreed to decisions. In terms of projecting that democracy outward, political candidates for all offices routinely sought meetings with the communities to explain their platforms and ask for votes. Communities, however, often resisted pressure from outside organizations to vote in particular ways. Candidates representing Pachakutik, for instance, faired poorly in the communities since the 2006 election cycle, despite most communities in Otavalo being affiliated with FICI and CONAIE, which supported Pachakutik. This pattern suggested that community members made their own political decisions, like for whom to vote, rather than listening uncritically to leaders of larger organizations.

Although these processes played a significant role in the development of wider participatory initiatives at the municipal level in Otavalo and particularly in Cotacachi, there were also less democratic processes at play within the communities. Entrenched leaders often employed coercion and pressures to ensure favorable results. Colloredo-Mansfeld (2009) documented the use of list-making as a means for keeping track of participation, fines, and other sanctions for those who did not comply. This sort of bureaucratization of community life by Indigenous organizations mirrored some state practices. Another controversial tactic employed by some community leaders was to punish noncompliance by cutting off people's water. Pacífico Fachamba, a long time organizer for UNORCAC and president of Peguche's *junta parroquial*, criticized this practice, noting that although the *juntas de agua* ought to be technical commissions, they were

> sometimes used for political ends and as a means of oppression. We should not operate this culture of repression, using fines and cut-offs of water for non-participation; instead we should invite people and convince them to participate. The issue of water has been very manipulated in our territories and at times it is a precise and lethal weapon of repression. It should not be; it is a right; it is life (Interview, Peguche, December 10, 2011).

In this statement the tensions between individual and collective rights and the right to dissent and not participate in community activities such as *mingas* or protests came into conflict with the desire of some leaders to enforce their authority. Fachamba, in this case, was advocating a more measured approach to encouraging participation, noting that convincing, rather than threatening, people was both more effective and built longer lasting and more coherent organizations.

Authoritarian structures within communities, however, were not uncommon. Commenting on his support for Rafael Correa's sometimes heavy-handed approach to Indigenous organizations, one Kichwa-Otavalo leader (and Correa supporter) noted, "after so many years on the *hacienda*, my people are used to the lash. They need to be told what to do sometimes, and what Correa is trying to do is overall good and necessary" (Interview, Otavalo, September 6, 2013). As an educated and politically savvy professional, Manuel explained, "all of the political parties come out here and ask for votes. The people (in the community) get confused and ask us whom we should vote for. So we tell them" (Interview, Otavalo, October 3, 2011). His position within the community clearly illustrated some of the class and educational divisions that have arisen within rural communities and the responsibility that he saw to inform his fellow community members of their best choices.

My point is not to cast judgment on particular community leaders or practices but rather to highlight the tensions that run through not only Kichwa but also many communities to a greater or lesser extent. Kichwa communities were not derived from whole cloth but were in a constant state of transformation in which members negotiated their relative positions just as the communities were also engaged in their own creation and re-creation in relationship to the rest of the world. Rural communities, furthermore, were not simply collections of people who happened to live near each other, nor were they idyllic, conflict free, completely egalitarian associations. They were created through dynamic processes of internal negotiations, inequalities, and tensions between members over leadership and direction. At the same time, as institutions they exercised important functions in the everyday lives of their members. Most notably they were the primary vehicle through which members found their voices in decisions that affected them and through which they represented themselves to the outside world.

Besides common history, practices, and beliefs, shared territory has been one of the components by which people defined their communities. Land was always both an economic and cultural resource to Indigenous communities. Historians Marc Becker and Silvia Tutillo (2009) reported that even before land reform "many Indigenous people were willing to work for lower salaries in order to have their own parcel of land, because it was a central element of their Indigenous culture and their ethnic legacy" (61). Even small parcels of land helped provide sustenance against uncertain times or the contingent nature of exclusively salaried work. Furthermore, being connected to a particular place outweighed the potential of earning more money elsewhere. The Indigenous movement prioritized territorial control because it represented not only an important economic resource, but also a key ideological component linking Indigenous people and differentiating them from Mestizos. The connection between territory and identity was one of the reasons that Don Roberto was concerned that some younger people in newer communities, for instance, did not know or seem to have much interest in the borders of their territory. Ancestral knowledge about medicine and agricultural productivity as well as the calendar of festivals was rooted in the land. The mass mobilizations of the 1990s were triggered, in large part, by the government's slow pace in carrying out land reforms promised in the 1970s by failing to break up large landholdings or recognize Indigenous land claims. At the same time, however, economic and population pressures made it increasingly difficult to maintain a community-based subsistence agriculture, putting into doubt the ability of communities to continue to maintain meaningful control over their territories.

We were standing on Don Pablo's roof, darkness falling quickly, in the Iltaquí community in the hills above Cotacachi. Lightning reflected off Imbabura and the mountains to the east.

> This is all of my land, beautiful isn't it? From that tree over there, over to the road is all ours. Mostly corn. It's good soil here. Up above, the community is building the soccer field; the president said they would fix the road if I gave them some land. Those cold winds come down from Mamá Cotacachi. It's about a two-hour walk up the mountain, if you don't stop to pick things to eat or rest. The water is good up there (Interview, April 5, 2014).

Like many people in the communities of Otavalo and Cotacachi, despite the land belonging to Don Pablo, he also belonged to the land. Also, like many people in these communities, his and his family's relationship to the land was quickly changing. Although his land was filled with corn and beans ready for harvesting, his main work was construction in Cotacachi, Otavalo, Ibarra, or even as far away as Quito, "wherever there is a job." His situation was quite the norm for the region, where weekdays saw a mass exodus of working-age men because subsistence farming was not a viable livelihood. Furthering the transformation of land tenancy, each generation's individual allotment of land dwindled as families' plots were subdivided into increasingly smaller plots, and as a result many physically left the community altogether. Don Pablo's children, for instance, all lived in the nearby towns of Quiroga and Otavalo, and one daughter even lived in Spain. Although the nearby ones came to tend their crops, they did not live there anymore.

While the economic dislocations of globalization were certainly nothing new to Indigenous people, the physical and cultural reproduction of the community had become increasingly tenuous as people's relationship to their land changed (Sánchez Parga 2007). Subsistence farming was a decreasingly viable option for families, who increasingly grew crops for their own consumption but had little left over to sell. Many farmers, like Don Pablo, were forced to either seek work in the city, in distant countries, or in large agribusiness operations—particularly flowers in the Northern Sierra. One Kayambi organizer, Miguel, an agricultural educator and leader of a production cooperative in his community which had sought to create markets for traditional crops, lamented the difficulties in maintaining the lands for which they had fought so hard over the past generations. He told me,

> It's impossible to make ends meet with those lands. We want some things: education for our children, a TV, things like that. I have had to sell some of my land to the flower *hacienda* because, although I want to keep it, if I can't produce on it, I can't keep it. I need to make some money to survive. All the families are doing it [...] and what happens is that people go to work with the flowers, particularly at their busy times because they pay a salary. It's terrible pay, but it is something. And then they don't produce the traditional crops anymore, so they have to buy their food from

outside the community, which means they have to sell more of their land because they don't have enough time to work on it. It's a cycle that keeps getting worse, and gradually people forget how to work their own land (Interview, Ayora, November 18, 2013).

People in these circumstances were seeing their social relations transform from people tied to their land to becoming a rural proletariat, increasingly dependent on a salary. This transformation came even at the expense of their own land, which many clearly acknowledged as not only their ancestral inheritance, but also key to passing on their culture and potential wealth to their children. Intimately connected with the economic difficulties of making a living off of the land, or even in some cases being able to hold onto one's land, was the concomitant loss of knowledge that goes with it. As people worked in the flower *haciendas*, for instance, they "forgot," in Miguel's words, how to grow traditional crops and became increasingly dependent of food grown and processed elsewhere, leading not only to poorer nutrition, but also to a loss of ancestral foods and knowledge about their preparation.

Another significant loss originating from the changes in community members' relationship with the land was the slow death of the *minga*, or collective work group, as an integral part of community practice and social identity. At one time *mingas* were how people reciprocated labor, working in each other's fields, helping to build houses, or community infrastructure, such as roads and water systems. As times changed, however, money often replaced reciprocal labor; it being more convenient, for instance, to hire laborers at harvest time, or skilled workers to build houses. This change was in part a reflection of rural people becoming more integrated into wage labor, where they did not have the time to work outside of their jobs, and where money, instead of reciprocal labor, became the medium of exchange. Road construction and repair, water systems, and environmental restoration projects were still carried out through *mingas* in many rural communities. Participation was expected and communal authorities kept track of who attended and who did not, often levying fines for failure to comply. Yet most community leaders reported that these work parties were rapidly disappearing. Pacífico Fachamba, President of the Miguel Egas (Peguche) Parish summarizing the perspective of many Kichwa leaders, said bluntly, "The *minga* has been lost. It is a festival and it has been lost, especially in Peguche" (Interview, Peguche, December 20, 2011). It is notable that this tradition has been particularly lost in Peguche, whose population has been actively involved in national and global artisan and commerce circuits and is perhaps less dependent on agricultural production than other communities.

Even in communities that were still primarily dependent on agriculture, the increasing importance of wage labor over subsistence agriculture created a different social relationship among community members. One Kichwa-Otavalo environmental leader, Frank Gualsaqui, explained:

> The flower plantations here threaten the entire social organization that there was before. Here the organizational base was very strong and everything was resolved around organizing the *minga*. Now we are in a moment in which that is tending to disappear, or at least there is a great risk of it ending, because the people are trading the logic of organizing for the logic of money. For example, in the community you have to go out to work in the *minga*. If not, you get fined. "No, I'm not going anymore. I'll pay; here take it, bye. No problem." So the organizational issue is sort of complicated because now people, 16, 17 years old, have chosen to work and they have their money and live their independence. So, yes, the issue of flower production has brought employment, but it has brought all of these social and organizational problems, too. So, yes the communities are fairly complicated: how do they sustain their ideals or the conception that they had of the community nowadays? (Interview, Tabacundo, October 28, 2011).

People's relationship to each other, therefore, as expressed through the willingness to work with each other was substantially changed by their livelihoods being dependent on salaried labor. As money became the key medium of exchange, and employment took individuals physically out of the community, shared work lost its value.

One former community president, Milton, from one of Cotacachi's rural communities, explained that this had implications beyond the economic.

> No one comes out for the *mingas* anymore. It's really quite sad. Before it really was a party. You had your project to do and everyone worked hard together at it, but all the families also brought food and drinks, *mote, fritada, habas*[corn, pork, beans], everything. And everyone would come. Now it's two or three of us and, if we remember, someone brings some bread and some Coke. It's not like it used to be. People would rather pay the fine. But, the *minga* was more than just the work. It was a way of bringing everyone together. You got to know people better. It was hard work, but it was also fun (Interview, Cotacachi, January 6, 2014).

The *minga*, therefore, besides being necessary to get large projects done, was also an important element in the construction and reproduction of a particular form of community. It reinforced Andean notions of reciprocity and provided an opportunity to build camaraderie by engaging in a common project. The *minga* tradition also distinguished them from the Mestizo population by emphasizing a collective over individualistic ethos.

"No one is going to tell us how to develop"

Faced with drastic changes and admitted losses, however, rural Kichwa communities in the area did not disappear but rather were in a process of adapting to their new normal situations. Just as they negotiated internal differences and coped with new methods of exchanging value and labor, they also sought out different relationships with urban areas to stay on their land and maintain their families and their cultures. Despite enormous pressures on them, they managed this process while redefining what it meant to be rural Kichwa communities in the twenty-first century, rather than abandoning those identities. Breaking with past development models, many Kichwa communities questioned the agendas of outside agencies, which historically had pressured them to assimilate into nationalist and capitalist modes of production at the expense of their own traditions. Building on the organizational strength and the self-confidence coming from the successes of the movements of the late twentieth century, communities were careful not to forsake their Kichwa identity even as they realized that being Kichwa meant adapting to changing circumstances. Rumiñahui Anrango, President of UNORCAC, very clearly stated that "nobody from outside is going to tell us how develop" (Interview, Cotacachi, April 19, 2007).

In Cotacachi, UNORCAC's political success was due, in no small part, to its leadership in designing development projects that improved the standard of living for rural people and provided for economic activities that supplemented subsistence agriculture, by building on and strengthening inhabitants ancestral knowledge and Indigenous identity (Rhoades 2006). A key element of UNORCAC's philosophy of "development with identity" was an understanding that economic development was necessary and that communities would not survive with the economic model of past generations. At the same time, however, they resisted the kinds of developmental practices that lead to the atomization of strictly capitalist development. Instead they encouraged development that not only brought economic benefit, but also simultaneously strengthened the community as a viable twenty-first century entity.

Keeping people on their land and active in collective projects were two of the underlying goals of many UNORCAC initiatives, including the issue of nutritional security. Families in the region faced a multiplicity of problems in guaranteeing adequate nutrition, including dwindling plot size, changing weather patterns that yielded hotter temperatures and less water for irrigation, and dependence on salaried work that resulted in the purchase of less nutritious, processed foods. If families could neither grow nor buy enough food to feed their families, they could not stay where they were, endangering the very existence of the rural community. In order to help support those communities meet their nutritional needs, UNORCAC focused on two primary strategies that combined traditional knowledge and practice with engagement with the outside world: namely, improving production and developing alternative forms of income.

UNORCAC project manager, Hugo Carrera, noted that the Cotacachi area is one of the most agriculturally bio-diverse regions in the country, containing twelve of the country's twenty-six varieties of corn along with numerous varieties of beans, root crops, and Andean fruits. He added that, "this diversity obeys the permanent relationship between agriculture and a millenarian culture of farming" (Interview, Cotacachi, October 27, 2011). Generations of experimentation adapted these crops and local cultural practices to the microclimates of the Cotacachi mountains and valleys. UNORCAC sponsored periodic workshops for family farmers to share their knowledge and adaptation strategies. These conversations often highlighted organic and agroecological practices, which both protect the area's biodiversity and help farmers avoid the financial burdens of industrial inputs. Another important initiative was the seed fair held shortly before the annual planting. UNORCAC encouraged families to keep their locally developed seeds after harvest to share with other families. This fair served to not only propagate local varieties, but also became an important community-building event where people, mostly women, exchanged knowledge about local crops and food preparation. The seed exchange provided alternatives to agribusiness-produced seeds, which had higher yields but were more expensive and had dubious long-term effects. Furthermore these exchanges encouraged people to continue to consume traditional, locally grown foods.

In addition to improving productivity by deepening ancestral and contemporary scientific knowledge, UNORCAC worked with communities on developing value-added products and local markets. Working with international microcredit agencies, they assisted communities in the creation of small agribusiness endeavors to produce dehydrated *uvilla* (ground cherry), native fruit jams, and *ají* (spicy pepper) paste. While they could sell these products locally, they also began to export them, taking advantage of their fair-trade, certified organic status. Locally, they also organized weekly agroecological markets in Cotacachi and Quiroga to sell their products directly to an urban population increasingly concerned about the harmful effects of pesticides and chemical fertilizers on their health and environment. These weekly gatherings, besides providing a modest boost to income, also constituted important social time between women from different rural communities, which in turn contributed to the production of a broader community.

Although agriculture continued to be an important economic activity, most rural people in Cotacachi were also involved in other types of work, and UNORCAC recognized that community development also meant exploring other ways to earn money while strengthening local identities and social relations. Tourism and health care were two fields in which development and community building took root. Building on Otavalo's success and realizing that many tourists were interested in Kichwa culture, UNORCAC formed its own tourist agency, *Runa Tupari* (Meeting Indigenous People). While providing many similar services as other tour groups, Runa Tupari sought to connect local people with tourists by arranging short visits and overnight stays in rural villages. It served as a means through which Kichwa communities could maintain control over their territories, earn money, and find a motivation to maintain their own cultural traditions. It also represented a fundamentally intercultural project in that it was dependent on interactions between Kichwa and other peoples, resulting in a constant exchange of experiences and ideas, while circulating a particular discourse of Kichwa community to outsiders. A second project, *Sumak Hampi* (Good Health), in conjunction with the Ecuadorian Red Cross, hoped to systematize ancestral knowledge of medicinal plants for use within the community and to market to a wider audience. Toward that end, they founded a small business, *Sumak Jambina* (Good Medicine), led by women, that was devoted specifically to "strengthening ancestral medicine" and marketing their products to the outside world as a safer and more ecologically sound alternative to Western medicine (Interview, SJ, Cotacachi, October 5, 2011).

Many of these efforts involved not just agricultural and employment innovation but also reflected local labor mobility, particularly that of men. It was no coincidence that many of these projects focused on women, in part because working-age men often left during weekdays for paid work elsewhere. Many rural communities in Cotacachi and Otavalo, therefore, acted as a sort of bedroom community, with men commuting to the nearby urban areas and flower plantations (Ortiz Crespo 2012). This notable daily or weekly absence of many men meant substantial changes in gender roles, particularly in terms of earning family incomes. Along with UNORCAC's advocacy of women's rights in general, therefore, special attention was paid to how women managed their family fields and found other types of income more closely related to their communities.

This mixed approach to development corresponded to UNORCAC's community advocacy by helping members maintain and transform their cultural identity. Kichwa identity was strongly linked to land and territory as both a source of income and as an important symbol. Projects designed to keep control of land, therefore, represented an intercultural approach to development. Using both ancestral knowledge and practices, as well as greater integration into urban and global markets, UNORCAC facilitated the transformation of rural Kichwa communities. UNORCAC's success and systematic efforts represented only one example of rural processes to simultaneously maintain an identity of difference, based on community cultural practices and social organization, while finding ways to interact with and take advantage of broader opportunities from other communities, urban areas, national agencies, and transnational organizations. Just as changing political contexts demanded new forms of organization in the articulation of community, changing economic circumstances also required new ways of organizing economic and social activity to sustain and reproduce those communities.

"I'M FROM OTAVALO NOW. I'M OTAVALEÑA."

The reorganization of rural communities represented only one of the multiple ways in which Kichwa people approached issues of change and continuity as they redefined their communities and their cultural identities. The abolishment of *huasipungo* under land reform, the impacts of globalization, and the increased participation in public life as a result of the successes of the Indigenous movement led many Kichwa people to reconsider community. Instead of just a face-to-face, geographically limited phenomenon, "the community" now also included people living in urban areas and other parts of the world, as well as in local villages. Not only did national and global discourses bump up against local and ancestral ones, but the heterogeneity brought about by social stratification, religious differences, and political disputes challenged the basic assumptions of sameness that would seem to underscore the definition of community. And yet, for the most part, people did not abandon their Kichwa identities, although what it meant to be Kichwa was not the same as their parents' or grandparents' sense of self and community. Jorge Sánchez Parga's (2009) "metamorphosis of the *ayllu*," was the result of an almost constant dialogue of a "multivocal community" (Wibbelsman 2009) that was constantly re-creating itself.

Extraordinarily high levels of migration and urbanization—sometimes permanent, sometimes circular—characterized the Otavalo population, which meant that members of Kichwa communities now crossed between rural, urban, local, and global spaces, challenging the historic groundedness of cultural discourses and practices. Language, dress, and other outward cultural markers, for instance, were frequent points of contention and usually overlapped with other generational issues. As the community spread further and further from the valleys around Imbabura and Cotacachi Mountains, technology played an ever greater role in not only keeping people connected, but also in defining the community itself. Although some practices and knowledge may have been lost, there were also many efforts to adapt knowledge and practice to the contemporary.

And yet, despite the seeming deterritorialization of at least part of the Kichwa-Otavalo community, there remained important ties to place and people made efforts to return to home to celebrate them.

Throughout Latin America, patterns of rural migration to the cities since the late twentieth century have been different than in earlier eras because moving to the city no longer necessarily meant abandoning the countryside, connections to rural communities, or cultural identity (Albó 2008; Bengoa 2000). The city of Otavalo represents a microcosm of this phenomenon, as Kichwa people interacted at all levels with Mestizo people, came and went from their ancestral communities on their way to Quito, Barcelona, or New York, appropriated cultural artifacts and practices from their travels, and yet maintained a distinctive sense of being Kichwa (Sobczyk and Soriano Miras 2015b). Just as changes in the countryside often revealed rifts within the community as sometimes painful debates about identity, change, and adaptation, urban residents (or people passing through urban spaces) also confronted questions about how to define their community. At the same time, becoming urban did not mean cutting ties with communities of origin, as family extended into the nearby rural communities and trips to the country for planting, harvesting, weddings, or the occasional soccer game or volleyball tournament were frequent. Cultural change, while different in the country and the city, was, therefore, at the same time intimately connected with the fluid relationships between them.

In the city of Otavalo, Kichwa people created a vibrant, diverse community that, while wielding a great deal of economic and political power, also constantly negotiated a series of contradictions in cultural models and sociability. Although it would be impossible to capture the diversity of that community, the contrast between two of my neighbors in a newer development in the northern part of the city in the years between 2006 and 2014 helps illustrate some of the disparities in Otavalo's Indigenous community. Both families consisted of a married couple in their twenties and thirties with several children. Their parents and extended families continued to live in smaller towns and own and work land in the outskirts of Otavalo or Cotacachi, and an important part of their social lives took place in those communities, to which they made frequent visits. They dedicated long hours to their various jobs and businesses, valued education for their children, and, although not politically active, followed local and national events, voting for candidates and policies that seemed to most directly affect them. They had Kichwa, Mestizo, and foreign friends and considered Indigenous traditions and knowledge to be important. At the same time, they followed usual standards of dress for urban (and increasingly rural) Kichwa people. The women wore traditional clothes, *anaco, blusa,* and *alpargatas* outside of the house, particularly to work, church, and social events. The men used Western dress, flannel shirts and jeans or athletic wear, and running shoes except in the most formal of occasions, where they would wear the more traditional white pants, shirt, and (rarely) blue poncho and felt hat. The children tended to use Western dress, although the girls would wear their "Indigenous clothes" for school and church. They preferred leggings and t-shirts.

Participating in traditional community celebrations proved challenging for both families. They were reluctant, for instance, to hold parties or become godparents for rural relatives because their living space would not accommodate the large numbers of people who would be expected to attend baptism or marriage celebrations. At the same time the expectation of reciprocity (exchanging potatoes, guinea pigs, chickens, and other goods) was difficult for them. Because they did not produce or keep these things in their household, acquiring them to give away represented a great expense. They did participate in family affairs but were also very much aware of the cost of these things to their individual family budget, where marginal surpluses were dedicated to investment in their businesses or the needs of their children.

The similarities between these families tended to end there, however. The Flores family, Atik and Luisa, would be considered middle class. From Peguche, Atik's family had been a merchant family for generations, and he spent many years from his late teens to early thirties traveling to and living in the United States, selling handicrafts in New York City and Chicago and on the craft fair and Pow-Wow circuit throughout the US. His father lived abroad, and his mother, after spending years in New York, worked on small commercial and tourist ventures in Otavalo and Peguche. Luisa's father was the first person from his rural community to attend university and he was a regional leader in the Indigenous movement in the 1980s and was later employed in various educational and development agencies, meaning that she spent a good part of her childhood and adolescence in Quito. Upon the family's return to the Otavalo area, her mother became a prominent community leader and eventually an activist in the Alianza PAIS political movement. Both Luisa and Atik finished high school and began their professional lives with Atik traveling to the US to sell and Luisa setting up a small textile store with a mostly Indigenous clientele. They bought land from Atik's family in Otavalo and built a house. They also owned rental property in another part of town. In their thirties, they began their university studies in management and business. Their hard work enabled them to undertake regular business trips to the United States, acquire a car and other consumer goods, and provide supplemental educational opportunities for their children. As small business owners, however, they were always concerned about the long-term viability of their finances.

Atik and Luisa also represented part of a cultural shift of Kichwa people in urban areas. Their parents were all bilingual Kichwa-Spanish speakers, equally comfortable in either language. They, however, generally spoke Spanish and Luisa described her Kichwa abilities as limited, claiming to mostly understand it, but unable to converse beyond basic formalities. They also both spoke English. Their children were, for all intents and purposes, monolingual Spanish speakers. This multi-generational language shift echoes a similar shift in other cultural practices as well, shaped by the exigencies of urban life. Inti and Luisa identified themselves as "*Indígena*" and "Kichwa," and maintained many cultural markers, such as long, braided hair for Atik and their boys and traditional dress for

Luisa and their girl. They were also enmeshed, however, in national and transnational consumer and media culture and envisioned a world where their children would move easily between Ecuador, the United States and Canada, where they had extended family.

In contrast, their neighbors, the Leyma family, lived an economically more precarious life and, like most of their extended family, neither Julio nor Marta had attended school. While they had held a variety of jobs, these were all in the informal economy and were low-paying. During the past decade they worked for a wealthier Kichwa family, making sweaters, hats, and cloth for scarves. The house in which they lived, owned by the *dueño* (owner), was mostly workshop with some living space. Mechanized looms and spinning machines, along with discarded spindles, spare parts, scraps, and boxes of imported threads filled the main rooms and the covered space of the courtyard. The family, four children and the parents, shared a room and three beds, with the kitchen and bathroom on the other side of the courtyard. With a decline in demand for the traditional sweaters and hats sold by the *dueño*, Marta and Julio took advantage of the extra time they had and bought two sewing machines on credit and began making synthetic fleece pajamas, sweatshirts, and jackets. The *dueño* bought some of these to sell in his stores in Otavalo and the parents travelled by bus most weekends to Quito or various fairs throughout the country to sell their products directly. On good weekends, they made enough to cover their travel expenses, buy more bolts of cloth for the next weekend, make their payment on the sewing machines, and pay their weekly bills. On bad weekends, they came home hungry.

They would have liked to buy their own place in the city. Although they had land and family in the country, they showed little interest in living there anymore. "No, our life is here now," Marta explained to me when I asked her one day, "the *wawas* (children) are used to it here. The schools are better and there is more opportunity for them when they grow up. We have our business here, too. It would be too hard up there." Their nineteen-year-old daughter, who married a Mestizo, and was often visibly uncomfortable with her parents' community and extended family in the country, most of whom she did not know well, put it bluntly, "I'm Otavaleña now—that's what it says on my identity card, and my voting card." Marta owned a small piece of land in her community that she inherited from her parents, along with an abandoned house. She reluctantly thought about selling them. She thought she could get about a thousand dollars, but that would not be enough to buy anything in the city. While they appreciated that the *dueño* let them live in their house, they would rather have had their own, so that he could not simply decide he did not need them anymore and make them move, leaving them both jobless and homeless. Their working relationship with the *dueño* was informal, and they were paid under the table for their work. As they were not recognized employees, he did not pay into social security or insurance for them. Without a legal contract they would have had little recourse if he should have made them leave. Land was expensive, however, in Otavalo and finding an affordable place proved impossible. By the end of 2015 they decided to open a stall in a market in Quito and moved the family there.

Much like with the Flores family, there was an education and language shift occurring, although perhaps a generation later. While Julio and Marta supported their children attending school, because they had no experience of it themselves, they often found it difficult to help them with class assignments. Unlike with the Flores family, the Leyma children did not have access to after-school enrichment programs, but instead were expected to work in the family shop. The language shift in the Leyma family was also notable and mirrored that of the Flores family by a generation. Julio and Marta were native Kichwa speakers and learned Spanish as a second language. They conducted their household business in Kichwa and used Spanish to communicate with people outside of their immediate community. Their children were also bilingual Kichwa-Spanish speakers, and while they used Kichwa with their parents and grandparents, they were more likely to use Spanish with each other. The younger children attended a bilingual elementary school, but Kichwa instruction was uneven, and they had little opportunity to polish their Kichwa language skills.

From my time in Otavalo from 2006–2016, there seemed to be no singular way of being Indigenous. While internal differences caused problems at times since religious conflicts and economic inequality could generate mistrust and charges of exploitation or of not being sufficiently or authentically Indigenous, a distinct "urban Indigenous" community and identity were developing. In her study of changes within Otavalo's Kichwa community, for instance, Otavaleña sociologist Gina Maldonado (2004) concluded,

> One cannot speak, therefore, of social and economic homogeneity among Kichwa-Otavalos. Differentiation is real. Nevertheless, it should not direct us to a simplistic solution based on cause and effect that privilege the factors of social differentiation of the ethnic. ... The new social organization tends to construct differentiation through the playing out of roles and status, but by examining the totality of the Indigenous population one can still appreciate that all of them, including young people, participate in the same system of values and are subjected to the same norms and obligations that the structure imposes on them (76).

This urban identity was multifaceted: connected simultaneously to rural communities and to a global one; marked by social differentiation in terms of class and educational background; open to the possibility of mobility; and yet, still distinctly Kichwa.

CHAPTER 5

CONSTRUCTING KICHWA
IN A DIGLOSSIC WORLD

The Indian, no matter how much he wears Adidas shoes, is going
to keep being Indigenous.

—Pacífico Fachamba

Communities, be they local, regional, national, or global in scope,
constantly build and change their cultures based on their changing
circumstances and their contacts with other ways of thinking and being
in the world. Some of this happens through deliberate attempts to create
particular hierarchies of order and meaning. Some of it occurs more
organically, seemingly through happenstance and beyond the conscious
control of participants. In the case of the intercultural processes that
were taking place in Otavalo through the early years of the twenty-first
century, the dialogues between global and local, ancestral and cybernetic,
Spanish and Kichwa, individual and collective, were creating a dynamic
situation in which Kichwa people were re-defining what it meant to
them to be Kichwa. Kichwa-Otavalos have a long history of interaction
with people from all over the world, and global circuits of travel and
commerce have resulted in numerous types of mixed cultural practices

and beliefs, as well as tensions, within Kichwa communities between adaptation and assimilation. While most cultural activists saw change as inevitable and beneficial, they also worried that ancestral knowledge and practices were being discarded to the detriment of future generations.

Kichwa people, particularly young people, navigated a world simultaneously constructed by ancestral knowledge and practices and the logics of a dominant, Western, consumerist society in which they were enmeshed. The cultural terrain, however, in Ecuador continued to be uneven and marked by inequality between groups and a long history of racism. Despite the local and national advances of the Indigenous movement, therefore, many Kichwa experienced immense economic, social, political, and linguistic pressures to conform to Mestizo-dominant norms. The inequality in power between cultural groups results in a sort of cultural diglossia (Sinnigen 2013), in which interactions between groups is defined and reinforced by often unconscious hierarchies. In sociolinguistics, diglossia refers to societies with unequal bilingualism, with one language being considered more prestigious than the other. The dominant language is used in official domains like schools, public administration and the like, whereas the minority language is the domain of home, village, or neighborhood. While not all members of diglossic societies are necessarily bilingual, bilingual speakers understand the proper domain for language usage and rarely confuse domains. When the "wrong" language is used in a particular domain, it is considered marked and inappropriate. In a similar manner, and despite the important gains of the past generation, Ecuador still lives in a culturally diglossic (sometimes called dicultural) situation in which there are high and low prestige groups, in which one cultural and linguistic norm is acceptable and "normal" (Aikman 1997, 468). At times these inequalities are governed by official policies, but often they are also habitual practices, and commonsense ways of understanding the world. Obviously, interculturality, understood as mutual respect, conviviality, and sharing among equals, is impossible in such a situation, which reinforces inequality of difference. Part of the struggle in the intercultural process, therefore, is not only to affirm the value of subaltern cultures, but also to define ways in which members of those cultural groups participate with and influence members of the dominant group as well.

Specifically, this chapter examines physical and virtual space, language and festivals as fields of struggle in Kichwa efforts to be part of, but distinct from, dominant society. Travel and internet technology were significant influences in the articulation and deployment of discourses of identity, particularly in creating a community that, although anchored in the Otavalo Valley, was not limited to it. Over the past generation, the use and revitalization of the Kichwa language became a contentious issue in defining and maintaining a distinctive culture and its relationship with Spanish exemplified the struggles between Kichwa and Mestizo cultures. Cultural festivals such as *Inti Raymi* and *Pawkar Raymi* became not only points of ethnic pride, but also ongoing, dialogic attempts to revalorize Kichwa culture and engage the wider world. Recognizing that cultures and identities are processes and not static entities, people blended their experiences to create new ways of being Kichwa, which were admittedly different than their grandparents' way of being Kichwa.

"I CAN BE *RUNA, WAMPRA* AND REGGAETONERO ALL AT THE SAME TIME"

Community is often associated with a particular territory. As Kichwa people have moved out into other spaces, and as people from other spaces pass through the Otavalo Valley, the connection between those particular spaces in which community and cultures are constructed are recast to include people's diverse experiences of the global. The distinction, of course, between local and global is often an artificial one as local spaces are thoroughly shaped by global forces, and people from local spaces contribute to constructing global realities. Chilean sociologist Beatriz Cid Aguayo (2008) argues that by focusing on large, cosmopolitan global cities, many analysts ignore the important role that small, rurally connected towns and cities have with global relationships, thus failing to understand them as "global villages" also thoroughly enmeshed in the processes of globalization. As a global crossroads that both sends and receives travelers, Otavalo offers a unique perspective into the construction of Cid Aguayo's global village. Otavalos historically have appropriated numerous cultural influences from around the world altering their local cultural practices and manifestations. At the same time, however, by spreading out around the world while maintaining ties to the *llakta*, or home territory, they have contributed to global culture through the selling of Otavalan products and the creation of a transterritorial community that reproduces Kichwa-Otavalo cultural practices, particularly festivals, in distant lands.

Otavalo, perhaps more than most cities of its size, plays an important role in connecting rural life with the global stage and transnational connections have long characterized Otavalo economics and culture. As early as the late 1550s, colonial records mention a class of specialized traveling merchants, *mindaláes,* who paid taxes in cloth and precious metals and were exempt from the usual labor tribute demanded of most Indigenous subjects (Maldonado 2004, 61–62). With this history as part of their cultural heritage, Otavalo merchants began traveling the country to sell local weavings and other handicrafts in the 1940s. By the 1950s, they had branched out to the rest of Latin America, arriving in Europe and North America by the 1970s. Traveling in the other direction, since the late 1970s, when the Pan-American Highway was paved from Quito, tourists have flocked to Otavalo, making it one of Ecuador's prime tourist attractions, driving product innovation and infrastructure improvement (Meisch 2002). What began as small-scale artisan production to supplement family incomes became, by the end of the twentieth century, a sophisticated, transnational enterprise, able to match new designs to new demands and to quickly replenish inventory throughout the world (Kyle 2000; Moncada Landeta 2016). Furthermore, the Ecuadorian government held up Kichwa-Otavalos as the "ideal" Indigenous group, since at least the 1940s, and used them as an example to international audiences of Ecuadorian citizenship and cultural diversity (D'Amico 2011).

Traveling, selling, and negotiating with people of different backgrounds, therefore, represented an important part Kichwa-Otavalo culture. While that is not to say that *every* Kichwa-Otavalo person travelled, most families had someone connected to international travel. Gina Maldonado reports that many of the young people she interviewed "shared the conception that *traveling* was a particularity unique to Otavalo identity. For many of them, traveling and commerce had become a way of living, a distinctive sign of what it is to be *Otavalo*" (2004, 48 (emphasis in original)). Working with Otavalo migrants in both Spain and Ecuador, Sobcyk and Soriano (2015a) observed that economic success abroad both brought "social prestige to the figure of the migrant" and contributed to "pride in belonging to an economically successful Indigenous group" (463). In my discussions, Otavalo travelers expressed pride in their accomplishments and often saw themselves as embodying the spirit of the *mindalá*. For many young men, and some women, traveling far was a rite of passage and a way of increasing one's and one's family's prestige. Many people, now in their thirties or forties, talked about their late teen selves and the "fever" they had to go to the United States or Europe to sell goods or play music. One Otavalo traveler bragged, "there are Otavalos in every country in the world, Europe, the United States, Canada, Australia, Japan. Someone has gone everywhere, I think, except North Korea. I'm sure someone is trying to get there, too. He will be a hero when he does" (Interview, Otavalo, 21 January 2007).

These young (and sometimes not so young, anymore) travelers, who spent months or years living abroad interacted with and brought back cultural practices and items from their experiences. Importantly, however, they generally did not lose themselves in their new environs. One of the motivations for travel, after all, was pride in their heritage and their culture, which was often reinforced by their experiences in other countries, as people were interested in their music, their items for sale, and them as culturally distinct (Sobczyk and Soriano Miras 2015b). At the same time, they learned new languages, customs, ways of living, fashion, and music. When they returned, they brought with them these new discourses and practices, which they appropriated and made their own. Clothes from New York, California, Japan, or Europe were signs of success and prestige, a testament to the risks one ran and the successes achieved.

This willingness to experiment with new and different ways of being Kichwa-Otavalo sometimes created generational conflicts. Activists that came of age in the 1970s and 1980s, for instance, fought hard for the right to be recognized as different. Prominent among their demands were the right for men to wear their hair in a long braid and to wear their traditional clothes. In the early years of the twenty-first century, although many young Otavalo men continued to wear their hair long as an outward sign of their ethnic identity, they tended not to wear the traditional felt hats, preferring baseball caps or none at all. Some also adopted the dress and postures of global youth culture, particularly that of hip-hop and reggaetón. For these young men, cutting their hair short and wearing the latest fashions—baggy shirts, New York Yankees caps, sunglasses, and jewelry, did not make them any less Indigenous. There was no contradiction between being a *wampra* (young indigenous man), a *runa,* and a reggaetonero (Runakuna 2007). I attended the *Runa Kay* (Being Kichwa) festival in Otavalo in 2007. Filled with traditional music, a fashion show of traditional dress and calls for pride in Kichwa culture, one of the most popular acts of the night was a young Kichwa-Otavalo boy dressed in traditional poncho, hat and white pants who brought down the house with a spirited hip-hop number in Kichwa. It was possible to belong to both Kichwa and global youth culture. When I discussed this issue with an older, prominent activist, he became increasingly and visibly agitated as he talked about the betrayal that these members of his community were showing toward the "authentic" culture that he and his comrades had fought so hard to have accepted (Interview, Quito, May 14, 2014). Another woman in her 60s lamented, "some of the boys today cut their hair, and no one is even *making* them" (Otavalo, October

14, 2013). This generational conflict demonstrated some of the painful processes of cultural change as people adapted to, appropriated, and were transformed by the contexts in which they lived.

While these changes also took place in the rural communities, it was in the towns and cities, particularly Otavalo and Peguche, where differences between traditional cultural markers like clothes, hairstyle, occupation, and other practices of younger people became more evident. Commenting on Otavalo, and its subsequent influences on smaller, nearby towns like Peguche, Pacífico Fachamba, Parish President, observed:

> I go around wondering who is Mestizo and who is Indigenous because now you can't tell who is who. A lot of times you realize with the hair—it's a little longer or darker. But today, you can't guess who is who; you have boys without braids. But, here we are. Maybe by the last name? Honestly, it is being lost. There is a long disruption—language, food, clothes, traditions, and customs (Interview, Peguche, December 11, 2011).

The blurring of Indigenous and Kichwa cultural appearances was not a new phenomenon. Status-conscious youth and returning travelers were very much aware of the latest fashions and were willing (and able) to pay for brand-name clothing. Ironically, perhaps, one of the outcomes of the Indigenous movement—greater integration (at certain levels) of Mestizo and Kichwa societies, combined with the economic success of some Kichwa-Otavalo families through the selling of a particular image of traditional society—resulted in dramatic changes to that imagined traditional society.

Change itself is inevitable as societies do not live in a-historic bubbles but are rather constantly adapting to internal and external processes. And, despite the reservations expressed by some Kichwa-Otavalo critics of changes within their communities, many Kichwa youth easily defined themselves as still Kichwa, just in a different way than their parents and grandparents (Célleri-Endara 2011). This adaptability and willingness to incorporate outside influences *into* Kichwa-Otavalo culture, rather than assimilation into mainstream Mestizo or global culture highlighted the intercultural construction of this experience. Because of their travels, many of these contemporary *mindaláes* comfortably adapted what they, or their friends or family, acquired abroad or through transnational social media into their ever-changing Kichwa culture. Many of the young people with whom I interacted did not express a need to preserve a particular moment of their culture because for them their culture was always changing, and rather than being *forced* into accepting outside cultural markers, they sought to make those cultural practices distinctly theirs. Even if, as Fachamba contended, it was increasingly difficult to tell the difference just by looking, younger ethnically Kichwa people did not identify themselves as Mestizo.

Travelers not only brought back cultural influences from abroad, but they also established relatively stable communities around the world. There are large communities of Kichwa-Otavalos, for instance, in Bogotá, Barcelona, and New York (Atienza de Frutos 2009; Kyle 2000, Ordóñez et al. 2014; Sobczyk and Soriano Miras 2015b). Unlike many other diasporic communities, however, most Kichwa-Otavalos who have traveled to and perhaps now live permanently in these enclaves did not generally leave Otavalo out of economic desperation. They maintained close personal, economic, and cultural contact with the *llakta*. They depended on their networks in Otavalo to keep them supplied with merchandise and they communicated frequently about design and supply issues. They also frequently sought to reproduce various cultural practices in their new homes. Luz, for instance, a middle-aged woman from Peguche, lived in New York for many years. One year she and her family were the *priostes*, or sponsors, of the *Inti Raymi* celebration that the community held in Central Park. "It was weeks and weeks of organizing and cost us a lot of money. But it was worth it," she explained to me. "It was important for those of us who could not get home for the festivals. Every year we had our own little *Inti Raymi* in New York" (Interview, Peguche, June 5, 2007).

This change in the space of community represented an important adaptation to Kichwa-Otavalo discourses about identity. Land and territory were key components of identity and cultural practices, but the Otavalos who now lived far away from, but still connected to, the homeland were creating a trans-territorial community. It would not be useful to call it de-territorialized because although the community that they were creating was not *dependent* on actually living in the ancestral spaces of the Otavalo Valley, the members of this globally dispersed community continued to be focused on life there, and there was much travel in and out of Otavalo and its communities. Just as global influences helped to shape the ways in which Otavalos created their sense of self and developed their cultural discourses and practices, so the influences of the *llakta* continued to mold and shape the transnational experiences of Otavalos traveling or living abroad.

Partially in response to that reality, a small group of young people, mostly living at least part of the year abroad, launched otavalosonline.com first as a means of publicizing the 1998 *Pawkar Raymi* (Festival of the Flowering) and developed it later to be a portal for Otavalos to share information about events, promote *runa shimi* (the Kichwa language), and to keep in touch with each other in the region and around the world. According to Sacha Rosero, a co-founder and administrator of the site, "Otavalosonline is a meeting place for all Otavalos, where people can chat with their friends, families, look at photos of Otavalos around the world, inform themselves of news relating to Otavalo and Andean *runas*" (Interview, e-mail, July 10, 2010). The website contained a mixture of news, downloadable Kichwa lessons, media, and links to cultural workshops and videos of festivals taking place in various Otavalo communities, both locally and globally. The website was emblematic of both the changes within the Kichwa-Otavalo community as well as those values and traditions that held it together because it was created by individuals with ancestral knowledge as well as training in information technology and marketing.

> Just like the rest of the world, technological advancements are generating a change in society, especially in the new generations, making communication more open and free, and access to them is always cheaper and get to more people. Over last two decades, I believe we have been in the midst of very accelerated changes in world society and, of course, we are also part of these changes (Interview, Sacha Rosero, July 10, 2010).

Otavalosonline.com was explicitly created by and for a generation that could make ample use of technology to define community in ways that were not necessarily tied only to territory. The proliferation of social media and ever less expensive means of communicating internationally with services like Skype and WhatsApp made communication with globally distant friends and relatives increasingly easy and commonplace.

The Kichwa communities of the twenty-first century, particularly young people, were influenced by information technologies and connected to people and ideas from around the world (Villacrés Roca 2016). This connection to the rest of the world, however, did not necessarily mean being absorbed into a homogenous transnational society. Rather, the use of technology provided a means to reimagine and fortify Kichwa culture.

> One of the things that we believe that OtavalosOnLine has contributed over the past 12 years, besides being a virtual place to communicate among our people is to strengthen our values, our culture. The celebration of *Inti Raymi*, for instance, we now call by its original name because before it was called the feasts of San Juan. Now whenever a group of we Otavalos meet abroad and get together, we celebrate *Inti Raymi* and some of them get published on OtavalosOnLine, which is something that didn't happen twelve years ago. Now there is a sort of small competition to see who can make the best *Inti Raymi* outside of the *llakta*. And this makes you feel closer to your culture and makes you feel more identified as a Kichwa *runa* (Interview, Sacha Rosero, July 10, 2010).

A reality of Kichwa-Otavalo community was that members were spread over the world and technology facilitated a new kind of community that simultaneously circulated discourses of the past with structures created by contemporary relationships. Kichwa-Otavalos appropriated technologies, values, and knowledge from others and put them to use to define themselves. The use of information technology allowed members to keep in touch with each other and recreate the community both within and outside of their traditional territories. This process, however, was based not in abandoning a collective past but rather promoted and circulated an ever-evolving, *Runa Kichwa* identity in relationship to other groups.

"I've been dancing all month"

As the interview with Sacha Rosero about the virtual Kichwa-Otavalo community suggests, the cycle of ancestral festivals, particularly *Inti Raymi* in June and *Pawkar Raymi* in February, played an important role in the continual construction of Kichwa-Otavalo identity. These festivals brought people physically and metaphorically back to the community. They represented not only an opportunity to remember the past and to celebrate both the material and symbolic ties that Kichwa people have as a community to the land and the growing cycles, but also the chance to continually create and transform those meanings. And although people traveled far from home, for many, returning to dance the *Sanjuanes* was rarely far from their minds and family members looked forward to their return.

Throughout the Andes, *Inti Raymi*, the celebration of the June Solstice, has become one of the predominant festivals celebrated by Indigenous people as a symbol of their ethnic history. Dating back to at least Incan times, *Inti Raymi* was the high holiday of the empire, designed to give solemn thanks to *Taita Inti* (Father Sun) for making life possible. With the arrival of the Spanish, clerical authorities appropriated many of the sun images into rites associated with Corpus Christi, which fell at about the same time on the calendar (Gareis 2007). Celebration in the northern Andes fell specifically on Saint John's and Saint Peter's Days, but over the past generation those names have fallen into disuse, and the festival is *Inti Raymi*, once again reflecting the resurgence of Indigenous pride and self-identification throughout Ecuador.

Celebrated with music, dancing, and community offerings of "*castillos*" (food tied onto wooden frames), *Inti Raymi* is a joyous time in Kichwa communities and ties them to their collective past. For weeks before the end-of-June celebrations, groups of friends and family get together and begin practicing their instruments and their dance steps. During the week of *Inti Raymi*, these groups, wearing costumes, go out into the streets to perform for neighbors and passersby. They are led by the ancestral figure of *Aya-Huma*, who wears a colorful mask, representing a rainbow, with a face on both sides, to see both north and south at the same time, and carries a whip to keep everyone moving, There is also a solemn side to the celebrations, in which people reflect on their gratitude to *Pachamama* and *Taita Inti.* In Peguche, on the night of the solstice many men bathe silently in the waterfall to purify themselves, recharge their energies, and to humbly face their gods and spirits. It is a time to contemplate community history and human relationships with nature and with each other

Pawkar Raymi, the Festival of the Flowering, does not seem to have been widely celebrated before the late 1990s. Organized in large part by migrants and timed to coincide with Carnival, the week before Lent begins, *Pawkar Raymi* has become the second most important Kichwa festival in the Otavalo Valley. The highlights of *Pawkar Raymi* include a ten-day-long soccer championship, the *Mundialito* (Little World Cup), made up of migrant Kichwa players from around the world, a series of shows with nationally and internationally known Andean musicians, and night-long festival, *Runa Kay* (Being Indigenous), originally presented bilingually, but eventually transitioned into Kichwa only. Over the years, it also grew to include traditional food and handicraft sales as well.

Although it might not have the historic roots of *Inti Raymi, Pawkar Raymi* also provides a space for reflection on individual and community relationships and connections with the Earth. It is explicitly a time to celebrate being Kichwa and represents an attempt for the worldwide Kichwa-Otavalo community to maintain its connection to the homeland, the *llakta.*

Besides symbolically tying today's ever-diverse Kichwa community to their historic roots and keeping the transnational Otavalo community focused on home, these festivals were part of an ongoing dialogic process of identity and group building. At the 2007 *Inti Raymi* in Otavalo, a young media and political activist, Carlos Yamberla, told the audience,

> They, the academics, the anthropologists, the sociologists used to say that traditions were a thing of the past, that they made us think only about the past. But now we know that our traditions are alive. The *practice* of the indigenous pueblos shows that traditions also point us to the future. Traditions connect the past and the future, because the indigenous *pueblos* are the *pueblos* of the future" (Otavalo, June 25, 2007)

For him, ethnicity was not an idealization of the past but a continuous creation of the present community to form a foundation for facing the future.

Michelle Wibbelsman (2009) argues that the various festival cycles in the Andes serve as a means through which ethnic identity is continually reconstructed through ongoing, multivocal conversations aimed at shoring up old and forging new relationships in an increasingly deterritorialized community. Locally based people and migrants negotiate the details of the festivals with various groups contributing ideas and funds to make them successful. The festivals also attract non-Kichwa visitors from all over. Therefore, part of the planning process, which begins for the next year shortly after the conclusion of the current year's activities, includes discussions about how to communicate the meaning of rituals with non-natives, advertising events, and making outsiders feel welcome. Besides sharing their cultural history, these are, after all, also a chance to make money. Wibbelsman (2005) contends that community is created in two important ways through the planning of these festivals. First, the need to meet, plan, and carry out a common project builds and fortifies various networks of people and gives them a common purpose, something that the increasing diversity of the population makes difficult in other terrains. Secondly,

> these festivals are celebrations and displays of diversity and affir-
> mations of community. Beyond embodying the ability to articulate
> different perspectives fleetingly, the processes of signification
> behind ritual performance produce the cultural institutions that
> make alternative forms of expression and collective utterance
> possible in the first place. As such, they enable conceptual frame-
> works that potentially extend beyond the ritual event and affect
> more broadly Otavalan ways of relating socially, styles of conver-
> sation, and symbolic repertoires for interpretation and action
> (Wibbelsman 2005, 156).

They represent active attempts among Kichwa-Otavalo people to define for themselves who they are by simultaneously noting their connections to the past (both real and imagined) and creating cultural expressions that have meaning not only for the immediate community but also for wider audiences.

That conversation, however, was not without its ambiguities. Talking about *Inti Raymi*, Pacífico Fachamba observed:

> But surely it is changing, too. The ways of celebrating *Inti Raymi*
> were something that was organized alone. You didn't need cash
> or anything. Today, you need people to organize it so that *Inti
> Raymi* functions in Otavalo. But, before it was spontaneous, you
> didn't need anyone to organize it. Your uncles, cousins, fathers,
> grandfathers got together, grabbed their guitars, *quenas*, flutes,
> "let's go, boys, to dance at the houses, to go visit." That was
> spontaneous. Now it's like obligatory. They go to dance. On such
> and such a day we'll get together. Not that, it was a kind of rule.

The twenty-first, you went to bathe in the river, which was more private then. No, now it is folkloric. *Inti Raymi* has not been lost, but it has become folkloric, now tons of people go. Before, it was a ceremony with Mother Nature, you bathed and everything was good. Now it is more folkloric, because you have to let people come and see. It's ok that they let people come and see, but it has changed its form. So, you realize that the connotation has changed the meaning of the celebration. It has changed, but has not been extinguished. Of course, there are changes; sometimes necessary. But, sometimes there should not be. It's ok; it's ok that things are transformed. What worries me most is that things will be lost (Interview, Peguche, December 11, 2011).

Fachamba was worried that there was often a thin line between changing and losing cultural practices. Fachamba's ambiguity about how the celebration of *Inti Raymi* has evolved points to a larger concern about how to maintain control over distinctive cultural expressions while also participating in the logic and institutions of Western, Mestizo society. Wibbelsman (2009) is correct to point out that festivals were very much part of a multivocal community and process, but all of those voices were not equal. As Kichwa institutions reached out to and interacted with those of other communities, many, like Fachamba, expressed an anxiety that they were not only changing, but also that they were becoming incorporated into the logic of a dominant system, rather than challenging that system in a meaningful way. They had clearly not abandoned their Kichwa principles but were wary of slipping into and supporting a system that saw their traditions as folkloric.

YANGA SHIMI, RUNA SHIMI:

While many other cultural markers, ideologies, and practices differentiated Indigenous and Mestizo communities, language was always one of the most important, and its role in constructing and revitalizing Kichwa communities and politics became a contentious debate about authenticity and belonging. Kichwa, or *Runa Shimi* as it is called by Kichwa speakers, was introduced to the region through the Inca conquest at the end of the fifteenth century and consolidated as the "Indian language," ironically, by Spanish missionaries through the sixteenth century, becoming the *lingua franca* of the Indigenous peoples of the Andes (Caillavet 2000, King and Hornberger 2006). In contemporary Indigenous communities in northern Ecuador, Kichwa served both an instrumental as well as a symbolic function. Although communities were becoming increasingly bilingual as more children attended school, Kichwa continued to be an important means of communication among community members. Symbolically, Kichwa served to differentiate Kichwa people from national society and to connect together an otherwise diverse Kichwa nationality throughout the country. Luz, a merchant from Peguche, who was active in the rights movement during the 1980s, explained to me that "our language is important; it allows us to talk to each other without them [the Mestizo authorities] knowing what we are saying" (Interview, Peguche, May 18, 2014). Many other political activists noted the apparent connection between Kichwa language and the cultural knowledge possessed by rural communities, insisting that some concepts simply could not be translated into Spanish. One language activist made explicit connections between the revitalization of Kichwa and continued political power, arguing, "if we lose our language, we lose our political power base. The constitution calls for territorial autonomy, but if we all speak only Spanish, how do we define our territory? How are we any different?" (Interview, Otavalo, December 15, 2011).

At the same time, many political and language activists believed that there was a real crisis of language continuity with many communities in and around Otavalo in the midst of a generation shift, where bilingual parents fail to transmit their native language to their children. Without systematic intervention, native speakers of Kichwa, they argued, will disappear within a generation or two, as the domains of Kichwa use become inexorably smaller. There are many reasons behind this phenomenon. One is the continued legacy of colonialism, and despite the advances of the Indigenous movement, particularly in this area of the country, many Kichwa speakers felt shame to speak their language in public. Writing about internalized racism, for instance, Kichwa-Otavalo linguist, Luis de la Torre, argued, "The so-called Indigenous began to name their things with connotations of prejudice and devaluation: their native language, for example, Kichwa, which was sacred and the *lingua franca* of America, was called '*yanga shimi*,' which means language that is good for nothing" (2006, 63). Despite the many efforts of cultural activists to raise the prestige of Kichwa, many native speakers still considered their language in such terms and avoided speaking it in public domains. One language activist related to me that even when he, a native Kichwa speaker, approached food sellers in the mainly Indigenous evening food market in Otavalo, speaking Kichwa, they would, out of embarrassment, only answer him in Spanish and chastise him for speaking Kichwa (Interview, Otavalo, September 14, 2013).

Beyond this immediate colonial problem, however, there was often a sense that Kichwa was for family and immediate community use only, with Spanish being the language of public domains. My neighbors in Otavalo, for instance, were bilingual, first generation transplants to the city. When they found out that I was learning Kichwa and that my daughter had Kichwa classes in the municipal-run elementary school, they were somewhat confused and taken aback. "How can you study Kichwa?" they asked. "It's not a language that you learn. It's just the way we talk." Many Indigenous families also made conscious decisions to emphasize Spanish over Kichwa. Sara, also a recent migrant to the city, explained:

> It was so hard for me to learn Spanish so that I could go to school and find work. I didn't want my daughter to have the same problems, so I decided that I would only speak to her in Spanish. I thought it would be best. I regret that now, and am trying to teach her Kichwa, too. But it is a little late [her daughter was twelve at the time] (Interview, Otavalo, February 2, 2014).

Although neither my neighbors nor Sara were politically active, their situation was not unusual even among many political and cultural activists. Pacífico Fachamba, who besides being president of his parish, served for many years as a technical advisor and project manager for UNORCAC and worked to implement its "development with identity" strategy. He firmly believed the Kichwa language ought to be preserved in order to maintain Kichwa culture and build healthy, sustainable communities. But, "my little ones, don't speak it. We are now putting aside Sundays as Kichwa only. I won't answer them if they speak to me in Spanish, so they are learning a little bit" (Interview, Peguche, December 11, 2011). His case was not the exception to the rule and pointed to the pressures of language shift.

Spanish, certainly, plays a central role in public life, and as Indigenous people become more integrated into that life, Spanish becomes increasingly important. Even individuals who would not necessarily be ashamed of their language often found that the need for the dominant language prevailed in their conscious and subconscious decisions on language use and transmission. In a diglossic environment, such as that between Kichwa and Spanish in this part of Ecuador, bilingual speakers tended to accommodate monolingual Spanish speakers because while many native Kichwa speakers were bilingual, very few native Spanish speakers were. These practices became ingrained. Sacha, one of the founders of *Kichwasisaraiy*, an organization dedicated to reversing Kichwa language loss through education and public outreach, related his epiphany about language use. While living with his sister in Barcelona, where he worked in computer programming and marketing, some Catalan friends, "asked me why we always spoke to each other in Spanish and not Kichwa. I hadn't really thought about it and didn't even realize that we did it. So, we started trying to speak to each other in Kichwa. It was strange at first" (Interview, Otavalo, September 7, 2013). As he became more conscious of his language use, he realized that Kichwa speakers always accommodated Spanish speakers, even in times, such as Kichwa cultural festivals, when Kichwa should have predominated. He recalled a meeting to plan an upcoming *Pawkar Raymi* that he attended:

> There were fifteen of us: thirteen from here and a woman from the Prefect's office and her assistant. We were all speaking Kichwa, until she came and then, without saying anything we all switched to Spanish. At the end of the meeting I said, "I don't mean to be rude or anything, but next time we meet, you will have to either learn Kichwa or bring a translator." Some of the *compañeros* thought I went too far; since we all speak Spanish too it's not a big deal to switch over. But I think if *we* don't stand up for our language, who's going to? It's just so automatic to speak Spanish, but that's how we're going to lose our language. Colonialism is still alive. If people come here they should have to learn to talk like us, too. It shouldn't be up to us to always make them feel comfortable (Interview, Otavalo, September 7, 2013).

Educational institutions are also prime shapers of language use. Spanish is the medium of instruction in Ecuador, and as education has become more universalized and Indigenous children attend state schools in ever greater numbers and for longer period of times, their formal Spanish skills improve, while their Kichwa skills are not similarly refined. César Cotacachi, a politically active, bilingual professional from Peguche argued that Kichwa was being lost in part, because,

> we learn how to speak Kichwa without ever knowing the how or why. That's why many people, both foreign and national, think that because someone is Indigenous and speaks Kichwa that they know everything about it. So you see people that are speaking Kichwa on television or on the news, but it's a totally different way of speaking from everyday life and this causes confusion (Interview, Otavalo, April 11, 2014).

With the introduction of bilingual education in the late 1980s, it was hoped that education in native languages would allow children early school success, while providing a formal way of reproducing Indigenous cultures and ways of knowing. The bilingual education system, however, was always beset with numerous problems, including insufficient funding, a lack of qualified teachers, and politicization of appointees. As a result, it was seen as a second-class education, leading many Indigenous activists themselves to opt out of sending their children to bilingual schools (Martínez Novo and de la Torre 2010). "It's a disgrace," an activist and mother told me, "I refuse to send my children to the bilingual schools. They don't have enough resources, or good teachers, so then your kids end up disadvantaged. Is this what we have been fighting for?" (Interview, Quito, December 2006). Instead, many committed Kichwa activists with the economic ability chose to send their children to the regular or "Hispanic" system schools or to private schools because they saw that as the most desirable option for their children's futures. These choices also recognized that knowledge of the dominant society—Spanish, White-Mestizo cultural norms and technology—was crucial to future success and highlighted an implicit challenge to the intercultural processes shaping Indigenous communities.

Tensions over the role of language raised the question as to whether it was actually necessary to *speak* Kichwa in order to *be* Kichwa. Just as other aspects of community were rapidly changing, with some things certainly being lost, new narratives of community also challenged language use as a necessary marker. Jorge Sánchez Parga (2009, 65), for instance, contended that despite a marked and perhaps irreversible trend away from Kichwa and other native languages, there was a steady if not slightly rising number of people who self-identified as ethnically Indigenous. His finding, therefore, suggested that speaking Kichwa was not necessarily essential to being ethnically Kichwa. This attitude separating language from ethnic identity had many adherents in the area. One University of Otavalo student explained:

> I don't speak Kichwa. I don't wear traditional dress. I don't live in a rural community but here in the city, but I know that I am Kichwa. I feel it in my heart. I am proud of my people and everything that

my parents and grandparents and ancestors suffered through and accomplished" (Interview Otavalo, April 23, 2007).

This insight pointed to how contemporary ethnic/class discourse was evolving around what it meant to be Kichwa. He did not live in a rural community, but in the city. While a peasant identity may have been important to those Kichwa who continued that lifestyle, like many other Kichwa, this young man did not belong to that social class. Despite assuming non-traditional cultural markers, however, he still self-identified as Kichwa; he had not assimilated into a more homogeneous Ecuadorian identity. His pride not only in that ethnic identity, but also in his ancestors and all that they have accomplished cemented his identity to the historic continuity of the larger community.

Despite the efforts of activist and academic groups to better understand the dynamics of language shift and to promote the use of Kichwa through radio, television, and social media campaigns, spreading Kichwa language was an uphill battle. The inequalities between Mestizo and Kichwa cultural and linguistic groups remained sharp. Even though Kichwa people improved their socio-economic standing in Otavalo over past generations, Spanish was still the predominant language of public business in the city, and it was generally expected that bilingual Spanish-Kichwa speakers accommodate monolingual Spanish speakers in almost all situations. Access to state education, while seen as an imperative by most families for the future success of their children, also further eroded Kichwa skills among Indigenous children by providing them the means to perfect their Spanish, but largely ignoring similar writing and expressive skills in Kichwa. Nevertheless, for some ethnically identifying Kichwa individuals, speaking Kichwa was not seen as necessary to being Kichwa, which led to new ways of imagining an increasingly diverse community.

"I'M AFRAID WE'RE BECOMING TOO CONSUMERIST"

If Spanish as the hegemonic language pressures Kichwa, making it difficult even for those who wish to maintain it, the hegemonic global consumerist culture also pressures other forms of exchange, accumulation, and sociability. The allures of consumer society were strong and were broadcast constantly from television and the Internet. The logic of development shapes desires for a never-ending supply of goods and services; and even many new-left governments critical of neoliberal development still pointed to access to higher levels of consumption and growing the middle class as signs of success (Conaghan 2017; Gudynas 2016; Polo Blanco 2018).

It is no surprise, therefore, that many people in Kichwa-Otavalo communities and cities, who generally had fairly high levels of contact with national and global institutions and who had accumulated higher levels of economic and social capital than other Indigenous groups, interacted closely with global consumerist society. Although the economic heart of Otavalo might have been the Plaza de Ponchos and the shops selling and exporting handicrafts and textiles around the world, the blocks spilling way from the plaza were increasingly filled with stores selling brand name and expensive clothes, shoes, and electronic goods to both Indigenous and Mestizo clientele. Hollister sweatshirts, both original but often imitation, crowded into many storefront windows and were almost as ubiquitous as embroidered blouses for many young Otavalo women. Nike and Adidas shoes had long replaced the traditional sandals of young men, who often wore North Face fleece shirts to fend off cool evening breezes. Trade was not a one-way process for Otavalo merchants, who may have left Ecuador loaded down with bundles of sweaters, shawls, and instruments, but who returned with brand-name jeans, baby clothes, and shoes that found their way into the shops along Otavalo's main streets.

Participating in national and global circuits of commerce and consumption was part of what it meant to be economically and culturally active and should not be held up as a critique of the choices that people made. Nor does it suggest that changing fashion and an affinity for outside influences necessarily meant that people were no longer being Kichwa. In fact, as I have been arguing throughout this book, just the opposite is true. Adapting to changing contexts and changing what it meant to be ethnically Kichwa was an integral part of being Kichwa in the twenty-first century. Rather, in my conversations, many Kichwa individuals warned that the *logic* of consumerism represented a threat to other cultural logics. None of my interviewees advocated a fundamentalist rejection of the West or of modernity. In fact, when I would sit down with people for interviews, they mostly used "Western" clothing and checked their phones frequently for messages. In one case, an interviewee spoke to me in flawless English, one of the five languages that he spoke fluently. For them, there was not necessarily a contradiction between being Indigenous and participating in global society, but as one of my interviewees noted, despite all of the efforts that she and her family had made to maintain their Kichwa identity, "I think that we are all becoming too consumerist." Realizing what was happening, however, did not necessarily mean that it could be avoided. (Of course, this does not apply to just Kichwa people.)

It was not the hybrid cultural practices and changes in outward appearance that were a point of major concern for most Kichwa people, but rather succumbing to the logic of consumerism and extreme individualism. Prestige and status were often demonstrated through possessions and having new things, at the expense of older forms of demonstrating status through reciprocity such as sponsoring festivals, weddings, and other publicly shared events. Segundo, a young Kichwa professional from Peguche, explained:

> There is not much interest in history or traditions because what interests people the most is money. This is very understand-able, because the system that we live in too much is a system of consumerism, a capitalist system that, like it or not, we have to accept. The famous saying, "tell me how much you have and I'll tell

you how much you are worth," is still around. At the Indigenous level, including the urban level, the economic question weighs heavily. People want to see how many houses you are building, and how many cars you buy, and what brand of clothes you wear. That's why I don't like it when festival times come around like *Pawkar Raymi, Inti Raymi, Kolla Raymi*; during the week or two that the parties last, all of the Indigenous talk about spiritual matters and *Pachamama*, how you have to take care of her, and blah, blah, blah. But as soon as it's over, those same Indigenous are eating at Kentucky Fried Chicken, at McDonald's, they're shopping in the malls and leaving with bags of purchases. They want fashionable shoes; they want brand name clothes. More than a criticism, what's happening is a real problem; we can't deny it (Interview, Otavalo April 11, 2014).

The problem that he was describing was not that Indigenous culture is changing, but rather that the logic of the system in which Indigenous people increasingly participate was pushing out other forms of cultural expression in favor of the new forms of prestige. While the festivals, for instance, were important symbolic vehicles for tying the disparate community together and for recognizing the importance of ancestral knowledge, Segundo was concerned that the values and practices suggested by these relatively brief moments in time did not extend beyond into the everyday practices of many Kichwa people. Instead, according to him, many were following the logic of consumerism. Under the logic of consumerism and development the new is always seen as progress, resulting in the prestige attached to new cars and new houses. Segundo worried that as people moved into the city and bought houses, they would tear down the old ones and put up same-looking, concrete-block constructions, erasing even the architectural heritage of Otavalo, which he saw as contributing to the symbolic erasure of a distinctive Kichwa-Otavalo culture.

As with the pressures that lead to language shift, the pressures to conform to hegemonic cultural norms become naturalized and common-sense. Other behaviors become marked and, like speaking Kichwa in a

Spanish-language domain, expressing values or practices that go against the expected seem out of place. Many men did not wear traditional clothes, for instance, because they would feel ashamed and strange wearing those clothes except for special occasions. Young men cut their hair not because anyone forced them to, but because they wanted to fit in with classmates and did not want to stand out as different. The logic, therefore, of demonstrating social status was to purchase and display consumer goods, which had become signs of success and achievement and indicated one's ability to negotiate the risks and rewards of the world. Even individuals that expressed ambiguity toward this process participated in consumer culture because it is the dominant logic and way of living.

From an intercultural perspective, the concern here is not in change, but rather in lack of balance between cultural traditions. It is certainly the right of Kichwa people to participate as fully as they are willing and able in globalized social, cultural, and economic relations. The preoccupation that some Otavalos expressed, however, was that these relatively new ways of being were not so much a sharing with older ones, but rather a replacing of them to the detriment of creating a better society. Kichwa-Otavalo intellectual, Luis de la Torre, saw interculturality as the mutual borrowing from cultural groups to improve their lives and the development of Kichwa-Otavalos an overall success story. More than other groups, they created hybrid cultural formations and practices that helped them navigate the globalized world, while at the same time creating an ever-stronger sense of being Kichwa. This borrowing, however, was not always balanced, and "sometimes I am afraid my people may have learned a little bit too much from the West, and become a little too individualistic" (Interview, Otavalo, September 15, 2013).

As part of his critique of consumerism pushing out historic memory, Segundo blamed a lack of a leadership able to react to today's needs.

> Otavalo and her people are perhaps one of the groups most interrelated with the Western world, but when we return there

> is an effort to recuperate the identity issue, but unfortunately there is not a person or institution that has taken leadership on this matter to help the people who come back to reconsider or to strengthen the customs and traditions that in the old days served them one hundred percent (Interview, Otavalo, April 10, 2014).

Leadership, for him, meant reflecting on what it meant to be Kichwa-Otavalo in the twenty first century and to shape and adapt practices to new realities. Without such leadership, Segundo and others worried that instead of an intercultural society, there would be a slow and inevitable drift into a consumerist, Mestizo society, with Kichwa culture reduced to superficial folklore. To be successful, interculturality needs to be articulated as a integrated political project based in a commonly constructed vision of a better future; otherwise, hybrid practices become mostly superficial differences in support of consumerist culture and individualistic development.

The problem from an intercultural perspective becomes one of articulating a clearly decolonial discourse to avoid the acculturation into dominant cultural modes, as often happens in diglossic cultural situations. Concerns about the folklorization of festivals and ceremonies and the slide into consumerist culture to demonstrate prestige and status suggested that the hybrid cultural practices that characterized the everyday lives of many Kichwa-Otavalo people represented the possibility of shifting to dominant Western cultural norms. Many of the mid-level activists with whom I spent time lamented a lack of clear leadership from Indigenous organizations as they confronted new challenges. A common complaint of activists who came of age since the mid-1990s, was that they often felt blocked from rising to leadership positions in the organizations. They believed that their perspective and concerns about how to be Indigenous in the twenty-first century continued to be subordinated to the needs and desires of leaders still fixated on land and rights struggles, which they saw as largely settled. One leader from Peguche offered that, the organizations were born from these processes of the strong demands from the decade of the seventies. They were born principally to demand as ancestral, original peoples, because we were being stepped on by the colonizing people and all of that, and they began to become strong. But then, these organizations began to be reborn and restructured, because the struggle now is not against racism, and the struggle now is not against discrimination, although they continue to persist, not just in Ecuador but all around the world. So now they say it's time to think about how my people are going to be able to get ahead economically... But now I believe that the organizations should be restructured, they should be modernized, because they can't continue with these structures that date from the 1970s, which I'm sure in that era were good, but after forty years they have to change. Reality has changed, and we have new challenges to face (Interview, Peguche, December 18, 2011).

As the times changed, a common concern among younger activists was that much of the Indigenous leadership had failed to take into account the needs of people in their new reality, which also made it difficult to navigate the globalized, consumerist world that dominated cultural logics. If official discrimination had ended, and if Indigenous people could participate in public life as Indigenous people, and if the land disputes that fueled the agrarian revolt of the 1980s and 1990s had been largely (if imperfectly) resolved, how could Indigenous organizations and leaders orient their people to confront more subtle changes to their cultural heritage?

NEGOTIATING CHANGE

Ecuadorian political scientist Santiago Ortiz (2012) argues that the Kichwa communities of the early twenty first century demonstrated both collective and individualistic expressions, and that

> the communities are not the expression of an essentialist identity isolated in their immediate environment, they are the result of struggles and negotiations with dominant actors, of affirmations of identity, and necessary "modern" adaptation, that make it impossible to consider Indigenous peoples as pure subjects that only sustain tradition (137).

The idea of traditional community and traditional culture, even as a construction of contemporary thinkers and organizers, was plainly challenged by substantial changes to some of its key components. Land ownership as an economic and spiritual resource, while still important, did not represent a viable livelihood, and as family plots shrunk with every generation, people looked for work elsewhere. The resulting shift toward an economy based on the exchange of money altered the ways in which community members interacted with each other. Even the language that people used to speak to each other came under pressure as community members dealt increasingly with outsiders and Spanish became more "practical" and necessary to better integrate with the rest of the world. Constant negotiation between traditional Kichwa cultural practices and markers and national and global societies demonstrated that identity was negotiated not only within Kichwa communities, but also with non-Kichwa people as well. Community members alone did not determine the boundaries of community because they were also informed by interactions with other cultures. Relationships with other cultural groups, however, did not mean that Kichwa culture was simply being discarded for inclusion into a broader Mestizo culture.

Understanding these processes not as acculturation but as interculturality underscores how Kichwa communities were managing the new post-movement normal of cultural relations. There was a consciousness among activists and, importantly, non-activists that even as their communities and the world more broadly changed, they wanted to continue being Kichwa people as a part of that world. César Cotacachi, a university-trained professional who traveled internationally, while acknowledging the losses that came with change, also bristled at the notion that Kichwa people were somehow not supposed to change.

> Otavalo undoubtedly forms part of these cultures that have had direct contact with consumerism and globalization. So, from my point of view, to talk about the issue of identity, without even knowing where in the world we are unfolding our history, is completely absurd. If we were really focused or sure about what identity means and how we can relate to it from our world, if we can call it that, with the more globalized world. When we talk about identity, many people say, many people criticize us saying that you have lost your identity. And when I ask when you say identity what do you want? Only clothes. And when you refer to clothes, at what time period do you want me to go back to? The eighties? The fifties? The beginning of the 1900s? Or are you maybe referring to photos that you might have seen in some archives that are easy to get to now? To what identity and what epoch do you want me to relate? When we talk about this, many people lament the loss of a music style, of other things, but there is so much to talk about (Interview, Otavalo, April 11, 2014).

Instead of being frozen in time, or turned into folkloric representations of some cultural other, Cotacachi, while being painfully aware of how some cultural knowledge and practices were being lost, also insisted that Kichwa culture and communities adapt to and are part of the globalized world as well. He, like many Kichwa activists, took seriously that the globalized and consumer society, of which they now formed part, could very easily overwhelm them, particularly given the lack of clear leadership and dialogue about how to best adapt to new cultural realities. He argued that "we cannot bring everything with us, but at least we can recover certain elements or practices that might be adapted and allowed to survive." The point was not to advocate an impossible nostalgia to remain unchanged, but rather to change wisely and take advantage of the possibilities offered by national and transnational society without becoming just another cog in a homogenizing global culture.

Caught between seemingly different cultural matrices, Kichwa people actively participated in intercultural dialogues and debates not only about their own communities, but also about and with the larger communities to which they also belonged. The heterogeneity both within the face-to-face rural communities as well as within the larger imagined community of Kichwa nationality resulted in diverse approaches to transforming community and culture. Unlike acculturation, where members of minority groups assume the practices and identities of the majority group, the intercultural process in which many Kichwa engaged was a dialogic one. Although traditional agricultural communities, social practices, and even language were under pressure from dominant society and global economic alignments, the country's Indigenous movements insisted on the value of Indigenous culture and demonstrated the importance of Indigenous peoples and organizations in bringing about democratic reform. Change, in other words, was not just unidirectional, but rather comprised a complex set of internal and external influences, through which people constructed their relationships and their everyday lives. Some Kichwa organizations responded to losses by trying to find ways for people to stay on their land, to encourage collective action, and to promote the revitalization of the Kichwa language. At the same time, the processes of urbanization and migration further blurred the differences between ethnic groups, resulting in a productive reflection on what it actually meant to be Indigenous and how being Indigenous contributed to transforming the larger Ecuadorian community.

Defining and maintaining community-based identities is problematic, particularly when those communities find themselves in the midst of profound transformations. The cases from Otavalo and Cotacachi demonstrate that Indigenous communities were neither homogenously constructed 'others' from national society, nor had they become simply folkloric representations of some past cultural difference now subsumed into a nominally multicultural, national melting pot. Instead, members of these communities were seeking out ways of simultaneously participating in national and transnational society, not only by preserving their cultural differences, but also by offering the knowledge contained within those differences as part of an ongoing dialogue. If the combination of economic circumstances wrought by globalization and the political integration sought by the Indigenous movement led to the 'decommunalization' of traditional Kichwa society, new forms of community were emerging from the residuals of that communalization (Sánchez Parga 2009). These new communities were built from ancestral knowledge and from a shared history of cultural difference. The success of the country's Indigenous movement in the latter part of the twentieth century allowed these newly emerging communities to negotiate their relationships from a position of self-esteem, which permitted them to borrow and adapt to changing circumstances without being assimilated into those dominant communities. It was possible to construct intercultural, but distinctly Kichwa, communities.

This process, however, did not happen by itself, and contact with other cultures was no guarantee of a vibrant, intercultural society. Creating a new cadre of leaders that understood the cultural processes that Kichwa people confronted was one of the essential tasks facing Indigenous organizations as they moved forward into the twenty-first century. César Cotacachi observed:

> Money is not everything in life. You have to prepare here in your head, too, so that people, the new leaders of the future have the ability to decide, to make the best decision about the new path for their generation, from here in twenty, thirty, forty years. My children, for example are now growing up and the children of my children will have to see what kind of Otavalo they want to live in. The ability to adapt to circumstances is extremely important. More than that, the idea is to strengthen our survival strategies. Along those lines, when you are in a hard space, to survive, there is the law of evolution, Charles Darwin, natural law, where only the strongest survive. In the case of the cultural issues in Otavalo only the best prepared are going to bring their people, their population

along the right path. This is what we need (Interview, Otavalo, April 14, 2014).

For interculturality to be successful and for Kichwa people to avoid being assimilated into dominant society, they needed to be aware of their cultural heritage and conscious about the ways in which it adapts to changing circumstances, as part of an ongoing critique of a world where money is seemingly everything.

Perhaps one of the ongoing legacies of the Indigenous movements, beyond the winning of rights, was the notion that one could be Kichwa without being tied to the past. Communities constantly renegotiate their identities and the boundaries they share with other communities. In the case of these Kichwa communities they actively placed themselves in the contemporary world while redefining but not abandoning their ethnic identities. They built on and refined their multivocal and dialogical practices as they moved themselves away from and back to their ancestral homelands, their kin, and their (changing) traditions. As Sacha Rosero, from otavalosonline.com noted, one of the contributions that he believed that his site and his community in general made was to be outward-looking. Not only did the community reinforce Kichwa culture but also "just like any other society, we Otavalos are also in a process of evolution. By adapting to the different experiences that we have lived, learning from them, we can share some of our values with other parts of the world" (Interview, July 10, 2010). The dialogic process of the Andean community, therefore, was not limited just to the internal dynamics of community, but also to what that community offered to other communities in the world. That dialogue could only continue through a process of seeking equality and continuing to valorize Kichwa cultural practices and epistemologies.

CHAPTER 6

SOCIO-ENVIRONMENTAL DILEMMAS IN MOJANDA

We've done a beautiful thing here. A really beautiful thing.
—Don Roberto Tocagón

In this chapter, I turn to some of the stories of highland communities in Otavalo and neighboring Pedro Moncayo and their efforts at *páramo* (high grassland) and water conservation. In the late 1990s, people in these highland rural communities of the Mojanda Lakes' *páramo*, to the north of Otavalo, became alarmed that both the quality and quantity of their water supply was noticeably decreasing. While it might seem a bit of a detour from the narrative of the rest of this book, it actually demonstrates how community members created and negotiated intercultural exchanges within the context of urban and rural, global and local. Furthermore, debates about environmental protection and resource management in Ecuador (and elsewhere) revolve around intercultural questions about human/nature relationships, and conflicts between "development" and living well (Gudynas 2016). These competing discourses are enmeshed in unequal power relationships, and building meaningful and sustainable futures are not simply policy matters but also pose fundamental cultural questions. As with other cultural and political projects, each cultural group possesses incomplete answers, and the necessarily shared space of environmental and developmental concerns becomes a fertile ground for intercultural practices.

At the turn of the twenty-first century, the *páramo* of Mojanda, like most *páramos* in the country, was confronting a series of socio-environmental challenges, including the advancement of the agricultural/cattle ranching limit, regular field burnings, climate change, and demographic changes. The pressures created by these processes threatened the ability of the *páramos* both to reproduce themselves and to provide the biological functions that their ecosystems, including those ecosystems' human communities, needed to survive. Faced with broad social, cultural, economic, and political challenges, the primarily Kichwa communities in and around the *páramo* of the Mojanda lakes engaged in collective, intercultural efforts to design projects and policies to protect their water supply. These projects also sought to lay a foundation upon which to build a more sustainable environmental, social, and cultural future. Because environmental problems of water supply and sustainability could not be divorced from their complex sociocultural contexts, the processes of environmental remediation and restoration are fundamentally intercultural endeavors.

Socio-Environmental Crises in the *Páramo*

Although the *páramos* in Latin America are defined as those lands between Costa Rica and Peru with an altitude between 3,000 and 5,000 meters, they vary greatly due to microclimatic differences and human use of them. They are generally characterized as the grasslands above the tree line and are associated with slow growing but hearty vegetation, which is able to survive the daily extremes in temperature and sun exposure. Their soils collect, decontaminate, and regulate water flow to lower-lying communities. Since ground water in the higher elevations is scarce, major cities like Quito depend on water derived from the *páramos* as does almost all of the irrigation in the highlands (De Bievre, Íñiguez, and Buytaert 2011, 81–82; Farley and Bremer 2017, 373). In Ecuador, the *páramos* run the entire length of the country and occupy approximately five percent of the national territory (León-Yanez 2011, 25–27). While the *páramos* perform important ecological functions and contribute to the region's biodiversity, they are increasingly under pressure from four main, interrelated sources: farmers who push the agricultural limit to ever higher elevations; ranchers who allow their animals to graze unchecked through the highlands; fires, set by both farmers and ranchers, to clear territory and allow new green growth; and, in some locations, mining activity (Peyre et al. 2015). Despite these activities producing short-term benefits, they create long-term problems to which there are no easy solutions. Conditions in these regions, for instance, are so severe that plants grow slowly and their periodic destruction, even over the course of just a few years, makes it almost impossible for them to regenerate themselves.

Nieto and Estrella (2011) found that because of

> modern cultivation and animal husbandry techniques, the expansion of the agricultural frontier, and the changes in the populations' dietary habits, the rich native agro-biodiversity of these ecosystems has been subjected to processes of alteration and erosion, with remote possibilities of recuperation (43).

Over time, the foodstuffs that were originally developed in the region have fallen out of favor and have been replaced with crops that are more marketable to urban consumers. These crops, while providing greater income, are also more costly to maintain, requiring more water and inputs than their native counterparts (Harden et al. 2013). Furthermore, agricultural practices alter the physical and chemical composition of the soil itself, making it less conducive to retaining and filtering water, leading in turn to greater erosion and degradation (De Bievre, Íñiguez, and Buytaert 2011, 89). These processes, in turn, lead to greater pressure on communities to open up more land to produce more crops for relatively distant markets, putting yet more pressure on the delicate balance of the *páramo* ecosystem.

Ranching also poses serious problems for maintaining the ecological integrity of the *páramos*. In addition to burning fields to create better grazing, the cattle themselves cause immense damage to existing plants either through eating them or trampling them. Furthermore, as cattle gather by open water sources, their waste contaminates downstream drinking water supplies. Finally, the weight of the cattle causes compaction of the soils, which in turn impedes the ability of the *páramos* to absorb water, leading to erosion and gradual loss of highland water sources, as rain water more quickly runs down the sides of mountains (De Bievre, Íñiguez, and Buytaert 2011, 92).

Fire is another of the challenges to the *páramos*. Farmers burn their fields to clear them for planting and ranchers burn fields to rid them of undergrowth and dead grasses and to promote new green shoots for their animals. Some also burn highland areas in the belief that the smoke released will start the season's rains. Unfortunately, it is not unusual for planned fires to get out of control and burn much greater areas than expected. Furthermore, even in the planned burn areas, the repeated damage done to native plants is virtually impossible to replace and detailed studies of the region show a marked difference in the types of vegetation and other abrupt changes to grassland ecosystems (León-Yanez 2011, 29–31; Martson and Bart 2014). Although fires promote short-term growth of new grass once the rainy season begins, they create longer-term problems by destroying the biological material within the soils, which degrades the ability for the soil to retain and replenish water supplies. Lastly, a burgeoning ecotourism sector represents a potential threat to the ecological sustainability of the *páramos*. In lieu of using the *páramos* for farming or ranching, tourism could provide many benefits to *páramo* communities. In addition to providing much-needed economic support, simply having outsiders spend time in the *páramos* helps to negate the widely held opinion that they are a sort of wasteland "up there." Instead city dwellers and foreigners would be able to see first hand the beauty and dynamics of these areas, seeing them as environmental regions worth maintaining for their own sake and perhaps creating a positive feedback in conservation efforts to support them (and the people who live there). At the same time, however, unregulated tourism often leads to the construction or improvement of roads up to and through the *páramos*, with the negative impacts that kind of development can bring with it. Finding a balance between access and maintaining a sustainable number of visitors so as not to disrupt delicate systems is often an elusive process (Villacís Mejía et al. 2016).

There is little doubt about the fundamental role that the *páramos* play in providing reliable and clean water for both agricultural production and human consumption to the region's populations. Furthermore, there is a fairly broad consensus among government officials, scientists, NGOs, and local communities that the high grasslands are under threat and that many of them have witnessed a marked decline in their environmental functions. Some of them have lost, perhaps irrevocably, their ability to successfully reproduce themselves due to biodiversity depletion, loss of native plants, degradation of soils, and erosion (León-Yanez 2011; Nieto and Estrella 2011; Ortiz-T 2008). Where there is little consensus, however, is in how to conserve the remaining *páramos* and begin recuperating damaged areas. Besides differing political agendas and policy prescriptions, the conflicts and possible resolutions to some of those conflicts also represent sometimes vastly different cultural understandings of nature, community, and human relationships (Ramón 2008). Many government agencies and NGOs, for instance, promote market-based solutions to these problems, based on a model of valuing the environmental services the areas provide (Moreano Venegas 2012; Stolle-McAllister 2015; B. Walsh 2011). While such initiatives often provide short-term funding to encourage communities to protect their resources, it also strengthens dominant modern and colonial understandings about the relationships between humans and nature.

The Mojanda *páramo*, in particular, represents an area of rich diversity, both in terms of its natural and human attributes. It also shares many of the risk factors seen throughout the country and region more generally. Covering approximately 28,000 hectares, the *páramo* varies between 2,500 and 4,250 meters in altitude, which allows for a wide variety of vegetation. The area includes several volcanic peaks, including the Fuya Fuya Mountain, three large lakes, and numerous streams including the headwaters of the Mira and Guayllabamba rivers (Villota, Behling, and León-Yanez 2017). Politically, it lies between the provinces of Pichincha and Imbabura, the cantons of Pedro Moncayo and Otavalo and the parishes of Tupigachi, Tabacundo, La Esperanza, Tocachi, Malchinguí, Otavalo, Eugenio Espejo, San Rafael, and González Suárez. A detailed study of the area by the NGO EcoCiencia in 2008 found 8,300 families distributed in 52 communities living in the area. Among that population, 62 percent consider themselves Indigenous, 37 percent Mestizo y 1 percent white or other. About 65 percent speak Spanish as their primary language and 35 percent Kichwa (Proyecto Páramo Andino 2008, 38–42). As the report concludes, "there exists only one *Páramo* of Mojanda and many people, organizations and institutions interested in using and preserving it" (120).

Like many areas in rural Ecuador at the turn of the twenty-first century, the population in Mojanda was experiencing transition brought about by environmental, socio-economic, and political changes. Urbanization was an increasingly important phenomenon as people migrated to the growing urban areas of Otavalo, Tabacundo, Cayambe, and Quito to work in a variety of professions, leaving behind agriculture. Furthermore, the floriculture industry, particularly in Pedro Moncayo, had a profound impact on communities throughout the area. Despite concerns about working conditions and wages, many young workers were attracted to regular pay and relatively steady employment. In the first decade of the twenty-first century, it accounted for 16 percent of all employment in the region, and was the first or second most important source of employment for many predominantly Kichwa communities (Proyecto Páramo Andino 2008, 45).

The shift to paid work for younger people had a profound effect on local communities. Not only did many in this group stop working in their families' fields, they were also less likely to want to participate in other community activities, such as *mingas*, contributing to a change in logic from communal responsibility to individual responsibility and opportunity (Sánchez Parga 2007). Loss of knowledge was a second and equally challenging implication of this transition in the underlying relationships within the community. As individuals became more oriented toward the market economy and their livelihoods no longer depended on ancestral agricultural and specific place-based knowledge, many community organizers and elders feared that as the current holders of that knowledge aged and passed on, it would not be transferred to new generations. This loss was particularly problematic for the continued protection of the *páramos* because the older generation that first identified the problems believed solutions were, in part, embedded in traditional community practices.

As an organizer of efforts to conserve the *páramos*, Frank Gualsaqui insisted that local successes to document and protect the *páramos* sprung directly from communities' ability to draw from and build on their knowledge and organization.

> There is a very conscious fight for people and for the thirty some years they've struggled with the floricultural industry, still not one social organization has disappeared. That's good, right? It's good because there are many problems, but they still have not disappeared. And, in many cases they have helped a lot to strengthen some areas (Interview, Tabacundo, October 28, 2011)[1].

In his opinion, community-based knowledge and organization, adapted to changing circumstances, provided the essential means to enact change.

These challenges in the population of Mojanda were intertwined with the environmental issues facing the *páramos*. By the late 1990s it had become apparent to many living in the area that a number of environmental issues, particularly water supply and quality, were beginning to be detrimental to people's lives and were precipitating inter- and intra-community conflicts. Through a participative process of community consultation, and with technical support from the NGO *Proyecto Páramo Andino* (Andean Páramo Project, PPA), degradation of soils around the micro-basins that collect and regulate water supply was identified as the immediate source of the water problem. The report found that agricultural and cattle grazing pressures at increasingly higher elevations, decreasing family land holdings, repeated burning of the *páramo* to clear land and produce green fodder for cattle, a gradual switch to monocultural production of non-traditional crops, and global climate change all contributed to the problem (Proyecto Páramo Andino 2008).

Over the generations, the agricultural frontier was consistently pushed higher as people were forced off of better lands at lower elevations, first by colonial settlers and then more recently by cattle *haciendas* through the first half of the twentieth century (Becker and Tutillo 2009). By the end of the twentieth century, those cattle *haciendas* were converted, for the most part, into the large flower operations. Although some of the *hacienda* lands were awarded to communities as a result of land reform laws of the 1960s and 1970s, they were almost always the less fertile, higher elevation plots. With no other place to go to support themselves, Kichwa and poor mestizo families moved increasingly higher in search of land to plant and space to graze their animals. PPA reports an average 140-meter upward push of the agricultural boundary since the 1970s (2008, 92).[2]

As families moved and worked up at higher elevations, they began altering the ways in which those delicate ecosystems functioned. Lands were plowed for crops and/or cleared for cattle grazing. Although generations of Kichwa farmers adapted certain crops to be successful under the conditions of the *páramo*, recent years witnessed a greater market demand for other crops. Farmers responded by developing monocultural fields (of particular types of maize, for instance) that required ever-greater amounts of inputs and quickly burned out the limited natural fertility of the soil (Ortiz-T 2008). As in other *páramos*, cattle grazing caused numerous, interrelated problems. Burning to clear brush and to stimulate new grass growth to support cattle grazing would regularly get out of control and destroy vast areas of grasslands, bushes, and trees. The repeated burnings and the compaction of the soils from the presence of the cattle eventually led to the incapacity of the micro-basins to retain and filter water leading to quick runoffs from rainfall and little retention of water for later use (Keating 2007).

Finally, climate change played an increasing role on both the environmental as well as social processes in the region. Many farmers reported that, historically, the rhythm of rainy and dry seasons were very predictable. Over the past thirty years, these cycles have become less reliable, starting late, abruptly stopping and then starting again, or bringing heavier than usual rains resulting in flooding and erosion, stronger winds, more intense hail storms, higher daytime temperatures and new diseases that can only be controlled with chemical suppressants. In a study of the meteorological records for Otavalo from 1980–2006, EcoCiencia confirmed the observations of the region's farmers, noting an increasing variability in the beginning and ending of the rainy season and greater variability of precipitation, particularly during the rainy season (Proyecto Páramo Andino 2008, 86). Noting many of these same climatic changes, former FICI President Marco Guatemal commented on their socio-cultural impacts:

> Today we can no longer calculate the planting season according to our Andean calendar. Instead it is becoming very difficult to apply our planting system according to the Andean calendar because global warming makes this era that we are living in difficult. This meant that there is less food for the individual to live on and with that we are no longer guaranteeing a healthy life in our territories to the next ones, or the new inhabitants that will come after us (Interview, Otavalo, August 22, 2011).

Adapting to global climate change, therefore, also brought with it challenges to the region's culture and natural resource management. Furthermore, because the *páramos* are an important source of water for the wider region, their protection played an increasingly important role in national and global discussions about conservation strategies.

ARTICULATED CONSERVATION EFFORTS IN MOJANDA

In the 1990s many of the rural inhabitants of the Canton of Pedro Moncayo began to notice that the gradual deterioration of water flow and quality were becoming increasingly acute. Frank Gualsaqui, an Indigenous man from Otavalo with a degree and experience in forestry management, came into the community as part of *"Poblamiento forestal de las microcuencas del Cantón Pedro Moncayo"* (Forest Population of the Micro-Basins of the Pedro Moncayo Canton) project in 1998, financed by a Swiss NGO.

> When I arrived, one of the first analyses that we did was defining the problem, right? So we could first identify that the issue of the *páramo* is very related for people with the issue of life, connected by water. So, the *páramo* is always going to be a compelling issue, an important issue, a high priority issue... We went to every community and talked with every community in its entirety with all of the time and materials we needed. Of course, we just reinforced what they already knew. They know what the problems are up there. So the idea was to make connections between the community, the project, and the institutions like the municipal government to do something together. I believe that this made the situation much, much stronger (October 28, 2011).

This strategy allowed Gualsaqui and his team to gather important information and to lay the foundation for an inclusive process through which local community members, local government, and NGOs would all contribute to developing and enacting conservation policies and practices.

Because they understood better than anyone else the dire predicament that they were facing and because they had deep cultural attachments to the *páramo*, most community members were enthusiastic about carrying out projects of reforestation in the basins. Gualsaqui described it:

We said, "ok, if the idea is to conserve water, the idea is to conserve the *páramo*, so, what do we do?" Then something very interesting began. It was very interesting because here in the Cantón Pedro Moncayo, between '98, '99, 2000, 2001 a canton-wide *minga* was carried out that involved mostly the communities from the rural sectors: Indigenous and campesino. The urban sector was like, "this isn't really my problem, right? I open the tap, water comes out—no problem." So there was not too much involvement from the urban sector or from certain institutions or organizations like the neighborhoods and the clubs that didn't have this level of consciousness. But in the communities, yes. So, this idea of cantonal planning came about. And, it was very interesting, because the project proposed the idea that together people could take concrete actions for conservation. And conservation was translated into planting native plants in the areas that we had thought technically prudent. It was incredible because from January to December, from *January* to *December* the trips from the communities were quickly planned...And, they filled; we had to say from here no more, no more. We'll wait until the following year to have a super strong plan. I began understanding from this logic that there is a community commitment to conserve. I was witnessing in practice that this idea of an Indigenous cosmovision is *really* practiced; it's really valued. It's in their way of life; it's in their politics of life, to take care of *Pachamama*. And, it's also an interesting issue because they are thinking about the future, right? In future generations. So, I was *feliz de la vida*, happiest I could be. Added on to this was the political will to support it, so I believe it was a super, super interesting experience (October 28, 2011).

In his recollection of the initial organizing to address local water problems, Gualsaqui touched on several important dynamics affecting the communities as they began thinking about how to address them. He noted, for instance, a difference between rural and urban dwellers in terms of relative awareness of the underlying water issues. In many rural communities in the Mojanda watershed, as is common throughout Ecuador, *juntas de agua*, or water governing boards have been established to capture and distribute water for both domestic and agricultural use

(Armijos Burneo 2012). These *juntas* are labor-intensive and demand much attention, time, and effort from all members of the community. City dwellers, however, are not generally required to put in labor to lay pipes, clean cisterns, or maintain their own water systems, but instead pay a monthly usage bill to the municipal government. Many higher-altitude, rural community members complained that their efforts in maintaining adequate and safe supplies of water for everybody were not recognized by most urban residents, often leading to feelings of resentment. Secondly, and as one of the keys to the successful efforts in Pedro Moncayo, Gualsaqui pointed to the importance of the collective effort. Certainly, the communities were enthusiastic and supportive of the plans they developed, but they were working in clear partnerships with the NGO and with municipal agencies. Finally, his epiphany of the importance of Indigenous culture and practice governing people's lives, and not just a folkloric backdrop to their organizations, struck him as immensely important not only because of its knowledge of social organizing and of natural systems, but also because of its forward-looking orientation. Indeed, this understanding that they were working for future generations stands in contrast to the ways in which Indigenous peoples are sometimes cast as nostalgic and backward-thinking.

In addition to the enthusiastic support of local communities, the Municipal Government incorporated the communities' conservation plans into its own five-year development plan, with the idea that it would not only result in better control of the canton's water supply, but also provide a means to educate the populace about the links between water service and environmental stability and open up new, more sustainable development practices. In 1999, the municipal government declared areas over 3,600 meters to be a protected forest zones and off limits to exploitation. Although it was not clear at the time if the municipal government actually had the authority to make such a decree, it nevertheless began a process of institutional support for conservation efforts (Interview, José Rivadeneira, Quito, September 20, 2011). In 2002, the municipalities of Pedro Moncayo and Otavalo signed a *Ordenanza Bicantonal para la*

Protección y Conservación de la Zona de Mojanda (Bicantonal Ordinance for the Protection and Conservation of the Mojanda Zone), which was composed of municipal government officials as well as representatives of the various *cabildos, juntas del agua,* and the Ministry of the Environment. In 2004, the municipal government declared that the *páramos* were part of the intangible patrimony of the municipality's people and specifically forbade burning, using ravines and basins for dumping of any sort, and encouraged citizens to denounce any of these activities to the authorities (Proyecto Páramo Andino 2008, 114). The state, in its various forms, in other words, became visibly involved in promoting the conservation of the *páramo*.

Similarly, in the *parroquias* of González Suarez and San Rafael, in the municipality of Otavalo, a dialogical relationship between municipal and local governing structures resulted in a dynamic and effective program to simultaneously protect the *páramo* and provide for local, autonomous development projects. As discussed in chapter 4, one of the main actors in these efforts was Roberto Tocagón, a Kichwa-Kayambi man from the community of Culuquí in González Suarez. Don Roberto was an important fixture in his community, serving in various official roles including community president as well as a project leader and intermediary between local communities and several NGOs and governmental agencies.

The story of conserving the *páramo*, like all social stories, is one complicated by political considerations, alliance building, and the constant work of convincing others that a particular project, or particular strategy is worth the investment. I quote at length here from a conversation that I had with Don Roberto about some of the motivations and struggles he had in beginning the work of restoring the *páramo*, and, as part of that process, restoring balance between the *páramo* communities and *Pachamama*.

> *Chuta*[3]—that was the most difficult part for me. Something I always regretted, but finally said, "Okay I've lost a lot of time here, but I'm not going to get stuck because somebody is going to help

me." Here when we would talk about deforestation, when we would talk about taking care of the *páramos*, people would say, "why should we go plant up there? That's crazy." We would say, "you shouldn't burn the *páramos*." And the leaders would be there saying, "of course, you need to burn them. Burning brings out new plants for the animals. The smoke is what calls on the rains." That is what they said. So, it was hard. Years went by and more years went by, and the springs began disappearing from top to bottom, the water supply was getting smaller, and the problem of the agreements between Otavalo and Tabacunda [attempting to regulate activities in the *páramo*], and then the people sort of woke up, and said, "yes, Don Roberto was right."

Little by little, there was no water, and people were beginning to fight at the tanks because there was a drop in the water pressure, trying to grab the last bit of water. Then they realized. And we said, "at least it's a beginning." They say that if there is, that is if we live through a third world war, it is going to be for water. We can see that. And this happened, and is still happening. You can see people from this community here and that community over there fighting over the same water. And, the communities' water supply was constantly getting smaller and smaller. So, as we had done before, some 10 or 12 years ago now, we built a catchment at a spring just a little bit above us here. Or, maybe it was a little earlier than that, maybe 18 or 20 years ago. So, as we were finishing building the tanks up there on the mountain, we finished by cleaning up the area. We cleaned up everything: the *chilcas*[4], the *auques*[5] that were there. Everything nice and neat. After three months, everything was ready. The water was hooked up and everything was ready to go.

But three months after that, when I went to see the water in the tank, there was hardly any. It was drying out. And after about a year, completely dry. We said after a while, let's bring this to the Assembly. We told the people we had done something wrong. That is when there was an elder who does rituals. So, this elder said, "Why did we not do the rituals? *Wambras* [young people], do the rituals." So, since I was the president at that time I said, "Okay, since we have a small fund, let's go buy some fruit, let's go buy

some *cuy* [guinea pigs] and some hens." We went up to the site of
the spring to do the ritual and to eat there, leaving some, half some
said, but at least a part there, and to ask *Pachamama* not to take
this water away from us. That is the truth. But, there was nothing...

From there we said, "*chuta*, but does this mean we should plant?
Or do something else?" And, again the elder approached me, and
said, "look, *wambras*, the waters are going to leave. I have dreams.
I have dreams." And, what are they asking? "You still need to
do something." So, once again we held another ritual, another
half, and now he said, "bring me sugar, a little sugar a little raw
sugar," and I don't remember what else he was asking me for. And
he did the ritual. And then, three days later, I went back to see,
and there was nothing left of the things that we had left there.
A tiny bit of the sugar and that was it. Now the, what do you
call it, the tank was ruined. The elder had been made to dream.
They had made him dream, and in his dream a *señor* appeared.
The *señor* was riding a horse, and he complained, "I want you
to go away now," he said, "or I will never appear there again."
But, the elder said, "I don't know why he would say that." He
really did not understand. He wasn't working there, remember,
he had only dreamed it. Then we said, "We somehow damaged
the spring." That is why the *señor* didn't go there anymore. It's
possible that just maybe if we were to bring him something... So
we held another ritual, we left him more sweets and we began
planting, the same plants that you find in other ravines, and since
it was raining we put them in right away.

Recently, with the PPA project we were able to complete more.
Now you, if you go up there, you will see a tremendous forest and
there is plenty of water. So, because of that, the people believe, and
so now if you say we are going to fight for the water, it doesn't
matter. If you say you need help, if someone says this, this and
this, people are willing. So, when there are fires in the *páramos*,
people go immediately. Young people more than anyone. They
run, like it's a sport. *Chuta.* So now we have everyone united
(Interview, Inti Culuquí, October 10, 2013)[6].

Don Roberto's story represents two important factors in developing conservation strategies: the ongoing struggles to convince people to act and the need to understand environmental issues within a cultural context that makes sense to them. Although he understood both from his Kichwa knowledge system as well as his training in Western science that the *páramo* communities were facing potentially existential problems, he encountered great resistance to his calls for change. Likewise, his attempts to foster participation with PPA's conservation efforts were met with skepticism, as the communities had all too often been the objects of others' development projects that led to personal enrichment and division and not the common betterment of the community. It is telling that the explanation of the well's failure derived from the elder's dream that the *señor* was not coming back because his space had been violated. Don Roberto interprets this in two ways. First, that, indeed, the natural order had been upended. In building the capturing tanks in the ways they had always done it, particularly by clearing away all of the vegetation around the spring, they had upset the spirits in charge of maintaining balance. In an earlier conversation, Don Roberto explained that,

> I believe there is a God up there, but I also believe that our gods are here, with us. Those are the ones who are raising us, nourishing us. Mother Moon gives us the calendar; Father Sun gives us warmth. So for us, everything is a system of reciprocity; we all must apply solidarity (October 5, 2013).

The elder noted that the work group forgot to carry out the proper rituals and forgot to leave the proper offerings that would be necessary to maintain reciprocity. Clearing the basin's plants, likewise, disrupted the reciprocity between soil, water, and vegetation, making it impossible for the spring to regenerate itself. By heeding the advice from the elder's dream and making amends for their disruption of the required order, the plantings stabilized the water supply and made the system functional. As Don Roberto commented, the success of that endeavor helped people see the effectiveness of his proposals and made them more willing to participate in the hard work of restoring the *páramos* and maintaining a harmonious and sustainable future. He was also able to convince community members to cooperate with PPA to document the various issues in the *páramo* and to propose solutions to those problems that made sense both to Kichwa sensibilities as well as those of outside funding agencies.

A second and equally important step was codifying the communities' rights and responsibilities toward the *páramos* in their territories. In 2008, after years of debate and consultation with residents, internal organizations, and outside agencies, the Community Assembly of Inti Caluquí approved its "Internal Regulations" (2008) that, among other things, directly addressed the use and protection of the *páramos* and other natural resources. Reaffirming community members' collective and exclusive rights to make use of the their lands and resources, the regulations clearly stated, "The grasslands, native forests and other resources, which may be in danger of deterioration, should be declared protected areas and construction or exploitation of any kind prohibited" (Article 24). Commenting on the *páramos*, the community declared that they are "the source of water, refuge for wild life and place of great cultural landscape value for the community" (Article 30). Community members, therefore, were charged to make "adequate" use of its resources, keeping in mind its limitations, to form and train fire brigades, build fire breaks, regulate outsiders' entrance into the *páramos*, build fences as necessary to keep animals out, ban all agricultural and grazing activity above 3, 200 meters, and coordinate future tourist development through the community council. To protect native forests, the assembly banned logging and cutting, but allowed community members to take advantage, in a sensible manner, of forest resources for firewood, medicinal plants, seeds, etc. Furthermore, they pledged to inventory existing flora and fauna and make outside researchers dependent on communal authorities to initiate activities. Finally, with an eye toward maintaining the sustainability and integrity of their lands, the internal regulations limited the introduction of new seeds and crops, instead encouraging community members to investigate and implement agroecological practices to avoid chemical inputs.

In writing these regulations, community members engaged with each other and with outside stakeholders to assert that their historic and collective rights to their land were dependent on protecting those resources going forward. Conserving the *páramo* was always linked to the rights and needs of community members to make "adequate" use of its resources. Unlike some conservation efforts advocated by organizations—primarily in the global north that seek to leave areas "wild," and off-limits to people—the approach taken all around Mojanda was better characterized as management. The internal regulations that operationalized the community's relationship with the *páramo*, and with each other, made clear that more than just an economic resource, the *páramo* constituted an integral part of their cultural identity. Instead of separating itself from its natural surroundings, the community sought a more harmonious relationship with *Pachamama* by articulating a set of rights and responsibilities for living there.

Sustainable agriculture was a prime example of working within the limits of their natural surroundings. To counteract newly-banned farming and grazing practices, Tocagón and other leaders organized the *Red de Productores Agroecológicas del Lago San Pablo* (Network of Agroecological Producers of San Pablo Lake) to promote agroecological production. Disavowing chemical inputs, local farmers sought to grow crops using natural fertilizers through a better understanding of the holistic, ecological functioning of their lands. "This is nothing new, of course. It's just a new name for our ancestral practices," one participant explained.

> I do compost; I do agroecology, so I don't lose. I give back to Mother Earth, because she also needs to be nourished, and because if I take and take, and take advantage of her, and don't give anything in return, Mother Earth is going to cry. She'll leave me needing (Interview, San Rafael, October 18, 2013).

Community leaders hoped that agroecology would help families not only to produce enough surplus to be able to sell to nearby urban markets, but also that it would reinforce the belief that rural communities could be sustainable, even in a world that would seem to be anxious to leave them behind. Don Roberto explained his role in the project:

> So, for me, there is too much work. Many people in the community say, "*Chuta,* I'm poor. I'm going to work in Quito, or for the flower company." *Chuta,* that's just not true, to say to an Indigenous person, I'm poor. No. We are not poor. In the community, we have everything. Instead we are lazy, we can't be bothered. We just want something easy. But, it should not be that way, because our parents consumed what they needed, they ate their own food, produced right here, made by their own hands. Now, what are we doing? We buy noodles, we buy rice, even though rice sometimes is worth it, but only associated with something else. And, they don't do that. They buy rice, late morning, if it's possible. They buy rice, noodles and they put it with some junk food, and that is what the young people who are going to work in the flowers eat. So what would be better: our proposal is that we want to create micro-enterprises, more than we already have. Building on these experiences with the markets, we have small businesses making jams from *jicama, mashra,* and *ocra,* so they are doing that. And with that they go out. And now that are also beginning to process grains. After growing the barley and the wheat, they are turning them into flour.

> See, before, I would produce, and I'm a good farmer in this area, I would produce 120, 150 *quintales*[7] of barley, maybe 200 of potatoes. Then, what would I do? I harvested it, saved some for seeds, and then turned it all over to an intermediary. And it was the intermediary who would profit. This is the bad thing about us. I wouldn't keep track of my work. My work is hard, but we never really paid attention to how much we were working. We didn't know if we were coming out ahead or if we were losing. I lost (October 10, 2013).

Agroecology, then, was not only a means to sustainably manage a delicate ecosystem, but also a way to nurture communities and create local autonomies as part of that management strategy.

Altieri and Toledo (2011) explain, "Agroecological production systems are biodiverse, resilient, energetically efficient, socially just and comprise the basis of a strategy of energy, production and food sovereignty" (587). One strategy for building resiliency is for communities to build out support networks. The local organization, for instance, was associated with the *Coordinara Ecuatoriana de la Agroecología* (Ecuadorian Coordinating Committee for Agroecology) and *Movimiento Agroecología de América Latina* (Latin American Agroecological Movement). They used these affiliations to learn from the experiences of other communities and organizations, to trade effective production and marketing techniques, and to improve their own standing in these larger associations. With the help of FICI and the Provincial Governments of Otavalo and Pichincha, their producers' network obtained tents and tables and permanent places in one of Otavalo's and Quito's weekly food markets. Selling directly to consumers, and bypassing intermediaries, allowed families to reap the full profits of their labor. In addition to providing a relatively stable income for the producers, they hoped that direct interactions with consumers would build better relationships with the urban sector and educate them about the communities that produced their food.

Communities involved in these projects could point to important successes, while still facing serious, ongoing challenges. Organizing around conservation and sustainability issues contributed to revitalizing the communities themselves. Drawing upon ancestral knowledge and internal organizing structures, they successfully partnered with outside organizations and agencies to plan and implement complicated and difficult projects. People showed immense pride in the success of their efforts, reporting, for instance, the satisfaction of taking their children up to the work sites years later to see the trees and other plants flourishing. They also defended their autonomy and asserted their rights to protect and manage their lands. Besides having a critical voice in articulating regulations and municipal-wide agreements, the communities steadfastly refused to let outside entities encroach on their territories. When grazing was banned, for instance, an *hacienda* refused to move its cattle from the protected zones. After local authorities refused to act, community members organized themselves and physically removed the cattle from the protected areas. Similarly in 2004, a private entity began a trout farming business on the major lake. When they would not cease operations, the community broke up the aquaculture infrastructure, making it clear that such endeavors would not be tolerated. While they received some criticism for acting unilaterally on these matters, it was an assertion of their autonomy and their rights to protect their territories.

That is not to say that everything was easy. Friction between rural and urban communities over responsibilities for maintaining a reliable source of water hindered relationships. Despite some outreach efforts to make common cause with urban organizations to involve them more in *páramo* protection, environmental issues were generally not a high priority for them. In addition to not providing bodies for different projects, urban apathy toward these issues also resulted in uneven funding commitments to various initiatives. Frank Gualsaqui, who was elected to the Pedro Moncayo Municipal Council in 2009, complained that he was generally unable to get his fellow council members or mayor to fund projects, noting that out of an annual budget of about five million dollars, only about five thousand was allocated to *páramo* conservation, despite binding agreements between Pedro Moncayo and Otavalo to protect and rehabilitate critical areas. Finally, population pressures, the loss of youth workers to the flower *haciendas*, and a changing sense of community among young people were continually seen as threats to the future of community-based projects.

LOCAL PROCESSES OF DEVELOPMENT

The *páramos* of Mojanda are not only a niche ecological landscape but also a fundamentally social and cultural space. Humans have lived and continue to live and work in these spaces, which contribute to their forms of social organization, their meaning-making practices, and the physical structure of the *páramos* themselves. Human and natural processes, in other words, have evolved together as people have shaped and transformed the *páramos*, just as living in them have shaped and transformed social relationships. Edgar Isch (2012) notes that the symbiotic relationship in general between humans and nature means that today,

> there practically does not exist any natural space that does not demonstrate influences or effects of human actions. Even less so, no human, who is a result of this natural dialectic, could exist without maintaining close relationships with their immediate and distant environment. An example of this can be seen in the Andean peoples, from hundreds and thousands of years ago, those who in interaction with natural forces went about constructing the *páramos* as we now know them and feel a need to protect them (54).

Human and natural evolution are mutually constitutive, meaning that when discussing environmental issues, we are also necessarily discussing social issues and vice versa. As Rossana Monosalva (2011) argues,

> There does not exist a single environmental problem, no matter how small or global it may be (global warming, pollution, loss and degradation of natural resources) that can be considered socially neutral, just as one cannot propose any sociopolitical argument that could be considered ecologically innocuous (130).

In the case of these communities in the Mojanda *páramo*, the solutions to preserving and improving the ecological functions of the *páramos* and to promote better and safer water supplies lay not in top-down prohibitions of certain activities, but rather in a dialogue between people living and working there. That dialogue also included a critique of the larger socioeconomic and cultural models that led to the degradation of their delicate ecosystems.

The communities of Mojanda developed intercultural approaches to their problems. Outside entities including NGOs, academics, and government agencies contributed both funds and knowledge to assessing the situation. EcoCiencia and PPA, using Western scientific techniques and knowledge, worked extensively on research projects that provided other kinds of evidence (water quality testing, species inventories) that backed local observations about the potential problems. The communities leveraged this technical support and information to augment their understanding of their situations and to efficiently reforest and protect their micro-basins and water supplies. As important as outside technical advice was, however, the initial diagnoses of problems as well as the concrete mechanisms for fixing them clearly came from the community and were based on local and ancestral knowledge and practices. José Rivadeneira, director of the *Coordinadora Ecuatoriana de Agroecología*, who worked extensively with the communities in Mojanda, noted that the successes in the area's conservation policies were due to an ongoing dialogue between various levels of government, from the ministry of the environment through the municipalities and the parishes, and, finally, the various levels and networks of local and regional organizations with which local community members are affiliated.

> At the end of the day, things get decided by the closeness that people have for these areas. And, in this sense, the internal community regulations have been important, because they incorporated, really in the best way, a series of environmental measures. So, the community managed to put its own people in order, they regulated grazing, they put limits on agriculture, they decided on how water is distributed. All of which is important. So here the lesson is how at these levels of decision-making, to protect a common good, the process of convincing and coming to community agreements at the level of their organization were all fundamental to its eventual success (Interview, Quito, September 20, 2011).

The need to build consensus and nourish acceptance of decisions was a constant task within the communities themselves even, as they reached out to and worked with outside actors and agencies. These projects were successful, in the end, because communities were able to incorporate multiple ways of knowing. Local leadership, knowledge, and persistence were fundamental to the projects' successes, as was their ability to operate within complex internal and external webs of relationships and networks.[8]

If internal actions were strengthened through relationships with outside agencies, it would have been impossible for those outside actors to have simply imposed new effective standards on the communities. Both local promoters as well as governmental and NGO organizers referred frequently to the need to "*socializar*" or socialize proposals. This process involved not only making a case for one's project, but also ensuring that people had the opportunity to discuss, debate, modify, and ultimately understand and incorporate the proposal into their social networks and their understanding of the situation. As Frank Gualsaqui observed,

> It is important to continue proposing this idea that the communities ought to play leading roles in the management of resources. From there they can confirm whatever contracts and agreements might be necessary, because the institutions like the municipal government don't have the capacity to manage the situation. Putting a forest ranger up there is not sufficient. Putting fifty rangers wouldn't be sufficient. But, there are 500, 800, 1000 people in the communities, and they are all being vigilant. If there is a fire, the community comes out. They organize and they head out. So, it seems to me that we could really advance this cause by arguing even more forcefully the need to turn the management of these zones completely over to the communities. I believe that would the socially and politically viable means to think about conservation (October 28, 2011).

The experience of the communities bore out this assertion. It was community members who organized themselves, at great personal risk, to remove cattle from the *páramos* and the fishing operation from the lake. It was up to community members and their elected authorities and assemblies to endorse and police their own internal agreements. Not only did the community see this internal regulation as in their own interests, but outside imposition of regulations and restriction would most probably have been rejected and outside enforcement would have been ineffective without sustained local cooperation.

Similarly, Roberto Tocagón, from González Suarez, saw the issue as one of dialogue between different cultural groups. Noting that, in the past, agency employees tended to stay in their offices,

> but now through our projects, we are signing contracts and making agreements so that they really come out to the communities and see the communities' needs so they can help solve them. For example, we might have a project to do a training workshop on *páramo* management, so we bring the technicians from environment, technicians from the provincial government and they help to train. But, we also train them about our conception of community, about our realities. So, teaching is shared: scientific level and local level (October 10, 2013).

Furthermore, he believed that the knowledge contained in what he called the local level was much more detailed and built on generations of observations and, therefore, had much to share with "scientific" knowledge.

> We, our parents, our grandparents, know a lot about the lunar calendar, and contact and communication with *Pachamama*. For us, for Indigenous people, *Pachamama* is a living being, she is living just like us. Because of this, life is increasing, the plants, the animals, us people, because everything is alive for us. And, what's more, everything goes together; nothing is separate. Scientific knowledge today, does not know, or maybe only knows a little bit about this reality [...] When I was at the university, they gave me these studies that said there were three altitudinal floors: the high part, the low part and the in-between part. There are

three. However, within the Indigenous worldview, we have *seven* distinct altitudinal floors that our elders, our ancestors had already identified. And at every level life is growing, right? So that's why we say when we are going to plant in the springs, we are going to have a beautiful experience. When we are going to plant, we first ask the oldest person, be it a man or a woman, that they go ask *Pachamama* that these plants grow. And we say that when we sow these plants that we are going to grow water. That is what we say. We call it growing water, because for us water is not just water. Very significant, no? First, it is blood, the blood that runs in the veins of our Mother Earth, of our *Pachamama*. Then, well, the water is for the needs and benefits of people (October 10, 2013).

His own approach to knowledge, therefore, was to build from his Kichwa cosmovision and incorporate the ceremonies of the elders, to learn from what he at another time referred to as their "library of knowledge," while at the same time taking from Western science what was useful to their situation.

Even the ways in which projects were organized reflected this move toward incorporating multiple ways of knowing, while not abandoning the local to the homogenizing tendencies of larger organizations. As much as they built out national and international networks for agroecological projects or sought funds from international agencies, the work also always centered around fortifying local organizations, developing projects that would be sustainable for the community in the long run, and ensuring local control over outcomes. They insisted, for instance, that government agencies come and spend time in the community in order to get a better understanding of the problems they faced because generic solutions did not map onto specific and complex problems. "Development" as an outside discourse and practice has been historically problematic and contradictory to the outlook of many communities.

Gualsaqui, for instance, rejected the notion of local development.

I don't believe in these histories of local development: from their conception they barely recognized us. An agency generates a document and says, "this is local development. This is what you have to do." So, one would open the memo and have to do this, that, and the other thing. From my experience, what I can say is that I don't support local development. What I *do* support are the *local processes* of development. The words change around a little, but the meaning is different. Here we are, I have witnessed that the local processes of development are oriented to the kinds of things I've been talking about. Not the other. Not the other. So, from the local perspective, strengthening our capacities has been one of the strongest issues I have worked on, and has been from where we have arrived. It is from where we try to achieve *Sumak Kawsay*, or whatever it is; it is our responsibility (October 28, 2011).

By insisting on "local processes of development," he hoped to ensure that local communities constructed economic, social, political, and cultural projects that conformed to *their* needs and desires and not, necessarily, the more destructive notions of development as articulated by dominant discourses. The projects of conservation and management of the *páramos* were inextricably connected not to outside notions of development, but to building on knowledge and organization within the communities to allow them to chart, as much as possible, their own course and their own internal and external relationships.

Perhaps one of the most interesting factors in this process was one that is missing. While there was much talk of developing micro-enterprises, strengthening producer-consumer market relations, and building up networks for community tourism as means through which the *páramos* could be sustainably used, there was no discussion of large-scale tourist development, or other attempts to induce outside capital to invest in local projects. Even local conservation strategies veered away from many of the market-based initiatives sponsored by the state and by international NGOs. An increasingly "green" strategy for many NGOs, governments, and even corporations has been to recognize the monetary value of environmental services, such as carbon sequestration and aquifer and biodiversity protection. Once a monetary value has been assigned, communities and individuals can be paid to protect those resources by not developing their lands or undertaking other types of activities that threaten their sustainability (Latorre Tomás 2011; C. Walsh 2011). Designed to help it integrate into the United Nations Reducing Emissions from Deforestation and Forest Degradation plus sustainability (REDD+) initiatives, the Ecuadorian government created a conservation program in 2008 known as *Socio-Bosque and Socio-Páramo* (Forest-Partner, Páramo-Partner) through which the state entered into long-term contracts with individuals and communities, providing them with funds for local development projects in return for the stewardship of their resources (de Koning et al. 2011; Farley and Bremer 2017; Karuse and Loft 2013; Stolle-McAllister 2015).

None of the communities of the Mojanda *páramo*, however, adhered to these programs, despite the fact that they could invest their payments in various types of projects. While funding and support from all levels of the state and NGO sources were helpful, the *incentive* for conserving and improving the *páramo* corresponded to a different logic. Despite some market-based solutions, particularly in identifying ways in which small producers using agroecological techniques could make a living by selling their products in nearby cities, or to promote environmentally friendly community tourism projects, there was no attempt to commoditize the environmental services that the *páramos* provide. The communities' conservation projects, although extremely thorough, sought neither to quantify the value of the *páramos* nor to market that value through transnational environmental services or other similar schemes. While more funding for programs would have been welcome, the idea of putting one's land into long-term agreements seemed unnecessary. Tocagón noted that participating in the national programs would have been a bureaucratic nightmare for his community because land titles were not clear and they already had a system that seemed to work. They agreed on enforceable rules about land use and saw their lands as inherently belonging to them, their communities, and their futures. Why potentially risk losing that in an environmental services-for-money agreement? The conservation organizing in Mojanda made clear that local people did not need to be told about their responsibilities toward conserving the lands and water upon which they depended. They already had been the stewards of those territories for generations. At the same time, however, they also demonstrated a remarkable willingness to engage state agencies and to enlist the assistance of outside technical experts to help develop conservation plans and proved they were willing to give up harmful practices.

INTERCULTURAL LESSONS FROM MOJANDA

The efforts in the Mojanda area suggest several important factors for analyzing other similar situations. First, the needs and desires of local communities are paramount in the success of any conservation effort. Landscapes, "environmental services," and conservation do not happen in vacuums, but in the spaces already occupied by people. Forcing conservation norms on others is another form of colonialism. No matter how critical an area may be for regional or even global climate stabilization, people living in those areas have rights to their use as well. As the case of the peoples living in Mojanda demonstrated, they also have a vested interest not only in seeing those areas preserved, but generally have practices in place (or are willing to put them in place) to ensure their viability. Secondly, local peoples have a deep knowledge of where they live. What is often referred to as "ancestral knowledge" in the Andes, which is based on generations of observation and experimentation, captures a wealth of information about specific ecosystems and specific ways of using them in ways that promote both production and conservation. A genuine dialogue between Indigenous and Western types of knowledge proved fruitful in the case of Mojanda and represented great potential for other situations as well. Thirdly, an intercultural approach to environmental issues can be productive and effective. Realizing that they had a deteriorating situation with their water supply, Indigenous communities in the Mojanda region were willing to cooperate with regional NGOs to analyze the problem and help them articulate a plan to reverse the worst processes. At the same time, the "Western" oriented NGOs and governmental agencies were open to dialogue with the communities and with the ancestral knowledge of their ecosystems to produce plans of action with them. The communities themselves, using internal decision-making processes, articulated rules for *páramo* use and enforcement mechanisms. They used the tradition of the *minga* to organize work parties to plant trees and they used the knowledge of the university-trained forestry technicians to decide on plant species and improve planting techniques. These were not minor issues and demonstrated both the hopes of intercultural encounters toward solving problems as well as the willingness of members of different cultural backgrounds to abandon the alleged superiority of a singular cultural paradigm without having to renounce their own.

Although the local communities were connected to broader political, cultural, and economic networks, they followed strategies that conformed to their needs, desires, and understandings of living well. These projects demonstrated a fundamentally intercultural initiative because they attempted to not only incorporate the knowledge and practices of distinct cultural groups, but also did so without accepting the logic of the dominant groups as a point of departure. Although they recognized that having close relationships with other types of communities was desirable, particularly for sellers' cooperatives, community tourism, and financial assistance for projects, they wanted to build those relationships within a framework that allowed them to maintain and strengthen their communities, their lands, and their ways of life.

Interculturality is more than just the mixture of ethnic-cultural groups. What made these projects intercultural was not just the interaction between the Kichwa majority of the Mojanda communities with Mestizo people and institutions, but rather their attempts to incorporate knowledge and practices for the desired ends of their communities. Despite the Kichwa communities' lower socio-economic position and history of marginalization, they insisted on the value of their knowledge and the appropriateness of their social organizations. They did not simply accept outside experts armed with answers for their problems. Outside agencies, therefore, had to earn the trust of the communities by working with them to frame their research questions and to articulate solutions to the problems they both encountered. For the communities, these projects were not just a means to conserve their natural environment, but also a means to strengthen their own organizations and identities. Cooperation, in this case, did not mean co-optation. Indeed, the success of these programs from an ecological perspective, based on the desires of the predominantly Mestizo NGOs and government agencies, *depended* on Kichwa knowledge, organization, and cultural heritage.

At the same time, the communities were building their projects at the margins of the dominant logics of development. By deciding not to participate in *Socio-Páramo*, for instance, they operated outside of the market influenced environmental services model of conservation promoted by the state. Their commitment to sustainable use of the *páramos* conformed to another logic, one that sees them as inextricably linked to their very specific histories and places in the world. Don Roberto Tocagón, for example, contended that "we will keep on working for conservation with or without money, with or without a project, because that's the way it should be. If we don't solve our own problems, no one else will be coming offering solutions, either."

All of which is not to say, as with interculturality in general, that this process was easy or without conflict. Structural inequalities between the communities, the urban centers, NGOs, and the state continued and could not be resolved by these projects alone. Young people continued to be lured away from ancestral homes and ways of knowing by the promise of more secure and consumerist futures. Urban inhabitants, who are generally Mestizo, tended not to understand or particularly care about the efforts of rural, highland communities to conserve the *páramos*, and thus, everyone's access to clean, reliable water supplies.

Nevertheless, the struggles around conserving the *páramos* demonstrated both the challenges and the promises of intercultural approaches to problem solving. Negotiations between cultural groups were fraught with histories of exploitation, misunderstanding, and belittlement of difference. The neoliberal context in which those negotiations occurred further destabilized attempts at creating genuine equality. At the same time, however, local communities, bolstered by the last generation of (sometimes turbulent) success of Indigenous rights, asserted their autonomy and engaged multiple possible solutions to their problems as a means to not only solve their immediate problem of resource conservation, but also to do so in ways they saw as desirable and beneficial by strengthening and transforming themselves.

Notes

1. Remaining quotations in this chapter from Gualsaqui are from interviews that took place from October 20–28, 2011 in the city of Tabacundo.
2. Ironically, it is now understood that these higher elevation lands are not wastelands but perform vital hydrological functions, which changes the social dynamics of understanding their value and, at times, leads to conflicts with local, regional, and national interests
3. *Chuta* is a colloquial expression used in Ecuador and Peru meaning roughly, damn! or Goodness!
4. A shrub native to the *páramos*. Its fruit is used to treat arthritis.
5. A plant native to the highlands.
6. Remaining quotations in this chapter from Tocagón are from interviews that took place from October 5–15, 2013 in the community of Inti Culuquí.
7. A quintal is approximately 46 kg.
8. See Armijos Burneo (2012) for a detailed analysis of the citizenship-making processes of negotiating water rights in Mojanda through the various first- and second-degree associations of the Mojandita community.

CHAPTER 7

BROADENING
DECOLONIAL STRUGGLES

Throughout *Intercultural Interventions*, I have examined how some Kichwa people, their organizations, and their Mestizo allies in Northern Ecuador have sought to bring cultural and political change to their lives by developing and adapting intercultural strategies in their struggles. The movement sought to destabilize the colonial order, to question the epistemic certainties of liberal modernity, and to navigate a cultural terrain carved out by global forces and local assertions of power. At a theoretical level, I framed the argument as a proposition to build a new social order based on profound respect for difference that could lead to the construction of narratives and institutions capable of a more equitable and sustainable future—in contrast to a dominant colonial order that, while malleable, is based on ethnic, economic, and epistemic inequalities. Indigenous organizations have contributed substantially to opening Ecuador to debates about cultural diversity, while also pushing the country toward a potentially different model of development. At the local level, people in the Otavalo Valley were interculturalizing their politics and their communities as they realigned power structures and built on regional and global networks of knowledge and cultural exchange.

This decade (roughly 2006–2016) of relative demobilization of the movement provided communities and individuals with the opportunity to assess, create, and adapt to the complexities of their new normal. That new normal was itself fluid and sometimes lacked the clarity of vision for positive change, which presented challenges to the aspirations of movement leaders. It also, however, allowed for flexibility in thinking and relationship-building that could be difficult in the more polarizing moments of intense mobilization. The interculturality being explored and practiced by many Kichwa people in this time period was characterized by what Philipp Altmann (2017) has called "radical localism," corresponding to the particular logics and practices of local communities rather than narratives established by outside thinkers and activists.

Those local intercultural processes were marked by ambiguity. As many intercultural theorists have argued, interculturality is not a linear process but rather one characterized by discussion, false starts, and ever-changing goals. Indigenous progress in securing political and cultural rights was uneven, as communities struggled with how to manage their new realities. Some change, of course, was brought on by Indigenous successes at transforming public discourse about the place of non-Mestizo people. Broader access to public education, while providing a foundation for greater opportunities for Indigenous children, also brought them into ever-closer contact with Spanish language use and other Mestizo cultural norms. Global travel and increasingly easier access to internet communication also substantially contributed to the ways in which Kichwa people defined and created their communities. Finally, economic restructuring provided both challenges and opportunities for many communities as people circulated more frequently between urban and rural spaces and money became the most common means of mediating economic exchanges. Some of these transformations were welcome and others accepted more warily, often highlighting generational rifts particularly when they appeared to threaten community continuity.

Kichwa people and communities, however, were certainly not passive recipients of change, but rather were active agents in interculturalizing their worlds. Many of the people I spent time with recognized that they (as all of us) needed to adapt to change. They did not see change as a bad thing but were also very careful to think about how they could use new ideas, technologies, and work-relationships in such a way that they improved their wellbeing without forcing them to cease being Kichwa. Voices of change were both explicit and implicit. Explicitly, Kichwa politicians and activists were regional and national leaders in efforts to dismantle colonial power relationships and to create new, more horizontal ones. Their successes were never complete, but their insistence on a new kind of inclusion advanced the debate and created more transparent and inclusive institutions. The work of mayors like Mario Conejo and Auki Tituaña demonstrated to outside audiences that Indigenous people could govern themselves and were also effective leaders and administrators of larger institutions. The normalization of multi-ethnic governance was an essential step toward interculturalizing politics and political institutions in the Otavalo Valley. Nationally, although the 2008 Constitution was not all that Indigenous advocates had hoped it would be, by explicitly recognizing the diversity of the country's population, along with its cultural and epistemological depth, it laid the foundation for the long-term continuance of the intercultural project. This project promises to be a contentious one, of course, with its share of advances and setbacks.

Beyond institutional politics, Kichwa families and organizations in the Otavalo Valley were able to invest economic success from textiles and trade to strengthen and revitalize cultural expression and traditions. Beginning in the 1960s, some families were able to send children to higher education. Many of these young people eventually became the political and intellectual leaders of various organizations and movements. Some went into politics. Others used their educational experiences in anthropology and linguistics to research their own histories and to develop programs to preserve and deepen ancestral knowledge. The ability to move between Mestizo and Indigenous contexts greatly interculturalized approaches to problem solving because they were able to use knowledge from both systems to make their work more effective. The revitalization of festivals throughout the region reflected their successes in understanding their pasts, interpreting and inventing traditions for the present, and communicating their importance to non-Indigenous people. Here too, however, intercultural processes also had ambiguous results. The increase in primary use of Spanish among Kichwa people alarmed many activists and, despite efforts at increasing its visibility and viability, the trend by the early 2010s was clearly toward increased use of Spanish to the detriment of Kichwa. Similarly, the reinvention of what it means to be Kichwa by many young people was troubling to many in older generations who had fought hard for the maintenance of a particular way of being Kichwa, particularly in terms of dress and social organization.

These intercultural processes, however, were taking place in a terrain still marked by great inequalities. Through their political commitments, economic choices, and ways of expressing their cultural identities, Indigenous people demonstrated openness to compromise, while borrowing from and changing their relationships with other groups. The challenge, however, was from groups in power that were unwilling to make similar gestures toward Indigenous cultural norms. For some, this was a conscious choice; for others it was more of an unexamined way of living. Many Mestizo individuals in Otavalo, for instance, often complained that Indigenous people were looking for special treatment, or did not want to follow the same rules as them, or insisted on being different. At a national level, leaders like Rafael Correa frequently rehearsed this sentiment (Conaghan 2017; Martínez Novo 2014). While recognizing the cultural difference of Indigenous people, for instance, he insisted that Ecuador was one country with one set of rules for everybody. Those rules were inextricably linked to White-Mestizo cultural and linguistic norms.

While not discounting continued racism and deliberate attempts to maintain power among dominant groups, much of the struggle for cultural equality was waged in a more subtle way. Despite the political advancement and the promotion of cultural revitalization, Indigenous groups nevertheless continued to face the dynamics of diglossia, in which the logic of the dominant group slowly and perhaps subconsciously weighs heavily on the decisions and actions of all. It makes more "sense" linguistically, for instance, for Indigenous parents to teach their children Spanish instead of Kichwa in order for them to succeed. Mestizo parents, however, never had to decide whether to teach their children Kichwa instead of Spanish. A similar dynamic is at work in the transmission of other cultural values and norms. Ancestral knowledge, particularly about local ecosystems, medicine, and community building are not generally part of discussions by Mestizo people and official institutions, even as Kichwa people confront, negotiate with, and adapt Western scientific knowledge, technology, and other cultural artifacts into their everyday lives. There is not an obvious answer to this challenge, and many of the Kichwa individuals that I interviewed struggled with how to preserve what they saw as important parts of their traditions while still moving forward in their relationships with the rest of the world. Intercultural theorists (Cruz Rodriguez 2013; Guerrero Arias 2002; Medina and Sinnigen 2009; Salazar Medina 2011; C. Walsh 2012) forcefully argue for equality between groups as essential for moving interculturality forward, specifically because it is too easy for smaller groups to eventually be assimilated into more powerful ones. In the case of early twenty-first century Ecuador, it was clear that equality was still an elusive goal.

The stories, arguments, and practices from these Kichwa community members not only document their struggles and efforts, but also contribute to a larger collective history. Colonial history, when not making Indigenous people invisible, often makes them either objects of others' machinations or folkloric remnants. The intercultural efforts of Kichwa groups and communities in the Otavalo Valley, however, demonstrated a decided resistance to colonial practice by insisting on

the abilities of Indigenous peoples to be active agents in their own histories. Over time, Kichwa communities broke the political and economic
power of the *hacienda* elites, occupied previously White-Mestizo urban
spaces, and successfully challenged the remnants of colonial political rule.
Electoral victories in Otavalo and Cotacachi at the turn of the century,
and the subsequent democratization of local state institutions, allowed
Kichwa people to prove that could they could not only amass electoral
support from their communities, but also build cross-ethnic alliances
and govern efficiently and transparently. Similarly, younger people
defined for themselves what it means to be Kichwa. They illustrated
their immersion into intercultural situations through their abilities to
adapt and integrate ideas, technology, and other artifacts from multiple
cultural systems. They used their experiences traveling abroad and their
access to transnational communication to change the way they dressed,
talked about themselves, and envisioned their futures (Atienza de Frutos
2009; Célleri-Endara 2011; Maldonado 2004; Ordóñez Charpentier 2014;
Sobczyk and Soriano Miras 2015b). Importantly, however, despite their
desire to change, they did not abandon seeing themselves as Kichwa.
Although these new sentiments sometimes created conflicts with older
generations, their distinct voices became important parts of Kichwa
narratives of self and success.

Intercultural theory contextualizes this multiplicity of Kichwa voices
and positions by moving the conversation beyond the simple celebration
of difference. Conflict constituted an inherent component of the political
and cultural realignments in the Otavalo Valley. Indigenous political
victories came about not only because Mestizo people were willing to
accept cultural others, but also because of long years – generations,
really—of struggle against oppression. Similarly,new or strengthened
confidence in cultural traditions, along with the ability to change those
traditions, was not just a broad acceptance of difference, but the result
of Kichwa insistence on inclusion and their successes in converting
economic capital into social and cultural capital. Kichwa people, along
with Mestizo and global allies, were protagonists in not only changing

their own cultural institutions, but also forcing those institutions into the public sphere more broadly. Intercultural dialogue is not a neutral meeting of cultures. Rather, it represents an often difficult and conflictive process in which historically marginalized groups insist on changing systems in order to be included in public conversations and institutions, without having to abandon their own identities and practices.

Because these dialogues and power alignments challenge the historic institutions built on exclusion, marginalization, and exploitation, they need to be considered as part of a decolonial project (Chaves et al. 2017; Cruz Rodriguez 2016; Escobar 2016; Polo Blanco 2018). This is a project, to be sure, that is nowhere near complete, and as much of the ambiguity about future directions would indicate, it is certainly not guaranteed. Nevertheless, by asserting their cultural and political rights in Otavalo and throughout the country, Indigenous people consistently contend that, while reforms are essential and the opportunity for individual advancement and improvement are important, the underlying relationships of inequality remain a painful and unhealed scar of colonialism. Dismantling the *hacienda* system and the political institutions that supported it, along with understanding their culture to be a living and ever-changing set of expressions, beliefs, and relationships (as are all cultures), represented a substantial step toward challenging the underlying matrices of power. By insisting that they, as Kichwa people, had the right to participate in the public sphere and to participate in local and global cultural interactions, they also defied the dominant cultural logic that posited that the Western, modern, and liberal model was the only acceptable form of public discourse.

Defining Living Well

One Kichwa intellectual, who had spent a great part of his career documenting ancestral knowledge, promoting bilingual education, and working with communities in culturally sensitive development projects, while looking out of his house onto his ready-to-be harvested corn, confessed, "I'm not sure that in four or five generations, we will be Kichwa people anymore. The economics of farming, the pull of the city, the constant change make it seem that we are becoming something else" (Interview, LT, Antutaqui, March 26, 2016). This assessment raises several important questions about how Kichwa people might construct themselves in the future. As Kichwa communities continue to become increasingly heterogeneous, what makes them a community? As various ways of living intermingle, how will a good life be defined? How does interaction with outside groups contribute to internal sense of self? How do the decolonial threads of the Indigenous movement resist the assimilationist pull of Western modernity and colonialism (including the best intentions of progressive allies)? How do Indigenous concepts of *Sumak Kawsay* and reciprocity communicate with other discourses and practices around issues of sustainability, equity, and anti-racism?

The construction of a good life was an underlying theme that ran through many of the conversations and observations that I had with people as they were sorting out the possibilities and the constraints of the new and fluid normal left in the wake of the intense Indigenous mobilizing of the turn of the century. Certainly, the concept of *Sumak Kawsay*, omnipresent as a political discourse after 2006, played a role in people's lives (Acosta 2012; Radcliffe 2012). What exactly it meant, however, varied widely. As a discourse wielded by politicians participating in Rafael Correa's Citizens' Revolution, it became interchangeable with more or less mainstream concepts of sustainable development (Busch 2016; Caria and Domínguez 2016). Its insertion into the 2008 Constitution and into subsequent state planning documents positioned *Sumak Kawsay* or Living Well as a means to discuss more equitable distribution of economic benefits while acknowledging the need to better manage natural resources. It did not, however, come to encompass a more radical approach to social relationships or question the underlying relationship between human society and the natural world constructed by Western, modernist thought (Alaminos Chica and Penalva Verdú 2017; Canelón Silva 2017; Oviedo Freire 2013).

Kichwa people had a more nuanced understanding of the concept. When I first began talking to people about their political and cultural projects in 2006, some would use the term *"Alli Kawsay"* which also means "living well." *Sumak* is a superlative to *alli* and quickly replaced it as it gained traction in political circles. The concept however, was more complex than simply an alternative form of development. In a 2011 interview, FICI President Marco Guatemal described the problem:

> With the state, every project is *Sumak Kawsay. Sumak Kawsay* this, *Sumak Kawsay* that. Every proposal has to have *Sumak Kawsay* until it doesn't have any meaning anymore. When really in the communities to speak of *Sumak Kawsay* means the we should have a high quality education, good levels of health, state guarantees in terms of respecting cultivation and use of my lands, respect for identity and culture and economic well-being. Today none of that exists in the communities. The only thing that exists is a principle in the constitution and in public policies everyone in the ministries talk about *Sumak Kawsay* (Otavalo, August 22).

Similarly, Pacífico Fachamba rejected *Sumak Kawsay* as "this phrase reinvented by Rafael Correa," and pushed endlessly by state agencies. Instead,

> *Sumak Kawsay*, the famous *Sumak Kawsay*, has always existed, just not with these words. It was a respect for *Pachamama*, a respect for nature, a respect for sacred spaces, ancestral spaces. That has always existed. It's not necessary for us to go around promoting it because it is an intrinsic part of us" (Interview, Peguche, December 10, 2011).

Many community members described *Sumak Kawsay* in terms of harmony, reciprocity, and respect beginning with the intimate relationships of family and spreading to neighbors and the larger community, eventually encompassing the more abstract (but no less important relationships) between humans and nature. As one Kichwa activist explained in critique of the developmental logic behind the state's interpretation of

Sumak Kawsay, "living well does not mean living better at the expense of others" (Interview, Otavalo, June 14, 2014).

These contentious interpretations of the phrase lead back to the intercultural premise underlying this study. Overcoming the dynamics through which outsiders impose meaning on the experiences of local communities, or even resignifying cultural terms and practices, requires a break in the colonial cycle of appropriation and structuring of inequality. These debates around what *Sumak Kawsay* means demonstrate that, without equality, the dynamics of coloniality obscure and appropriate meaning. Alban and Rosero (2016) contend, for instance, that the notion of development is intimately tied to the Western separation of the natural and the human, and to the political and social imposition and maintenance of colonial relationships. They suggest therefore that,

> perhaps we could think of interculturality in its relationship with sustainable development as a decolonial pedagogical praxis, which implies undertaking three fundamental actions: 1.) unlearning in order to relearn; 2.) pointing out the epistemic ties that bind us, and; 3.) breaking free of westernizing narratives (Albán and Rosero 2016, 34).

Thinking together about what "living well" might mean is fundamentally different than imposing a state-centered vision of sustainable development. As Albán and Rosero suggest, however, it also means unlearning the naturalized dynamics of coloniality.

A key step in this direction, therefore, is to recognize that local communities create their own narratives of who they are and how they interact with the rest of the world. In his "decolonial reading" of the debates around what it means to live well, for instance, Philipp Altmann (2017) posits that the "decolonial character of ... of *sumak kawsay* ... resides in its radically local nature—it is about a place-based everyday reality that is opposed to abstract and universalizing Western ideas of state, society, or public sphere" (750). Instead, he argues that

> the task of a decolonial theory ... is to look for decolonial thought
> "on the ground," that is, within the social movements in ques-
> tion and not to reduce it to some big thinkers who generally
> have a rather close, even if critical, connection to Western theo-
> ries and institutions... The logic of the local is invoked but not
> thought through. The indigenous movements, and most notably,
> the Ecuadorian one, have developed their own ideas of how capi-
> talist exploitation and ethnic or national domination, combined
> with racism, sexism, and other manifestations of discrimination,
> can be understood as one coherent phenomenon (751).

I would add to that argument that listening to and engaging with people
through the local logics that they develop and use to make sense of
their worlds often means challenging our (non-Kichwa) pre-conceived
notions of the world.

Many articulations of a good or better life were embedded in people's
stories from the Otavalo Valley. Sometimes, particularly from more
politically active individuals, a vision of the good life or of a different kind
of life was explicit. They articulated ways in which institutions could be
changed and past wrongs accounted for. Many people I came to know,
however, had more ambiguous senses of how they were negotiating the
complexities of their lives to create better ones. All were grounded in the
historic experiences of marginalization and a reliance, to greater and lesser
extents, on ancestral knowledge and organizing. This radical localness,
however, was never isolationist. People's networks traversed all manner
of boundaries. Those constant (and constantly evolving) connections
also sometimes challenged communities' abilities to articulate a vision
of difference. As global consumerist discourses, for instance, became
an increasingly stronger influence on people's values and decisions, it
became less clear how to counter them.

I do not offer that as a critique, but rather an observation that Kichwa
people's lives are governed by infinite complexity, and negotiating the
complexities of everyday life are difficult. A significant part of that

complexity was the changed and unstable cultural and political landscape left by the success of the Indigenous movement of the late twentieth and early twenty-first centuries. The movement opened new opportunities, changed the rules of engagement with White-Mestizo society, and created new challenges toward articulating what living well could and should mean. At the same time, it is important that those of us not from those communities understand and respect the process of making meaning and charting life courses which may intersect with, but not be subsumed by, our own understanding of the world. In other words, even those of us who are supportive of change ought to avoid the colonial practices of imposing our vision of the way life should be on those who are also decolonizing their lives.

BEYOND THE ANDES

The call for a decolonial, intercultural process should resonate beyond the borders of Ecuador and Latin America. The colonial matrix of power that the Indigenous movement has challenged and with which Kichwa communities engage, negotiate, and resist also structures a world-system based on economic exploitation, racism, and an epistemology that assumes the superiority of Western liberal thought over all others (Escobar 2010b; Mignolo 2011). As discussed in chapter 5, Sacha Rosero, one of the founders of Otavalosonline.com and a committed political and language activist, stressed the desire of many Kichwa people to participate as active agents in global transformations.

> Just like any other society, we Otavalos, are also in a process of evolution: adapting ourselves to the different experiences that we have lived, learning from them, and sometimes teaching some of our values that can be shared in some other part of the world (e-mail, August 7, 2010).

In his view, the interactions that Kichwa people have with the rest of the world are dialogic. It is not just that Kichwa communities are influenced by outside entities but, rather, that their values have a place in discussions with the wider world.

If those of us who are not members of Indigenous communities are to fully take part in this intercultural dialogue, we have to understand those values that Rosero mentions, along with the other kinds of ancestral knowledge about medicine, agriculture, and ecosystems that Don Roberto Tocagón referred to as "living libraries" (Interview, Inti Culuquí, October 10, 2013), and the social knowledge that allows communities to function in collective and democratic ways. This step is particularly challenging for many of us enmeshed in systems of power that discount other ways of knowing. The Indigenous movement and the ways in which Kichwa communities in the Otavalo Valley have engaged with other ways of knowing and being suggests that intercultural relations depend on a willingness to accept and to interrogate the other (Aman 2014). Economic and political inequality between cultural groups has to be part of that discussion because the voices of the marginalized groups often go unheard or there is a tacit assumption that they must adjust to dominant institutions and cultural norms. The point of intercultural dialogue, after all, is to include all parties in a meaningful process, to create, in the words of Fidel Tubino (2013), a "liberating" rather than a "functional" interculturality (608).

Beyond politics and culture, therefore, interculturality also represents a fundamental epistemological dilemma (de Sousa Santos 2016). It does not mean the abandonment of any particular knowledge system, rather the dialogue between various (Chaves et al. 2017; Cruz Rodriguez 2016). Many of the Kichwa individuals that I know, for instance, accepted other influences while not rejecting their own cultural/knowledge system. Rather, it meant being open to using others' discourses and practices when it was useful in advancing their political, economic, or cultural agenda. This posture represents a challenge to traditional liberalism in that the unrecognized assumption of liberal modernity is that it represents the end of the evolutionary chain of human civilization. By accepting the validity of multiple cultural and epistemological systems, decoloniality does not require the rejection of all of modernity's contributions (Mignolo 2017). Quite the opposite—it is an effort to find the ways in which our different cultural systems might work together to create multiple modernities based on what Arturo Escobar (2010a, 2017) connotes as the complexities of everyday life. The basis of genuine collaboration toward a social/cultural/political project relies on recognizing inequality and endeavoring to eliminate it. As many Kichwa individuals explained to me, the unequal terrain on which they negotiated with Mestizo and global projects lent itself too easily to assimilation rather than dialogue.

This project is not the domain of any particular cultural system but, rather, must be built from understanding the ways in which various cultural systems interact. Too often in Ecuador (as elsewhere), interculturality is seen as a project of Indigenous people. To be successful, however, it must also involve Mestizo, Afro-descendent, Asian-descendent, and Euro-descendent people as well. Because of global interconnectedness, decolonial, intercultural projects also involve critiquing larger structures of power that create and maintain inequalities between groups (Gudynas 2016). The openings for cultural pluralism and for seeing all of our fates as mutually interdependent seem grim as I write this in 2019. More than ever, our collective knowledge about the earth, its peoples, and their cultural and political systems are needed as we enter into uncharted territory brought about by climate change, mass migrations, rising authoritarianism, and uncertain economic futures. Those seeking to hold and consolidate power use, as effectively as ever, the tools of division, tribalism, and fear of others. Yet, as so many of the people I have talked to in Ecuador over the last decade make clear, sometimes it is adding one's grain of sand that makes a difference because the struggle is long and the results are not always obvious. Part of that process involves building unity by respecting differences. As Pacífico Fachamba made clear to me, despite his years of organizing experience, advanced degrees, and time spent both locally and internationally, he would have no idea how to organize the community across the lake because "they are so different."

Nevertheless, the struggles and processes of the Kayambis on the south side of Lago San Pablo made the Otavalos on the north side stronger too. Connecting in a meaningful way with movements for freedom and liberation from cultures and peoples distinct from one's own means working to decolonize the structures of oppression wherever one lives.

My hope is that this book not only contributes to knowledge and insight about Kichwa peoples' struggle for acceptance and equal participation in their local interactions, national debates, and global encounters, but also encourages those of us from far-flung places and different life circumstances to more fully understand our relationships with people who have too often been pushed to the margins. I see this not only as a righting of historic wrongs, but also as an important opportunity to better our own lives. I imagine that most of you reading this, like me, have grown up in a culture that assumes that, while imperfect, "our way of life" is the envy of the world and the natural progression forward. Many of us look critically on those assumptions and through genuine intercultural dialogue attempt to make our world, and ourselves, more complete and more resilient. I recall Don Roberto Tocagón's story about how he was taught in his university studies that the highlands where he lives have three ecological planes. His observations, based on generations of work, actually identified seven. What if, metaphorically speaking, by relying on our Western knowledge system we only see three levels of difference, when there are really seven? Would we not all be better served with a deeper knowledge? My hope is that despite the strong headwinds and seemingly bleak outlook, we can, as Don Roberto described his community's efforts, "do beautiful things, here. Beautiful things."

PHOTOGRAPHS

Photograph 1. Anita Chávez addresses crowd, San Roque, 2011.

Source: Author's photograph.

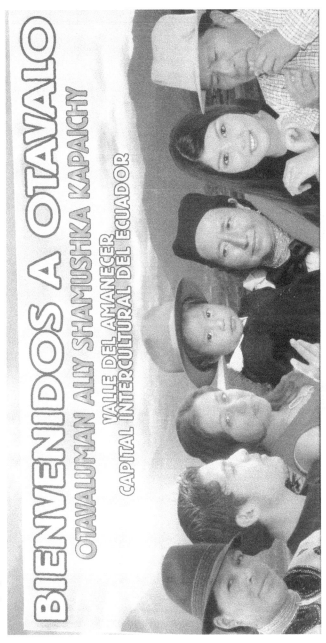

Photograph 2. Billboard at entrance to Otavalo, 2006.

Source: Author's photograph.

Photograph 3. Inaugurating new house, Luis de la Torre, San Roque, 2007.

Source: Author's photograph.

Photograph 4. Campaign poster for Mario Conejo, Otavalo 2014.

Source: Author's photograph.

Photograph 5. Aya Huma, Inti Raymi, Otavalo 2014.

Source: Author's photograph.

Photograph 6. Plaza de Ponchos, Inti Raymi, Otavalo 2014.

Source: Author's photograph.

Photograph 7. Castillo Offering, San Roque, 2011.

Source: Author's photograph.

Photograph 8. Entrance to Mojanda Páramo, 2011.

Source: Author's photograph.

Photograph 9. Crowd, Plaza Bolívar, Otavalo, 2014.

Source: Author's photograph.

Photograph 10. Family Outing, Otavalo, 2006.

Source: Author's photograph.

Photograph 11. Sunday in the countryside, Morrochos 2016.

Source: Photograph by Rowan Stolle-McAllister. Used with permission.

Photograph 12. Plaza de Ponchos, Otavalo 2013.

Source: Author's photograph.

References

Acosta, Alberto. 2009. *La maldición de la abundancia*. Quito: Editores Abya Yala; Comité Ecuménico de Proyectos.

———. 2012. *Buen vivir/Sumak Kawsay: una oportunidad para imaginar otros mundos*. Quito: Abya Yala.

———, and Esperanza Martínez. 2009. *El buen vivir: una vía para el desarrollo*. Quito: Abya Yala.

Acosta, Yamandú. 2015. "Emergencias de la trans–modernidad y refundación plurinacional e intercultural del estado: Ecuador y Bolivia en el siglo XXI." *Historia actual online* 37 (2):85–100.

Acosta, Alberto, and Esperanza Martínez, eds. 2010. *Agua. Un derecho humano fundamental*. Quito: Abya–Yala; Universidad Politecnica Salesiana.

Aikman, Sheila. 1997. "Interculturality and Intercultural Education: A Challenge for Democracy." *International Review of Education* 43 (5–6):463–479.

Alaminos Chica, Antonio, and Clemente Penalva Verdú. 2017. "Entre el Sumak Kawsay y el Buen Vivir Institucional. Los discursos sociales del Buen Vivir en las zonas rurales del Sur de Ecuador." *Revista de Paz y Conflictos* 10 (1):137–167.

Albán, Adolfo, and José R. Rosero. 2016. "Colonialidad de la naturaleza: ¿imposición tecnológica y usurpación epistémica? Interculturalidad, desarrollo y re–existencia." *Nómadas* 45.

Albó, Javier. 2008. *Movimientos y poder indígena en Bolivia, Ecuador y Perú*. La Paz: CIPCA.

Alimonda, Héctor, ed. 2011. "*La Naturaleza colonizada. Ecología política y minería en América Latina*." Buenos Aires: Consejo Latinoamericano de Ciencias Sociales.

Almeida, Ileana, Nidia Arrobo Rodas, and Lautoro Ojeda Segovia. 2005. *Autonomía Indígena frente al estado nacional y a la globalización neoliberal.* Quito: Ediciones Abya Yala.

Altieri, Miguel , and Victor Manuel Toledo. 2011. "The Agroecological Revolution in Latin America: Rescuing Nature, Ensuring Food Soveignty and Empowering Peasants." *The Journal of Peasant Studies* 38 (3):587–612.

Altmann, Philipp. 2017. "Sumak Kawsay as an Element of Local Decolonization in Ecuador." *Latin American Research Review* 52 (5):748–759.

Aman, Robert. 2014. "Why Interculturalidad is not Interculturality: Colonial remains and paradoxes in translation between indigenous social movements and supranational bodies" *Cultural Studies:* 1–24.

Anderson, Benedict. 1991. *Imagined Communities.* New York: Verso.

Arboleda, María. 2006. "Género y gobernanza territorial en Cotacachi y Cotopaxi." In *En las fisuras del poder: Movimiento indígena, cambio social y gobiernos locales,* edited by Pablo Ospina, 151–214. Quito: Instituto de Estudios Ecuatorianos; Consejo Lationamericano de Ciencias Sociales.

Armijos Burneo, María Teresa. 2012. "Negotiating Citizenship Through Communal Water Management in Highland Ecuador." PhD, Development Studies, University of Sussex.

Asamblea General de Comuneros. 2008. *Reglamento Interno de la Comunidad de Inti Caluquí.* Otavalo: Asamblea General de Comuneros de Inti Caluquí.

Atienza de Frutos, David. 2009. *Viaje e identidad: La génesis de la élite kichwa–otavaleña en Madrid, España.* Quito: Ediciones Abya–Yala; Universidad Politécnica Salesiana.

AUC. 2010. "Cotacachi en datos y cifras." Asamblea de Unidad Cantonal de Cotacachi, accessed 1 April 2014. http://www.asambleacotacachi.org/pagina.php?varmenu=110.

Barié, Cletus Gregor. 2014. "Nuevas narrativas constitucionales en Bolivia y Ecuador: el buen vivir y los derechos de la naturaleza." *Latinoamérica. Revista de Estudios Latinoamericanos* 59:9–40.

Barrett, Patrick S., Daniel Chavez, and César A Rodríguez Garavito. 2008. *The New Latin American Left: Utopia Reborn.* London: Pluto Press.

Bartolome, Miguel Alberto. 2006. *Procesos interculturales: antropología política del pluralismo cultural en América Latina.* Mexico City: Siglo XXI Editores.

Becker, Marc. 2008. *Indians and Leftists in the Making of Ecuador's Modern Indigenous Movements.* Durham: Duke University Press.

———. 2011 (a). "Correa, Indigenous Movements, and the Writing of a New Constitution in Ecuador." *Latin American Perspectives* 38 (1):47–62.

———. 2011 (b). *¡Pachakutik! Indigenous Movements and Electoral Politics in Ecuador.* Lanham: Rowman and Littlefield Publishers.

———. 2012. "Building a Plurinational Ecuador: Complications and Contradictions." *Socialism and Democracy* 26 (3):72–92.

———, and Silvia Tutillo. 2009. *Historia agraria y social de Cayambe.* Quito: Editores Abya–Yala; FLACSO.

Benavides, O. Hugo. 2004. *Making of Ecuadorian Histories: Four Centuries of Defining Power.* Austin: University of Texas Press.

Bengoa, José. 2000. *La emergencia indígena en América Latina.* Santiago: Fondo de Cultura Económica.

Bonilla, Inés, and Rosa Ramos. 2009. "La construcción e implementación del Reglamento de Buena Convivencia en Cotacachi." In *Mujeres indígenas y justicia ancestral,* edited by Miriam Lang and Anna Kucia, 136–139. Quito: Fondo de Desarrollo de las Naciones Unidas para la Mujer.

Bonilla, Nathalia, Ivonne Yánez, Ivonne Ramos, and Jaime Breilh. 2011. *Cambio climático: una mirada desde los derechos de la naturaleza.* Quito: Instituto de Estudios Ecologistas del Tercer Mundo.

Busch, Dominic. 2016. "What is Intercultural Sustainability: A First Exploration of Linkages Between Culture and Sustainability in Intercultural Research." *Journal of Sustainable Development* 9 (1):63–76.

Cabello, Joanna and Tamara Gilberston, eds. *No REDD: A Reader.* Hermosillo, Mexico: Editorial Tres Perros.

Caillavet, Chantal. 2000. *Etnias del norte: etnohistoria e historia de Ecuador.* Quito: Ediciones Abya Yala, Instituto Francés de Estudios Andinos, Casa de Velázques.

Cameron, John. 2005. "Municipal Democratisation in Rural Latin America: Methodological Insights from Ecuador." *Bulletin of Latin American Research* 24 (3):367–390.

———. 2010. *Struggles for Local Democracy in the Andes.* Boulder, CO: First Forum Press.

Canelón Silva, Agrivalca Ramsenia. 2017. "Marca País: una mirada crítica para América Latina inspirada en la filosofía del Buen Vivir." *Chasqui. Revista Latinoamericana de Comunicación* (134):61–83.

Caria, Sara, and Rafael Domínguez. 2016. "Ecuador's Buen Vivir: A New Ideology for Development." *Latin American Perspectives* 43 (206):18–33.

Castañeda, María Ecrilia. 2009. *Gobierno comunitario: el caso de las comunidades de la parroquia González Suárez.* Quito: FLACSO––Ecuador; Abya Yala.

Célleri–Endara, Daniela–Alexandra. 2011. "Jóvenes indígenas (kichwa-otavalos) entre etnicidad, clase y género." *Boletín Científico Sapiens Research* 1 (2):13–16.

Cervone, Emma. 2010. "Celebrating the Chagras: Mestizaje, Multiculturalism, and the Ecuadorian Nation." *The Global South* 4 (1):94–118.

———.2012. *Long Live Atahualpa: Indigenous Politics, Justice and Democracy in the Northern Andes.* Durham, NC: Duke University Press.

Chaves, Martha, Thomas Macintyre, Gerard Verschoor, and Arjen E.J. Wals. 2017. "Radical Ruralities in Practice: Negotiating Buen Vivir en a Colombian Network of Sustainability." *Journal of Rural Studies*:1–10.

Chávez M., José M., ed. 1989. *Imbabura Taita Parlan (recopilación de la tradición oral indígena: cuentos, leyendas, supersticiones, sueños y creencias).* Quito: Casa de la Cultura Ecuatoriana "Benjamin Carrión.

Cholango, Humberto. 2012. "Los pueblos y nacionalidades de Ecuador frente al extractivismo." In *Naturaleza y cultura en América Latina:*

Escenarios para un modelo de desarrollo no civilizatorio, edited by Eloy Alfaro, Katterine Enríquez, and Yolanda Flores, 75–84. Quito: Abya Yala; Universidad Politécnica Salesiana.

Cid Aguayo, Beatriz Eugenia. 2008. "Global Villages and Rural Cosmopolitanism: Exploring Global Ruralities." *Globalizations* 4 (4):541–554.

Clark, Kim A., and Marc Becker. 2007. *Highland Indians and the State in Modern Ecuador*. Pittsburgh: University of Pittsburgh Press.

Collins, Jennifer N. 2008. "Rafael Correa and the Struggle for a New Ecuador." *Global Dialogue* 10 (1/2):37–47.

CNE. 2014. Resultados oficiales: elecciones febrero 2014. edited by Comisión Nacional de Elecciones. Quito: Comisión Nacional de Elecciones.

Colloredo–Mansfeld, Rudi. 1999. *Tha Native Leisure Class: Consumption and Cultural Creativity in the Andes*. Chicago: University of Chicago Press.

———. 2007. "The Power of Ecuador's Indigenous Communities in an Era of Cultural Pluralism." *Social Analysis: The International Journal of Social and Cultural Practice* 51 (2):86–106.

———. 2009. *Fighting Like a Community: Andean Civil Society in an Era of Indian Uprisings*. Chicago: University of Chicago Press.

CONAIE. 2010. "Constitución del Parlamento Plurinacional ". CONAIE, accessed 2 July 2010. http://www.conaie.org/nacionalidades–y–pueblos.

Conaghan, Catherine. 2017. "Ecuador Under Correa." *Journal of Democracy* 27 (3):109–118.

Coryat, Diana, and Manuela Lavinas Picq. 2016. "Ecuador's Expanding Extractive Frontier." *NACLA Report on the Americas* 48 (3):280–283.

Creed, Gerald. 2006. "Community as Modern Pastoral." In *The Seductions of Community: Emancipations, Oppressions, Quandries*, edited by Gerald Creed, 23–48. Santa Fe: School of American Research.

Cruz Rodríguez, Edwin. 2012. "Redefiniendo la nación: luchas indígenas y estado plurinacional en Ecuador (1990–2008)." *Nómadas. Revista Crítica de Ciencias Sociales y Jurídicas*

———. 2013. *Pensar la interculturalidad: una invitación desde Abya–Yala/ América Latina.* Quito: Abya Yala.

———. 2016. "El Buen Vivir y la crítica del universalismo abstracto." *Cuadernos de filosofía latinoaméricana* 37 (115):177–198.

Dávalos, Pablo, ed. 2001. *Yuyarinakuy: díganos lo que somos, antes que otros no den diciendo lo que no somos.* Quito: Editorial Abya–Yala.

———, ed. 2005. *Pueblos indígenas, estado y democracia.* Buenos Aires: Consejo Latinoamericano de ciencias sociales.

D'Amico, Linda. 2011. *Otavalan Women, Ethnicity, and Globalization.* Albuquerque: University of New Mexico Press.

De Bievre, Bert, Vicente Íñiguez, and Wouter Buytaert. 2011. "Hidrología del páramo: Importancia, propiedades y vulnerabilidad." In *Páramo: Paisaje estudiado, habitado, manejado e institucionalizado*, edited by Patricio Mena Vásconez, Anabel Castillo, Saskia Flores, Robert Hofstede, Carmen Josse, Sergio Lasso B., Galo Medina, Nadya Ochoa and Doris Ortiz, 81–97. Quito: EcoCiencia; Abya–Yala; ECOBONO.

de Koning, Free, Marcela Aguiñaga, Manuel Bravo, Marco Chiu, Max Lascano, Tannya Lozada, and Luis Suarez. 2011. "Bridging the gap between forest conservation and poverty alleviation: the Ecuadorian Socio Bosque program." *Environmental Science & Policy* 14:531–542.

de la Cadena, Marisol. 2010. "Indigenous Cosmopolitics in the Andes: Conceptual Reflections beyond 'Politics'." *Cultural Anthropology* 25 (2):334–370.

de la Torre, Luis. 2006. "La interculturalidad desde la perspectiva del desarrollo social y cultural." *Revista Sarance, Instituto Otavaleno de Antropologia* (25):62–87.

de Sousa Santos, Boaventura. 2016. *Epistemologies of the South.* New York: Routledge.

Dosh, Paul, and Nicole Kligerman. 2009. "Correa vs. Social Movements: Showdown in Ecuador." *NACLA Report on the Americas* 42 (5):21–40.

Ellner, Steve, ed. 2014. *Latin America's Radical Left: Challenges and Complexities of Political Power in the Twenty-first Century.* Lanham: Rowman and Littlefield Publishers.

Escobar, Arturo. 1995. *Encountering Development: The Making and Unmaking of the Third World.* Princeton: Princeton University Press.

———. 2010a. "Latin America at a Crossroads: Altnernative Modernizations, Post–Liberalism or Post–Development?" *Cultural Studies* 24 (1):1–65.

———. 2010b. "Worlds and Knowledges Otherwise: The Latin American Modernity/Coloniality Research Program." In *Globalization and the Decolonial Option,* edited by Walter Mignolo and Arturo Escobar, 33–64. New York: Routledge.

———. 2016. "Thinking–feeling with the Earth: Territorial Struggles and the Ontological Dimension of the Epistemologies of the South." *Revista de Antropología Iberoamericana* 11 (1):11–32.

———. 2017. "Complexity Theory and the Place of the Now." *Cultural Dynamics* 29 (4):333–339.

Estay, Jaime. 2018. "Past and Present of Latin American Regionalisms, in the Face of Economic Reprimarization." In *Regionalism, Development and the Post–Commodities Boom in South America,* edited by Ernesto Vivares, 47–76. New York: Palgrave MacMillan.

Esteva, Gustavo. 2015. "The Hour of Autonomy." *Latin American & Caribbean Ethnic Studies* 10 (1):135–145.

Farley, Kathleen A., and Leah L. Bremer. 2017. ""Water Is Life": Local Perceptions of Páramo Grasslands and Land Management Strategies Associated with Payment for Ecosystem Services." *Annals of the American Association of Geographers* 107 (2):371–281.

García Canclini, Nestor. 1995. *Hybrid Cultures: Strategies for Entering and Leaving Modernity.* Translated by Christopher Chiappari and Silvia López. Minneapolis: University of Minnesota Press.

———. 2004. *Diferentes, desiguales y desconectados: mapas de la interculturalidad.* Barcelona: Gedisa.

García Linera, Álvaro. 2004. Asamblea constituyente y movimientos sociales. *Revista Aportes Andinos* 10. Accessed 1 November 2011.

Gareis, Iris. 2007. "Los rituales del Estado colonial y las élites andinas." *Bulletin de l'Institut Français d'Etudes Andines* 37 (1):97–109.

Gaybor Secaira, Antonio. 2010. "Acumulación capitalista en el campo y despojo del agua." In *Agua: un derecho humano fundamental*, edited by Alberto Acosta and Esperanza Martínez, 47–66. Quito: Abya Yala; Universidad Politécnica Salesiana.

Gerlach, Allen. 2003. *Indians, Oil and Politics: A Recent History of Ecuador.* Wilmington, DE: Scholarly Resources, Inc.

González, Miguel. 2015. "Indigenous Territorial Autonomy in Latin America: An Overview." *Latin American & Caribbean Ethnic Studies* 10 (1):10–36.

Grey Postero, Nancy, and Leon Zamosc, eds. 2005. *La lucha por los derechos indígenas en América Latina.* Quito: Ediciones Abya–Yala.

Gudynas, Eduardo. 2005. *Ecología, economía y etica del desarrollo sostenible.* 5 ed. Montevideo: CLAES – Centro Latino Americano de Ecología Socia.

———. 2011. "Buen Vivir: Today's tomorrow." *Development* 54 (4):441–447.

———. 2013. "Savitanretlayahon = no hay alternativas." *La linea del fuego*, 16 September. http://lalineadefuego.info/2013/07/17/savitanretlayahon–no–hay–alternativas–eduardo–gudynas/.

———. 2015. *Extractivismos: Ecología, economía y política de un modo de entender el desarrollo y la Naturaleza.* Cochabamba, Bolivia: Centro de Documentación e Información Bolivia (CEDIB).

———. 2016. "Beyond varieties of development: disputes and alternatives." *Third World Quarterly* 37 (4):721–732.

———, and Alberto Acosta. 2011. "La renovación de la crítica al desarrollo y el buen vivir como alternativa." *Utopía y Praxis Latinoamericana* 53:71–83.

Guerrero, Andrés. 2001. "Determinaciones del pasado y mentalidades del presente: un conflicto entre comuneros." In *De la economía a las mentalidades*, edited by Andrés Guerrero, 11-22. Quito: El Conejo.

Guerrero Arias, Patricio. 2002. *La cultura: estrategias conceptuales para entender la identidad, la diversidad, la alteridad y la diferencia.* Quito: Ediciones Abya–Yala; Escuela de Antropología Aplicada––Universidad Politécnica Salesiana.

———. 2004. *Usurpación simbólica, identidad y poder: La fiesta como escenario de lucha de sentidos, Serie Magister.* Quito: Universidad Andina Simón Bolívar, Sede Ecuador, Ediciones Abya–Yala, Corporación Editora Nacional.

———. 2011. "Interculturalidad y plurinacionalidad, escenarios de lucha de sentidos: entre la usurpación y la insurgencia simbólica." In *Interculturalidad y diversidad*, edited by Ariruma Kowii Maldonado, 73–100. Quito: Universidad Simón Bolívar, Sede Ecuador; Corporación Editora Nacional.

Guerrero, Fernando, and Pablo Ospina. 2003. *El poder de la comunidad: Movimiento indígena y ajuste estructural en los andes.* Buenos Aires: Consejo Latinoamericano de Ciencias Sociales.

Hale, Charles, and Lynn Stephen, eds. 2013. *Otros saberes: Collaborative Research on Indigenous and Afro–descendant Cultural Politics.* Santa Fe: School for Advanced Research Press; Latin American Studies Association.

Harden, Carol, James Hartsig, Kathleen A. Farley, Jaehoon Lee, and Leah L. Bremer. 2013. "Effects of Land–Use Change on Water in Andean Paramo Grassland Soils." *Annals of the Association of American Geographers* 103 (2):375–384.

Herring, Cedric, and Loren Henderson. 2015. *Diversity in Organizations: A Critical Examination.* New York: Routledge.

Hidalgo Flor, Francisco. 2011. "Buen Vivir/Sumak Kawsay: aporte contrahegemónico del proceso andino." *Utopía y Praxis Latinoamericana* 16 (53):85–94.

Huarcaya, Sergio Miguel. 2010. "Othering the Mestizo: Alterity and Indigenous Politics in Otavalo, Ecuador." *Latin American and Caribbean Ethnic Studies* 5 (3):301–315.

———. 2014. "Imagining Ecuadorians: Historicizing National Identity in Twentieth–Century Otavalo, Ecuador." *Latin American Research Review* 49 (3):64–84.

Ibarra, Hernán. 2010. "Conflictos rurales, violencia y opinión pública en los años cincuenta." In *Transiciones y rupturas: El Ecuador en la segunda mitad del siglo XX*, edited by Felipe Burbano de Lara, 411–464. Quito: FLACSO; Ministerio de Cultura.

INEC. 2014. *Población y Demografía*. .Quito: Instituto Nacional de Estadística y Censos.

Isch, Edgar. 2012. "Antropología, derechos y naturaleza: visiones no civilizatorias." In *Naturaleza y cultura en América Latina: Escenarios para un modelo de desarrollo no civilizatorio*, edited by Eloy Alfaro, Katterine Enríquez, and Yolanda Flores, 51–64. Quito: Abya Yala; Universidad Politécnica Salesiana.

Jameson, Kenneth. 2011. "The Indigenous Movement in Ecuador: The Struggle for a Plurinational State." *Latin American Perspectives* 38 (176):63–73.

Jones West, Karleen. 2015. "Decentralization, the Inclusion of Ethnic Citizens and Support for Democracy in Latin America." *Latin American Research Review* 50 (3):46–70.

Joseph, Miranda. 2002. *Against the Romance of Community*. Minneapolis: University of Minneosta Press.

Karg, Juan Manuel. 2014. Siete años de Revolución Ciudadana. *América Latina en Movimiento*. https://www.alainet.org/es/active/70500. Accessed 16 January 2014.

Karuse, Torsten, and Lasse Loft. 2013. "Benefit Distribution and Equity in Ecuador's Socio Bosque Program." *Society and Natural Resources: An International Journal* 26 (10):1170–1184.

Keating, Philip. 2007. "Fire Ecology and Conservation in the High Tropical Andes: Observations from Northern Ecuador." *Journal of Latin American Geography* 6 (1):43–62.

King, Kendall A., and Nancy H. Hornberger. 2006. "Quechua as Lingua Franca." *Annual Review of Applied Linguistics* 26:177–194.

Korovkin, Tanya. 2001. "Reinventing the Communal Tradition: Indigenous Peoples, Civil Society and Democratization in Andean Ecuador." *Latin American Research Review* 36 (37–67).

Kowii, Ariruma. 2006. "Propuestas y retos para la construcción del Estado pluricultural, multiétnico y intercultural del Ecuador." In *Desarrollo e interculturalidad, imaginario y diferencia: la nación en el mundo Andino*, edited by Hamilton Magalhães Neto, 157–174. Rio de Janeiro: Academia de la Latinidad.

Kowii Maldonado, Ariruma. 2011. "Diverisidad e interculturalidad." In *Interculturalidad y diversidad*, edited by Ariruma Kowii Maldonado, 11–32. Quito: Universidad Andina Simón Bolívar, Sede Ecuador; Corporación Editorial Nacional.

Kyle, David. 1999. "The Otavalo Trade Diaspora: Social Capital and Transnational Entrepreneurship." *Ethnic and Racial Studies* 22 (2):422–446.

———. 2000. *Transnational Peasants: Migrations, Networks and Ethnicity in Andean Ecuador*. Baltimore: Johns Hopkins University Press.

Kymlicka, Will. 2012. "Comment on Meer and Modood." *Journal of Intercultural Studies* 33 (2):211–216.

Lalander, Rickard. 2009. "Los Indígenas y la Revolución Ciudadana. Rupturas y alianzas en Cotacachi y Otavalo." *Ecuador Debate* 77 (3–5):185–219.

———. 2010a. "Between Interculturalism and Ethnocentrism: Local Government and the Indigenous Movement in Otavalo–Ecuador." *Bulletin of Latin American Research* 29 (4):505–521.

———. 2010b. *Retorno de los Runakuna*. Quito: Abya Yala; Universidad Politécnica Salesiana.

———. 2014. "The Ecuadorian resource dilemma: Sumak Kawsay or development? ." *Critical Sociology*:1–20.

———, and Maria-Therese Gustafasson. 2008. "Movimiento indígena y liderazgo político local en al Sierra eucatoriana: ¿Actores políticos o proceso social?" *Provincia* 19:57–90.

Larrea, Carlos. 2006. *Hacia un historia ecológica del Ecuador*. Quito: Universidad Andina Simón Bolívar, Sede Ecuador, Corporación Editora Naciona, EcoCiencia.

Latorre Tomás, Sara. 2011. *El pago de servicios ambientales por conservación*. Quito: Editores Abya–Yala; FLACSO.

Lema A., Germán Patricio. 2005. *Los Otavalos: cultura y tradición milenarias*. Quito: Abya–Yala.

León Bastidas, Arturo. 2011. *La plurinacionalidad del Ecuador*. Riobamba: Casa de la Cultura Ecuatoriana Benjamín Carrión núcleo de Chimborazo.

Le Quang, Matthieu, and Tamia Vercoutere. 2013. *Ecosocialismo y Buen Vivir: Diálogo entre dos alternativas al capitalismo*. Quito: Instituto de Altos Estudios Nacionales.

León-Yanez, Susana. 2011. "La flora de los páramos ecuatorianos." In *Páramo: Paisaje estudiado, habitado, manejado e institucionalizado*, edited by Patricio Mena Vásconez, Anabel Castillo, Saskia Flores, Robert Hofstede, Carmen Josse, Sergio Lasso B., Galo Medina, Nadya Ochoa and Doris Ortiz, 25–40. Quito: EcoCienica; Editorial Universitaria Abya–Yala; ECOBONA.

Lucero, José Antonio. 2008. *Struggles of Voice*. Pittsburgh: University of Pittsburgh Press.

Lupien, Pascal. 2011. "The Incorporation of Indigenous Concepts of Plurinationality into the New Constitutions of Ecuador and Bolivia." *Democratization*, 18 (3):774–796.

Maldonado, Gina. 2004. *Comericiantes y viajeros: de la imagen etnoarqueológico de "lo indígena al imaginario del kichwa otavalo "universal"*. Quito: Editorial Abya–Yala; FLACSO, Ecuador.

Martínez Dalmau, Rubén. 2016. "Democratic Constitutionalism and Constitutional Innovation in Ecuador." *Latin American Perspectives* 43 (206):158–174.

Martínez Novo, Carmen. 2004. "Los misioneros salesianos y el movimiento indígena de Cotopaxi." *Ecuador Debate* 63:235–268.

———. 2014. "Managing Diversity in Postneoliberal Ecuador." *The Journal of Latin American and Caribbean Anthropology* 19 (1):103–125.

———, and Carlos de la Torre. 2010. "Racial Discrimination and Citizenship in Ecuador´s Eduational System." *Latin American and Caribbean Ethnic Studies* 5 (1):1–26.

Martínez–Alier, Joan. 2003. *The Environmentalism of the Poor: A Study of Ecological Conflicts and Valuation* Northampton, MA: Edward Elgar Publishers.

Martson, E.C., and D.J. Bart. 2014. "Plant–community Responses to Shrub Cover in a Paramo Grassland Released from Grazing and Burning." *Austral Ecology* 39 (8):918–928.

Medina, Adriana, and Jack Sinnigen. 2009. "Interculturality Versus Intercultural Competencies in Latin America." In *The Sage Book of Intercultual Competencies*, edited by Darla Deardoff, 249–263. Thousand Oaks: Sage.

Mena Vásconez, Patricio, Manolo Morales, Pablo Ortiz, Galo Ramón, Silvana Rivadeneira, Esteban Suárez, Juan Fernando Terán, and Cecilia Velázquez, eds. 2008. *Gente y ambiente de páramo: realidades y perspectivas en el Ecuador.* Quito: EcoCiencia; Abya Yala.

Mena Vásconez, Patricio, ed. 2012. *Páramo: Páramo y políticas (II),* Quito: Grupo de Trabajo en Páramos del Ecuador.

Meisch, Lynn. 2002. *Andean Entrepreneurs: Otavalo Merchants and Musicians in the Global Arena.* Austin: University of Texas Press.

Mignolo, Walter. 2011. *The Darker Side of Western Modernity: Global Future, Decolonial Options.* Durham, NC: Duke University Press.

———. 2017. "Coloniality is Far from Over, and So Must Be Decoloniality." *Afterall* 43:38–45.

Mijeski, Kenneth, and Scott Beck. 2011. *Pachakutik and the Rise and Decline of the Ecuadorian Indigenous Movement.* Athens: OH: Ohio University Press.

Miller, Marylin Grace. 2004. *Rise and Fall of the Cosmic Race: The Cult of Mestizaje in Latin America.* Austin: University of Texas Press.

Moncada Landeta, Raúl. 2016. "Semiótica y mercancías en Otavalo (Ecuador) y El Alto (Bolivia)." *Comunicología ecuatoriana* 93:260–269.

Monosalva, Rossana. 2011. "Introducción: El páramo habitado." In *Páramo: Paisaje estudiado, habitado, manejado e institucionalizado,* edited by Patricio Mena Vásconez, Anabel Castillo, Saskia Flores, Robert Hofstede, Carmen Josse, Sergio Lasso B., Galo Medina, Nadya Ochoa, and Doris Ortiz, 129–134. Quito: EcoCienica; Editorial Universitaria Abya–Yala; ECOBONA.

Moreano Venegas, Melissa. 2012. "Socio Bosque y el capitalismo verde." *La linea de fuego,* 10 September http://lalineadefuego.info/2012/09/04/socio–bosque–y–el–capitalismo–verde–por–melissa–moreano–venegasi/.

Moreno, Camila. 2013. "Las ropas verdes del rey: la economía verde: una nueva fuente de acumulación primitiva." In *Alternativas al capitalismo/colonialismo del siglo XXI,* edited by Miriam Lang, Claudia López, and Alejandra Santillana, 63–100. Quito: Abya Yala; Universidad Polítecnica Salesiana.

Moya, Ruth, and Alba Moya. 2004. *Derivas de la interculturalidad: Procesos y desafíos en América Latina.* Quito: Centro Andino para la Formación de Líderes Sociales; Fundació Andina de Desarrollo y Estudios Sociales.

Nazarea, Virginia, and Rafael Guitarra, eds. 2004. *Ñaupa Rimaikunata Charishpa Katinamanta/Cuentos de la Creación y Resistencia.* Quito: Abya–Yala.

Nieto, Carlos, and Jaime Estrella. 2011. "La agrobiodiversidad en los ecosistemas de páramo: una primera aproximación a su inventario y sus situación actual." In *Páramo: Paisaje estudiado, habitado, manejado e institucionalizado,* edited by Patricio Mena Vásconez, Anabel Castillo, Saskia Flores, Robert Hofstede, Carmen Josse, Sergio Lasso B., Galo

Medina, Nadya Ochoa, and Doris Ortiz, 41–62. Quito: EcoCiencia; Abya–Yala.

Ordóñez Charpentier, Angélica. 2014. "'Como el agua vuelve al mar, volvemos'. La importancia de la comunidad en la migración kichwa otavalo (Ecuador)." *Amérique Latine Histoire et Mémoire. Les Cahiers ALHIM [on line]* 27.

Ordóñez, Juan Thomas, Fabio Andrés Colmenares, Anne Gincel, and Diana Rocío Bernal. 2014. "Migraciones de los Kichwas–Otavalo en Bogotá." *Revista de Estudios Sociales* (48):43–56.

Ortiz Crespo, Santiago. 2004. *Cotacachi: una apuesta por al democracia participativa.* Quito: Facultad Lationamericana de Ciencias Sociales––Sede Ecuador.

–––. 2012. *¿Comuneros kichwas o ciudadanos ecuatorianos? La ciudadanía éntica y los derechos políticos de los indígenas de Otavalo y Cotacachi (1990–2009).* Quito: Facultad Lationamericana de Ciencias Sociales––Sede Ecuador.

–––. 2013. "Comuneros y revolución ciudadana: los casos de Otavalo y Cotacachi en Ecuador." *Antropologica* 31 (3):81–100.

Ortiz–T, Pablo. 2008. "Páramos y agro." In *Gente y Ambiente de Páramo: Realidades y Perspectivas en el Ecuador,* edited by Patricio Mena Vásconez, Manolo Morales, Pablo Ortiz, Galo Ramón, Silvana Rivadeneira, Esteban Suárez, Juan Fernando Terán and Cecilia Velázquez. 2008. *Gente y ambiente de páramo: realidades y perspectivas en el Ecuador,* 53–82 Quito: EcoCiencia; Abya Yala.

–––. 2011. "Modelo de desarrollo, extractivismo, Buen Vivir y conflictos socio–ambientales (CSA)." In *Conflictos socioambientales, políticas públicas y derechos. Aproximación a un debate,* edited by Pablo Ortiz–T., 97–122. Quito: Ediciones Abya–Yala; Universidad Politécnica Salesiana; Secretaría de Pueblos, Movimientos Socialaes y Participación Ciudadana.

–––, ed. 2006. *En las fisuras del poder: Movimiento indígena, cambio social y gobiernos locales.* Quito: Instituto de Estudios Ecuatorianos; Consejo Lationamericano de Ciencias Sociales.

Ospina Peralta, Pablo. 2009. "'Nos vino un huracán político': la crisis de la CONAIE." In *Los Andes en movimiento: Identidad y poder en el nuevo paisaje político*, edited by Pablo Ospina, Olaf Kaltmeier and Christian Büschges, 123–146. Quito: Universidad Andina Simón Bolívar, Sede Ecuador; Universidad de Bielefeld; Corporación Editora Nacional.

Oviedo Freire, Atawalpa. 2013. *Buen Vivir vs. Sumak Kawsay: Reforma capitalista y revolución alter–nativa*. 3ra ed. Buenos Aires: Ediciones CICCUS.

Pachano, Simón. 2010. "Ecuador: El nuevo sistem político en funcionamiento." *Revista de ciencia política* 30 (2):297–317.

Parker, Charlie, Andrew Mitchell, Mandar Trivedi, and Niki Mardas. 2009. *The Little REDD+ Book*. Oxford: Global Canopy Foundation.

Peyre, G., Balslev H., D. Martí, P Sklenár, P. Ramsay, P. Lozano, N. Cuello, R. Busmann, O. Cabrera, and X. Font. 2015. "VegPáramo, a flora and vegetation database for the Andean páramo." *Phytocoenologia* 45 (1/2):195–201.

Philip, George, and Francisco Panizza. 2011. *The Triumph of Politics: The Return of the Left in Venezuela, Bolivia and Ecuador*. Cambridge, UK: Polity Press.

Polo Blanco, Jorge 2018. "Colonialidad múltiple en América Latina: Estructuras de dependencia, relatos de subalternidad." *Latin American Research Review* 53 (1):111–125.

Postero, Nancy. 2017. *The Indigenous State: Race, Politics, and Performance in Plurinational Bolivia*. Oakland: University of California Press.

Proyecto Páramo Andino. 2008. *Plan de manejo y desarrollo de la zona de Mojanda*. Quito: EcoCiencia.

Quijano, Aníbal. 2000. "Coloniality of Power, Eurocentrism and Latin America." *Nepantla: Views from South* 1 (3):533–580.

Radcliffe, Sarah. 2012. "Development for a Postneoliberal Era? *Sumak Kawsay*, Living Well and the Limits of Decolonisation in Ecuador." *Geoforum* 43:240–249.

———. 2015. *Dilemmas of Difference: Indigenous Women and the Limits of Postcolonial Development Policy*. Durham: Duke University Press.

Ramírez Gallegos, René. 2012. "Izquierda y "buen capitalismo": un aprote crítico desde América Latina." *Nueva Sociedad* (237):32–48.

Ramón, Galo. 2005. "Comentario sobre política e interculturalidad." In *Hacia un modelo alternativo de desarrollo histórico*, edited by Rafael Quintero López and Erika Silva Charvet, 53–62. Quito: Ediciones La Tierra.

———. 2008. "Conocimiento y prácticas ancestrales." In *Gente y Ambiente de Páramo: Realidades y Perspectivas en el Ecuador*, edited by Juan Sebastián Martínez, 11–20. Quito: EcoCiencia, Proyecto Párao Andino; Abya–Yala.

———. 2011. "La interculturalidad frenada: los límites de la 'revolución ciudadana'." In *Interculturalidad y diversidad*, edited by Ariruma Kowii Maldonado, 131–151. Quito: Universidad Simón Bolívar; Corporación Editora Nacional.

Rappaport, Joanne. 2005. *Intercultural Utopias: Public Intellectuals, Cultural Experimentation, and Ethnic Pluralism in Colombia*. Durham: Duke University Press.

Resina de la Fuente, Jorge. 2012a. *La plurinacionalidad en disputa: el pulso entre Correa y la CONAIE*. Quito.

Rhoades, Robert E., ed. 2006. *Desarrollo con identidad: Comunidad, cultura y sustentabilidad en los Andes*. Quito: Ediciones Abya–Yala.

Rice, Roberta. 2013. *The New Politics of Protest: Indigenous Mobilization in Latin America's Neoliberal Era*. Tucson: University of Arizona Press.

Roitman, Karem. 2009. *Race, Ethnicity, and Power in Ecuador: The Manipulation of Mestizaje*. Boulder, CO: First Forum Press.

Rosset, Peter, and Maria Elena Martínez–Torres. 2012. "Rural Social Movements and Agroecology: Context, Theory and Process." *Ecology and Society* 17 (3). doi: 10.5751/ES–05000–170317.

Runakuna, Redacción. 2007. "Reggaeton vs. Identidad." *Runakuna*, Mushuk pukuy (Feb/Mar)2007, 34–37.

Salazar Medina, Richard. 2011. "Derechos colectivos e interculturalidad: hacia la construcción del nuevo Ecuador." In *Interculturalidad y diversidad*, edited by Ariruma Kowii Maldonado, 101–121. Quito: Universidad Andina Simón Bolívar, Sede Ecuador; Corproración Editora Nacional.

Sánchez Parga, José. 2007. *El movimiento indígena ecuatoriano: la larga ruta de la comunidad al partido.* Quito: Centro Andino de Acción Popular.

———. 2009. *¿Qué significa ser indígena para el indígena? Más all de la comunidad y la lengua.* Quito: Abya Yala, Universidad Politécnica Salesiana.

———. 2011. "Discursos retrovolucionarios: Sumak Kausay, derechos de la naturaleza y otros pachamamismos." *Ecuador Debate* 84:31–50.

———. 2013. *Los indígenas y la política: representación y participación electorales: Ecuador 2013.* Quito: Universidad Polítecnica Salesiana; Abya Yala.

Santillana Ortiz, Alejandra. 2006. "Proceso organizativo y límites del proyecto político de Pachakutik." In *En las fisuras del poder,* edited by Pablo Ospina, 215–266. Quito: Instituto de Estudios Ecuatorianos; Consejo Latinoamericano de Ciencias Sociales.

Sawyer, Suzana. 2004. *Crude Chronicles: Indigenous Politics, Multinational Oil, and Neoliberalism in Ecuador.* Durham: Duke University Press.

Selverston–Scher. 2001. *Ethnopolitics in Ecuador: Indigenous Rights and the Strengthening of Democracy.* Boulder, CO: Lynne Rienner Publishers.

Sinnigen, John. 2013. "Introduction: Intercultural Practices in Latin American Nation States." *Journal of Intercultural Studies* 34 (5):604–619.

Sobczyk, Rita, and Rosa Soriano Miras. 2015a. ""El indígena tiene que estar siempre innovando": transformaciones de la etnicidad de la diáspora comercial de Otavalo." *Revista Española de Antropología Americana* 45 (2):457–476.

———. 2015b. "La dimensión étnica de la identidad: la diáspora comercial de Otavalo." *Mirador Latonamericano* 2015 (2):2017–237.

Stolle–McAllister, John. 2005. *Mexican Social Movements and the Transition to Democracy.* Jefferson, NC: McFarland Publishing.

———. 2013. "Intercultural Processes in Kichwa–Governed Municipalities in Northern Ecuador." *Journal of Intercultural Studies* 34 (1):1–17.

———. 2014. "Beyond Mestizaje: Andean Interculturality." In *Mestizaje and Globalization: Transforming Identity and Power in the Americas*, edited by Stefanie Wickstrom and Philip D. Young, 234-248. Tucson: University of Arizona Press.

———. 2015. "Environmental Services in Ecuador: Extractive Development versus Intercultural Intervention." *Capitalism, Nature, Socialism* 26 (2):8–26.

Telles, Edward, and Denia Gracia. 2013. "*Mestizaje* and Public Opinion in Latin America." *Latin American Research Review* 48 (3):130–152.

Tituaña Males, Auki. 2000. "Autonomía y poder local: el caso de Cotacachi, Ecuador." In *Las sociedades interculturales: un desafío para el Siglo XXI*, edited by Fernando Garcia, 107–118. Quito: FLACSO.

Torres, Víctor Hugo. 2011. "Políticas públicas, interculturalidad y conflictos socioambientales. Una aproximación." In *Conflictos socioambientales, políticas públicas y derechos. Aproximación a un debate.*, edited by Pablo Ortiz–T., 21–58. Quito: Abya–Yala; Universidad Politécnica Salesiana; Secretaría de Pueblos, Movimientos Socielaes y Participación Ciudadana.

Torres–Dávila, Victor Hugo. 2003. "Desarrollo local: ¿alternativa o discurso neoliberal?" In *Desarrollo local: ¿alternativa o discurso neoliberal?*, edited by Lola Vázquez, 57–69. Quito: Universidad Politécnico Salesiana.

Tubino, Fidel. 2002. "Interculturalizando el multiculturalismo." In *Intercultural. Balance y perspectivas*, edited by Yolanda Onghena, 181–194. Barcelona: Centro de Estudios y Documentación Internacional de Barcelona.

———. 2005. "La praxis de la interculturalidad en los estados nacionales latinoamericanos." *Cuadernos Interculturales* 3 (5):83–96.

———. 2013. "Intercultural Practices in Latin American Nation States." *Journal of Intercultural Studies* 34 (5):604–619.

UNORCAC. 2008. *Shuk Yuyaylla, Shuk Shunkulla, Shuk Makilla/ Un solo pensamiento, un solo corazón y una sola mano.* Cotacachi: Unión de organizaciones campesinas e indígenas de Cotacachi.

Van Cott, Donna Lee. 2008. *Radical Democracy in the Andes.* Cambridge: University of Cambridge Press.

Vélez Verdugo, Catalina. 2006. *La interculturalidad en la educación: reformas curriculares de Ecuador, Perú y Bolivia, Serie Magíster.* Quito: Universidad Simón Bolívar, Abya–Yala, Corporación Editora Nacional.

Villacís Mejía, María , Cantos Aguirre Enriqueta, Roberto Pons García, and Luis Ludeña Villacís. 2016. "La Eco Ruta Cultural Mojanda–Cochasquí: Una Propuesta De Desarrollo Turístico Sostenible Para La Zona Rural De La Provincia De Pichincha." *Revista Turismo Y Sociedad* (19).

Villacrés Roca, Juio Ricardo. 2016. "Incidencia del uso de las tecnologías de información y comunicación (TIC) en los hábitos y costumbres de jóvenes de cultura kichwa en Ecuador." *Asian Journal of Latin American Studies* 29 (1):109–131.

Villavicencio R., Gladys. 1973. *Relaciones interétnicas en otavalo: ¿una nacionalidad india en formación?* México: Instituto Indigenista Interamericano.

Villota, Andrea, Hermann Behling, and Susana León–Yanez. 2017. "Three millennia of vegetation and environmental dynamics in the Lagunas de Mojanda region, northern Ecuador." *Acta Palaeobotanica* 57 (2):407–421.

Wade, Peter. 2005. "Rethinking mestizaje: ideology and lived experience." *Journal of Latin American Studies* 37 (2):239–57.

Walsh, Bryan. 2011. "Paying for Nature." *Time,* 21 February 2011, Special Section 1–4.

Walsh, Catherine, ed. 2005. *Pensaminento crítico y matriz (de)colonial: reflexiones latinoamericanas.* Quito: Universidad Andina Simón Bolívar; Ediciones Abya–Yala.

———. 2009. *Interculturalidad, estado, sociedad: luchas (de)coloniales de nuestra época.* Quito: Universidad Andina Simon Bolivar; Ediciones Abya–Yala.

———. 2011. "Afro and Indigenous Life–Visions in/and Politics. (De)colonial Perspectives in Bolivia and Ecuador." *Bolivian Studies Journal* 18:49–69.

———. 2012. *Interculturalidad crítica y (de)colonial: Ensayos desde Abya Yala.* Quito: Abya Yala; Instituto Científico de Culturas Indígenas (Amawta Runakunapak Yachay).

———, Álvaro García Linera, and Walter Mignolo. 2006. *Interculturalidad, descolonización del estado y del conocimiento.* Buenos Aires: Ediciones del signo.

Webber, Jeffery R., and Barry Carr. 2012. *The New Latin American Left: Cracks in the Empire.* Lanham: Rowman and Littlefield Publishers.

Weismantel, Mary. 2006. "Ayllu: Real and Imagined Communities in the Andes." In *The Seductions of Community: Emancipations, Oppressions, Quandries*, edited by Gerald Creed, 77–100. Santa Fe: School of American Research Press.

Werbner, Pnina. 2012. "Multiculturalism from Above and Below: Analysing a Political Discourse." *Journal of Intercultural Studies* 33 (2):197–209.

Weston, Burns, and David Bollier. 2014. *Green Governance: Ecological Survival, Human Rights and the Law of the Commons.* Cambridge: Cambridge University Press.

Wezel, A., S. Bellon, T. Doré, C. Francis, D. Vallod, and C. David. 2009. "Agroecology as a Science, a Movement and a Practice." *Agronomy for Sustainable Development* 29 (4):503–515.

Whitten, Norman, ed. 2003. *Millennial Ecuador: Critical Essays on Cultural Transformations and Social Dynamics.* Iowa City: University of Iowa Press.

———, and Dorothea Scott Whitten. 2011. *Histories of the Present: People and Power in Ecuador.* Champaign, IL: University of Illinois Press.

Wibbelsman, Michelle. 2005. "Otavaleños at the Crossroads: Physical and Metephysical Coordinates of an Indigenous World." *Journal of Latin American Anthropology* 10 (1):151–185.

———. 2009. *Ritual Encounters: Otavalan Modern and Mythic Community*. Ubana, IL: University of Illinois.

Wickstrom, Stephanie and Paul D. Young, eds. 2014. *Mestizaje and Globalization: Transforming Identity and Power in the Americas*. Tucson: University of Arizona Press.

Zamosc, Leon. 2009. "Ciudadanía indígena y cohesión social en América Latina." In *Los Andes en movimiento*, edited by Pablo Ospina, Olaf Kaltmeier and Büschges, 13–40. Quito: Universidad Andina Simón Bolívar; Universidad de Bielefeld; Corporación Editora Nacional.

Zúñiga Paredes, Luis. 2011. "Cultura e interculturalidad en el Ecuador." In *Interculturalidad y diversidad*, edited by Ariruma Kowii Maldonado, 123–130. Quito: Universidad Simón Bolivar; Corporación Editora Nacional.

INDEX

CPSIA information can be obtained
at www.ICGtesting.com
Printed in the USA
BVHW030225160319
542842BV00004B/41/P

9 781621 964254